JAPANESE GARDENING IN SMALL SPACES

DISTRIBUTORS:

UNITED STATES: Kodansha America, Inc., through Oxford University Press, 198 Madison Avenue, New York, NY 10016.

CANADA: Fitzhenry & Whiteside Ltd., 195 Allstate Parkway, Markham, Ontario L3R 4T8.

AUSTRALIA AND NEW ZEALAND: Bookwise International, 174 Cormack Road, Wingfield, SA 5013 Australia.

ASIA AND OTHER COUNTRIES: Japan Publications Trading Co., Ltd., 1-2-1, Sarugaku-cho, Chiyoda-ku, Tokyo, 101-0064 Japan.

First edition, October 1996, 9th printing April 2007

Printed in Japan.

ISBN : 978-0-87040-977-6

ACKNOWLEDGMENTS

My grateful appreciation to the following individuals for their encourgement and patience throughout the many months it took to compile this book.

Junnichi Kato, Yoshihiko Koshizuka, photographers
Yoko Ishiguro, translator
Akira Sakurai, constructor for photograghy
Ogihara Planning, book designer
Toshie Kozakura, illustrator
Akira Naito, chief-editor
Satoru Shimura, editor

Isao Yoshikawa

PREFACE

The term *tsuboniwa* seems to originate from the *Heian* Period (794 - 1191) when Japanese arts flourished. In those days the small courtyards of the Imperial Palace or the mansions of high-ranking ministers were called *tsuboniwa*, which literally meant alcoves or enclosed spaces. The term *tsubo* later acquired different meanings such as tea gardens, small quadrangles, or inner gardens. Nowadays *tsubo* is only used as a unit of measurement (one *tsubo* is equivalent to 1.8 square meters or 5.5 square feet), and most people indentify *tsuboniwa* as any small scale garden regardless of whether it is enclosed or open.

People often ask me how to define a "small" garden. There is no rule of how small it should be. The concept of size varies from country to country, or from city to city, and garden designers each have their own definitions of what a "small" garden should be. I myself think any garden under 20 *tsubo* ($66m^2$ / $71yd^2$) could be called a small garden.

One of the notable characters of Japanese gardening is its versatility in size. Even the smallest patch of land can be transformed into a beautiful landscape as shown in this book.

I presume people's need for small gardens will increase especially in the cities. I will attempt to introduce the basic techniques of *tsuboniwa* construction using as many practical examples as possible.

Isao Yoshikawa

CONTENTS

TSUBONIWA OR SMALL GARDENS

***Tsuboniwa* or small gardens can be made in spaces of one *tsubo*, or thirty six square feet. The smaller the area, the easier it is for the garden creator's taste and individuality to be reflected in the garden. The point to keep in mind when making a small garden is to carefully select the materials and strive for quality - not quantity. For example, if you place an inappropriate shaped stone lantern in the garden, the garden will lose something in character, no matter how much work you put into it. Aim for a tasteful and elegant garden.**

1

A small garden constructed with *Kenninji-gaki* and *Kinkakuji-gaki* bamboo fences which serve as a partition from the front yard on its left. An *Oribe-toro* lantern is set on a grassy mound of dwarf snake's beard serving as the focal point. *Ise* gravel is used to cover the ground. See page 107 for instructions.

2

The central part of the small garden constructed on the balcony of a condominium, on the third floor. *Tsukubai* or a washing basin front plays a dominant role in this garden, by arranging a mortar shaped washing basin and a *Sunshoan* style lantern. *Koka-seki* stones, a kind of pumice, are used to reduce the weight. See page 108 for instructions.

3

An example of a small-scale dry waterfall as the main feature of *karesansui* or the dry stream garden . For the stone arrangement, *Sanba* blue stones are used to symbolize each traditional role such as the water source, distant mountains, or a stream divider. See page 109 for instructions.

4 (Left)
A compact *tsuboniwa* of 5m^2 (6yd^2) made beneath the outer stairway of a concrete house. This is a view from the front doorway, and it is accented with a basic style water basin and *Bushoan* stone lantern, surrounded by two-sided original bamboo fence.

5 (Left)
Koetsu-gaki bamboo fence divides this tea garden from the front yard, to be viewed from the living room. *Tsukubai* featuring *Shihobutsu* basin as a focal point harmonizes with the small scale *Oribe* stone lantern. Hairmoss and the flowers add colors to the stones including the muted stepping stones. See page 110 for instructions.

6 (Left)
The detail of a small garden: *Sode-gata* stone lantern is purposefully positioned utilizing the curved border of hairmoss and *Shirakawa* gravel. See page 111 for instructions.

7 (Above)
Kyoto's typically small *tsuboniwa* called *"Totekiko"* of *Daitokuji* Temple. A narrow, rectangular space is simply filled with *Shirakawa* gravel that sets off the perfectly balanced five-stone arrangement. The simplicity of a *Zen* temple is finely expressed here. See page 112 for instructions.

TSUKUBAI GARDENS

Tsukubai **literally means a hand-washing facility where you bend your knees to reach the low basin. The basin is accompanied with a drainage and a front stone to step on. Often more scenic stones are set as *yuoke-ishi*, or stone for dipper, and *teshoku-ishi*, or lantern stone.**

8
A *tsukubai* example using an excellent *Kesa-gata* water basin, a model of the *Kamakura* Period. It is located in the front garden, with an L-shaped, flat green stone from a noted quarry. The ground is covered with hairmoss and bamboo grass. See page 113 for instructions.

9
A bleak, north balcony of a condominium is transformed into a small garden with true character. *Tsukubai* serves as a focal point with the small-sized *Teppatsu* water basin and the low *Kenninji-gaki* bamboo fence in the background. See page 114 for instructions.

10 (Left)
An orthodox example of *tsukubai*, constructed in front of a Japanese room. A variation of the *Ginkakuji* water basin is used to create a mood. The basin can be centered like this, when you want to make a larger *tsukubai* composition. See page 115 for instructions.

11 (Right)
Here a traditional *Teppatsu* water basin is added as an element to *karesansui*, or a dry stream garden, accompanied with irregular-shaped front stones. This is a unique design of *tsukubai*, for no other scenic stones are laid around the basin to make its beautiful outline stand out. See page 116 for instructions.

TORO GARDENS

***Toro*, or stone lantern, is one of the most important stone structures in a Japanese garden. Select an artistically shaped one out of the numerous designs, and consider its position carefully since this is not only a decoration but a light source in its origin. For this reason, stone lanterns are often placed to illuminate the water basins.**

12 (Above left)
A limited space on the basement is made into a small garden which is enhanced with a small *toro*. This square lantern, implanted in the ground, matches the cryptomeria bark fence in the background. The *Reiganji* water basin is also set in black *Nachi* pebbles.

13 (Above right)
An *Oribe toro* stands beside the basin front to illuminate the *Teppatsu* water basin. Since this stone lantern is made to be implanted in the ground, the impression can be changed depending on the height it is set. See page 117 for instructions.

14 (Below left)
A guide-toro placed to provide a dim light for the stepping stones . Its natural shape and practical setting together give an effect of quiet refinement to the garden pássage. This special style stone lantern was originated in the late *Edo* Period. See page 118 for instructions.

15 (Below right)
A dignified *Kamakura*-style *toro* installed in the front garden, right behind the gate. This type of large, traditionally designed lantern is most effective when placed in an important location, as in this case, where it is visible immediately upon entering the garden. This particular lantern is a copy of the famous one in Kawageta-Mikawabe Shrine, Shiga. See page 119 for instructions

PAVING & STEPPING STONE GARDENS

Paving stones and stepping stones were originally used in gardens for tea ceremony houses, and later started being used in regular gardens. Today these stone constructions are the essential elements of Japanese gardens. Originally stone-paved walkways led to a proper house whereas stepping stones led to an informal spot such as a garden house or a kitchen door. However, since pavement designs allow a great many variations, there will be numerous ideas for both types of stone setting.

16
A stepping stone layout in a small-scale garden surrounded by a bamboo screen fence. Large, *Chichibu* blue stones are effectively set to enhance the whole garden, leading to the step-up shoe stone of the house. See page 120 for instructions.

17
A paved walkway through the front garden, in the most appropriate style. Precisely cut paving stones are called *shin*-style, which is used for a proper space. Here, the wider space between the stones makes a beautiful contrast of its own. See page 121 for instructions.

18 (Below left)
Small stepping stones laid in pebbles, serving not only as a walkway but to accentuate the dry garden. The rusty color of *Tanba-Kurama-ishi* stone contrasts well with the white pebbles. See page 122 for instructions.

19 (Below right)
A challenging design for paving stones. Small *Awaji* pebbles piled up from the edges represent the traditional forms of clouds over the diagonally divided garden. White plaster is used between the pebbles to further resemble clouds. See page 123 for instructions.

STONE ARRANGEMENTS GARDENS

Stone arrangemenst play a dominant role in Japanese gardens. Especially when you have *karesansui*, or a dry stream garden, a stone arrangement is a must that defines the quality of the garden and the garden maker's sense of beauty. Some people think displaying well-shaped stones from famous quarries would do the work, but it is not always true. I suggest that you create your favorite landscape by combining stones of various shapes. Stones for this purpose would not cost much, and once you make a tasteful arrangement, you can enjoy it for a long time without frequent maintenance.

20

Local andesite stones enclose the original, coin-shaped water basin in this small dry stream garden. Smaller stones of different shapes create an interesting sight in contrast with the pebbles and the green.

21 (Above)

An old stone formation in the famous *karesansui* garden of *Daisen-in* temple completed in the *Muromachi* Period (14-16c). Although this is a small-scale garden for the period, it has a stream made of blue stones. This photograph shows the upper to middle part of the stream set off by the stone bridge.

22 (Below left)

A *karesansui* example using blue stones set on a green mound. *Tamaryu* grass(dwarf snake's beard)covers the smoothly curved mound to set off the depth of the stone formation. The plaster wall offers a contrasting background.

23 (Below right)

A five-stone arrangement made for a limited space of only 40cm(1.3') width. The high, oiled bamboo fence shows the clear lines of stones. A good example of how a stone arrangement can create a mood even in a narrow space.

24
Simple *karesansui* garden. In a rectangular space lined with *Shirakawa* gravel sits nothing but a three-stone arrangement called *Sanzon*, or the Buddha Three, the most basic formation. The key to success is to give a rising but stable impression.

25
Karesansui garden using the traditional,"7-5-3" style arrangement of 15 stones. Five stones are set in the raked gravel and seven stones in the greenery of *tamaryu* grass(dwarf snake's beard) , creating the sense of perspective.

26
Small *karesansui* garden to be viewed from the window. Among distinctive features are the grass-covered high mound raised on *Roppo-seki* stones and the *Sanba* blue stones combined to represent a dry waterfall, capturing the grandeur of nature in a small urban space. The fishnet bamboo screen sits atop the white concrete wall. Matches the arrangement.

27 (Above left)
Large blue stone behind a low, bamboo branch fence which symbolizes a boat floating on the sea. The Kyoto style *Kenninji-gaki* fence sets off the shape of the tall stone. See how fun free-style stone setting can be.

28 (Above)
Detail of a *karesansui* garden. The tall stone and mountain-shaped stone behind the *tsukubai* project a sense of force. The unique ridges of *Awa* blue stone give maximum impact. Tall stones are the most important element of Japanese gardens.

29 (Middle left)
Tsuboniwa in a Buddhist temple of Pure Land sect. I designed this *karesansui* to depict "*raigozu*", the descending scene of the buddha Amida. The standing stones represent Amida and his followers coming down on the clouds. One of his disciples sits seperately, which gives a sense of perspective.

30 (Below left)
This magnificent blue stone is a part of the famous *karesansui* in *Daisen-in* garden. The dry stream runs through the garden carrying this celestial ship towards the right ... or so it seems.

GARDEN ACCENTS

Stone lanterns, stone water basins, stone images of Buddha and pagodas give accents to simple Japanese gardens. For *tsuboniwa*, these stone structures are indispensable to creating the scene together with a bamboo fence in the background. It can be said that the quality of these works often determines the quality of the garden. Be generous with the price and severe with the artistic value especially when you select stone lanterns and water basins because once you set one, probably you will not replace it in your lifetime. As for bamboo fences, ready-made ones are availabe in small sizes, however, it is best to construct the most suitable fence yourself to match your garden.

***Kinkakuji-gaki* fence**

This low-lying, see-through fence originated in *Kinkakuji* temple, Kyoto, hence the name. Having another name *ashimoto-gaki*, or foot-level fence, this fence is often used to enhance the pathways in the front gardens. The most prominent feature of the *Kinkakuji-gaki* fence is the split-bamboo beading that runs along the top.

***Koetsu-gaki* fence**

Hon'ami Koetsu, a craftsman of many talents, lived in the *Edo* Period and his family temple, *Koetsuji* in *Kyoto*, is the source of this fence. Also called *Koetsuji-gaki* or *Gagyu-gaki* ("lying cow" fence), the *Koetsu-gaki* fence is similar to the stockade fence constructed with split bamboo lattice, but with round beading at the top made with bamboo branches and split bamboo.

***Kenninji-gaki* fence**

Kenninji temple in Kyoto is said to be the first to construct this type of fence. Nowadays the fence is the most commonly made screening fence in Japan, favored with its horizontal and vertical bamboo combination. Split bamboo is used to form the vertical design across which tiered bars add more solidity.

***Tokusa-gaki* fence**

Tokusa is the word for a kind of rush. The *Tokusa-gaki* fence is not in fact made of this plant, but is so named because the vertical poles of bamboo resemble rushes, so often found growing in gardens. This fence uses no front crossbars to secure the vertical poles. Instead, black hemp rope joins the bamboo in a variety of tying designs, making this fence special.

Bamboo Fences

Of all garden structures the bamboo fences are most favored by the Japanese. We treasure the textures and the subtle tones of bamboo that change as time passes. For its elegant beauty and flexibility no other materials suit tsuboniwa as a background. Although recently there are various imitation bamboo materials made of plastic, they look cheap when used in a small space like *tsuboniwa*. Only natural bamboo harmonizes the natural stone components.

Bamboo fences are classified into two categories according to usage, screen fences and see-through fences. The latter is used for partitioning gardens or bordering walkways and sometimes combined with the other screen type. Also, there is a narrower fence called *sode-gaki*, or wing fence, which extends from the house and is used mainly as a decorative screen . Bamboo fences include ones made of tree branches and tree bark but most of them have bamboo crossbars to hold them in place. Naming of each bamboo fence depends on numerous factors, such as an image from the shape or species of bamboo, or the name of the temple, person, or place.

Species of bamboo used for fences

Madake

The most widely used fencing material. *Madake* is a common species with an elegant look . Because of the thinness and length between joints it is the most suitable bamboo for processing. For a *Kenninji-gaki* fence, split *madake* is used as vertical poles.

Medake

Narrower than *madake*, *medake* is a general name for thin, flexible bamboo stalks, including *yadake* and *hakonedake*. *Medake* is processed into *sarashidake* and *shimizudake*, both of which are typical materials for the *Misu-gaki* fence.

Madake

Medake (Sarashidake)

***Takeho-gaki* fence**

Takeho literally means whole bamboo branches, but only longer and softer branches are suitable for bamboo fences. Species called *mosochiku* and *kurochiku* are readily available and used to make this type of screening fence by packing into a panel which is secured by crossbars. A variety of designs are known.

***Aboshi-gaki* fence**

One of the modern, originally designed fence, showing an old fishnet pattern called *aboshi moyo*. This fence became popular bacause of the bold design giving a fanned -out impression towards the bottom.

Original fences

Any exclusively designed bamboo fence can be called an original fence. It should be designed for a particular garden, therefore each fence has a different look. Introduced above is an example which combines the horizontal and diagonal panels.

***Misu-gaki* fence**

Misu is a word for a rolled, fine bamboo screen used in noblemen's houses, in order to hide the nobles' faces. Narrow bamboo stalks are joined together to make a panel of horizontal lines and secured with vertical bars and black hemp rope. Although it has a screening look, it is breathable because of some spaces between the horizontal bars. This fence is suitable as an under- the-eave fence since it is less sturdy than other fences.

***Sugikawa-gaki* fence**

A dark colored fence using *sugikawa* or cryptomeria (Japanese cedar) bark for the panels. The bark is cut into certain width and sold in two thicknesses. The strips of bark are attached to horizontal bars and secured with narrow bamboo stalks in the front. *Sugikawa-gaki* has the advantage of outlasting the fences that are entirely made of bamboo.

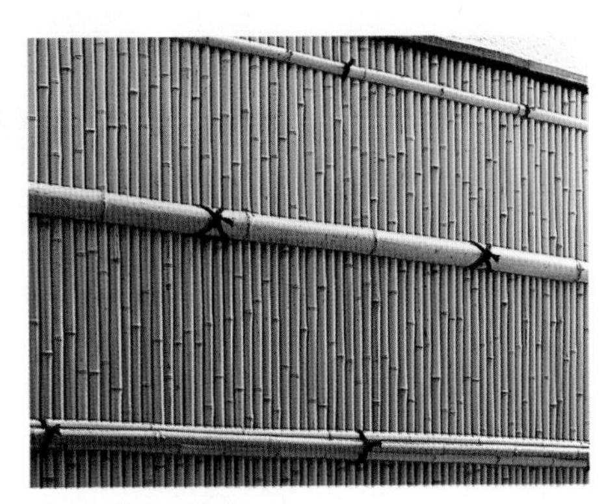

***Sarashi-gaki* fence**

This fence can be called *Tokusa-gaki* fence in its style, but for its material it can be called a *sarashi-gaki* fence because of the *sarashidake* bamboo used as the vertical poles. In the same way, a fence made of *shimizudake* bamboo can be called a *Shimizu-gaki* fence. *Sarashi-gaki* fences are more suitable as interior partitions rather than outside walls.

TORO

Generally, *toro* refers to stone lanterns, although there are also *toro* made of metal or wood. *Toro* were originally used to illuminate the front of the Buddhist temples, and had nothing to do with the gardens. In the *Kamakura* Period, many good quality *toro* were produced, and they started to be used in the following *Momoyama* Period when the tea ceremony was established and tea gardens needed a "highlight". People purchased fine *toro* from the temples or made copies of them. Later in the *Edo* Period, they started to order stone lanterns small enough for their gardens as *niwa-toro* or garden lanterns, in different styles than the traditional ones. These new *toro* include implanted *toro*, *toro* with base stone, and movable *toro*. The smaller, movable lanterns are ideal for small gardens. There are in fact many ill-shaped lanterns these days. Be sure to select one that can be enjoyed as a work of art.

Oribe Toro

The typical stone lantern of the *Momoyama* Period. It is said to have been designed by a master of tea ceremony called Oribe Furuta, but this is not certain. One of its outstanding features is the swollen top of the square pole implanted in the ground. Many fine examples are found in the *Katsura-Rikyu* Gardens, Kyoto.

Kawageta-gata Toro

One of the masterpieces (finest *toro*)made in the late *Kamakura* Period. The original model exists in the *Kawageta Mikawabe* Shrine, Shiga Prefecture. It has a dignified atmosphere, with a hexagonal pole standing on the base stone which has carvings of three-stemmed lotus, lion, and peacock. The whole structure is well preserved except for a minor damage in the lantern box.

Shikaku-gata Toro

Shikaku or square lanterns are implanted in the ground. Their outstanding features include the elegant line of the roof and the crown jem which is shaped like a lotus bud. The specimen above shows the characteristics well.

Sode-gata Toro

The name "*sode*" (sleeve) comes from the shape of the lantern box set in the thick pole which resembles the sleeve of *kimono*. The specimen above is a reduced model of the preserved original *sode-gata toro* which is 112cm(44") tall. Although most of the original models of garden lanterns are unidentified today, the original *sode-gata toro* still stands at the edge of a teahouse near the *Shugakuin Rikyu* Shrine, Kyoto.

Parts of *Toro*

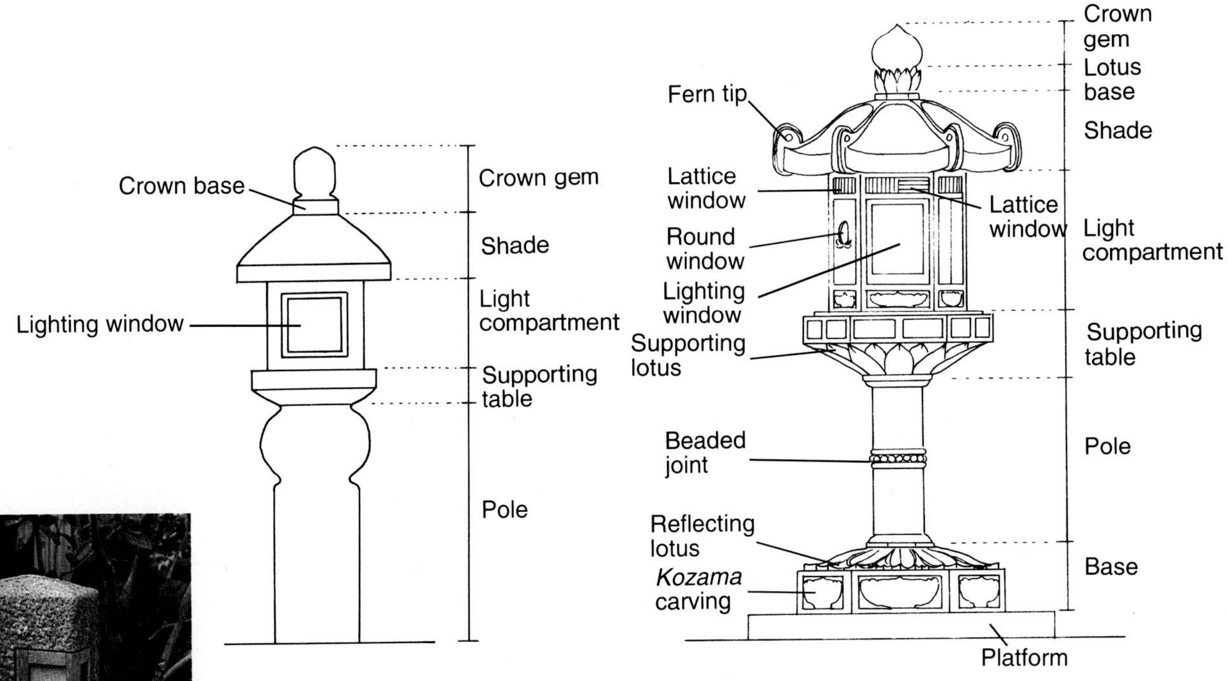

Michishirube-gata Toro
Guide stones were built at intersections of highways, pointing each direction with a place name. Originally it seems that some abandoned guide stones were reformed by chiseling out spaces to make the lantern compartments. Today, it is almost impossible to obtain an old guide stone and various imitations are made with letter carvings.

Sunshoan-gata Toro
The traditional *toro* once included hanging lanterns besides the common ones that were implanted in the ground or placed on the base stones. Hanging lanterns were made of metal because of the weight and hung with chains under the eaves. Later in the *Edo* Period, only the shape of this hanging lantern was inherited in the common stone lanterns to set on the ground. Regrettably, finely shaped examples are hard to find today.

Bushoan-gata Toro
As previously explained in the *Sunshoan-gata toro*, ground-set hanging lanterns have deteriorated from the original form. In order to restore the traditional style of hanging lanterns, I have designed a new model as shown above. This lantern is inspired by an old hanging lantern preserved in *Kasuga Taisha* Shrine, Nara, and is only 30cm(1') tall to be set both indoors and outdoors.

CHOZUBACHI OR WATER BASINS

***Chozubachi*, sometimes called *mizubachi*, is a general term for water basins set in tea gardens or other gardens. They were used as an adjunct to the tea ceremony, to be used by the guests to ritually "purify" themselves by washing their hands and mouths before entering the tea house. Most of them are made of stones although there are also metallic, earthenware, and wooden basins. Although the term "*tsukubai*" is often mixed up with *chozubachi* even among garden specialists, *tsukubai* does not mean the basin itself but rather the whole area surrounding a low-set *chozubachi*, including the drainage system and a scenic stone arrangement. *Chozubachi* were also used as the washing basin near a toilet. But eventually by the end of the *Edo* Period, people started to use them as a decorative element of residential gardens. There are numerous styles of *chozubachi*, which can be sorted into three categories: natural stone basin, recycled basin, and original basin. When selecting one, keep in mind that a good *chozubachi* has not only a refined shape, but also a deep, finely scooped hollow.**

Shihobutsu-gata Chozubachi

Shihobutsu are carvings of the Buddha made in the four sides of a stupa. Therefore, the origin of this style was in the stupas abandoned from Buddhist temples, which were made into water basins. Sanskrit words describing the Buddha may be carved in place of the images of Buddha.

Ishiusu-gata Chozubachi

Ishiusu, translated as either stone mortars or millstones, were widely used in everyday life in former times, and later started to be used as washing basins. This is also an example of a reformed basin. A millstone basin is made by carving a hole in a millstone in such a way as to preserve the ridges over the inner wall, while a mortar basin can be used as it is.

Kiso-gata Chozubachi

Another example of recycled basin using the old foundation part of various stone objects such as stone lanterns and certain kind of stupas. There are various shapes: square, hexagonal, octagonal, and round. *Kiso-gata chozubachi*, carved with reflecting lotus flower are especially prized. The typical examples of this type are the square basins made of *ho-kyo-in-to* stupas.

Ginkakuji-gata Chozubachi

A typical example of original *chozubachi* made for the purpose. All four sides of the square basin are carved with various lattice patterns. The original basin exists in *Ginkakuji* temple, Kyoto.

Teppatsu-gata Chozubachi

This is a basin shaped like *teppatsu* or a small iron bowl used by mendicant priests. Made from a balloon-shaped section of the *gorin* stone tower which appeared in the late *Heian* Period, this is another reformed basin. There is a variation which is carved with a Sanscrit letter.

Kesa-gata Chozubachi

First appearing in the *Kamakura* Period, a *Kesa-gata* basin is another reshaped example made from the body of a stone stupa. The name *kesa-gata* is derived from the fact that the pattern on the sides of this basin resembles *kesa,* a priest's surplice. It is interesting to know that in its origin, the pattern was supposed to show the simplified shape of doors, but no one called it a *to-gata* or door-pattern basin.

Tsukubai and *Chozubachi*

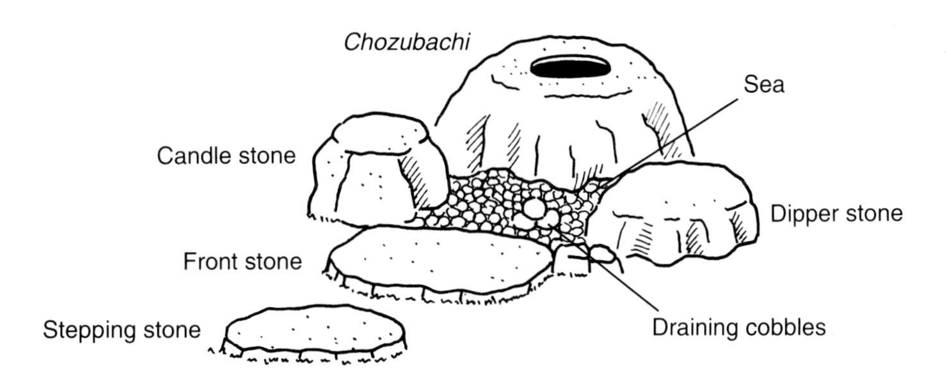

Soseki-gata Chozubachi

A general term for reformed basins made from *soseki* or disposed foundation stones of old wooden buildings. *Soseki* itself has a variety of styles, but basins made from natural stones are not included. Variations include *garan-seki*, *soban-gata*, and *Reiganji-gata* basins.

Rendai-gata Chozubachi

Most stupas and statues of Buddha have pedestals shaped like lotus petals, which are called *rendai* or *rengeza*. *Rendai-gata* basins are made from rendai abandoned by temples. The thick rims carved with blooming lotus petals facing upwards give a very elegant impession.

Reiganji-gata Chozubachi

This is my original basin named after the beautiful foundation stones of the famous stupa in *Reiganji* Temple, China. The outstanding features of this basin are the reflecting lotus flower carved on the octagonal base and the intricate carvings of the central bead loop, which set off the water surface inside.

Zeni-gata Chozubachi

Another original type of basin shaped to resemble *zeni*, or old coin with a hollow square center surrounded by carved-out letters. Two well-known examples are: *Fusen Chozubachi* inspired by an old Chinese coin, and *Chisoku no Chozubachi*, from *Ryoanji* Temple, Kyoto. Shown above is my creation named *Enyu no Chozubachi*.

MATERIALS FOR *TSUBONIWA* OR SMALL GARDENS

In order to make a garden of good quality, a well-planned blueprint and careful construction are most important as a matter of course. However, selecting the appropriate materials for your garden could also make the difference between success and failure. That is because a small garden, much more than a spacious garden, is designed to be viewed at close range. Garden materials can be sorted into two categories, plants and stones. There are several points which should be kept in mind when you purchase each of them. For the plants, visit the farms or nurseries directly and let the cultivators select what suit your garden. However, you should select stones according to your own taste, with the exception of gravel, which should always be natural and should be chosen according to the quality of the stone itself.

Trees and shrubs

Garden trees can be classified into two kinds: trees suitable for large gardens such as parks, and trees for residential gardens. Although there are trees common to both classifications, the number is limited when it comes to *tsuboniwa* or small gardens. Since it is essential in a small garden to use as few trees as possible, it is important to choose a careful assortment of evergreen and deciduous trees . Select sturdy, shade-tolerant, and easy- to-prune species since tiny gardens often have scarce sunlight. Since trees are apt to grow upwards seeking the sunlight, lower branches may move higher and out of sight of the room, if left untended. Try to select trees whose lower trunks grow slowly, and avoid fast-growing trees such as zelkova, Chinese parasol, gingko, or metasequoia that will spoil the whole *tsuboniwa*. Also pay attention to protecting the trees against diseases and pests, and select varieties that are resistant to such troubles.

AOKI

Aucuba japonica. Evergreen shrub. Native from Himalayas to Japan. One of the most shade-tolerant shrubs that accepts deep shades. Although rather fast growing, it can be kept lower by pruning. Perfect for *tsuboniwa* where year-round quality is essential. Lovely clusters of bright red berries from October to February. Varieties include variegated leaves and thin leaves.

ASEBI

Pieris japonica. Bog rosemary. Evergreen shrub with leathery, narrow leaves, somewhat like those of rosemary. Tolerates shade and can be shaped by pruning. Not adapted to areas with alkaline soil. Low ones are often added to *tsukubai* or basin front. Pest-resistant because of the poison in its leaves.

JAPANESE PLUM

Prunus salicina. Deciduous tree. A type of European plum. Favored for its early spring blossoms, sweet fragrance and fruits, along with the graceful lines of old trunks and branches. Best in well-drained soil and sunny site. Tolerates transplanting and pruning. Has a wide variety.

KUROGANEMOCHI

Ilex rotunda. Evergreen tree. Densely foliated, but slow growing. Excess pruning may damage the tree, unlike other ilex species. Adds a subdued atmosphere to the garden.

GOYOMATSU

Pinus pentaphylla. Japanese white pine. Evergreen tree. Name comes from "*Goyo*", five needles in a bundle. Thick trunk with very leafy branches. Suitable for garden because of its elegant figure. Shade-tolerant.

SUGI

Cryptomeria japonica. Japanese cedar. Evergreen tree. Angular, well proportioned form. Fast growing and tolerates pruning, good for hedges. Grows in nearly any soil, but weak against polluted air. Bark can be used for bamboo fences.

DAISUGI

Cryptomeria japonica, the same species as common Japanese cedar. Distinctive form is favored and suitable for gardens. Cut slightly above the root when the trunk is thick enough, and narrow trunks will grow into lovely forms.

CAMELLIA

Camellia japonica. Evergreen shrub and small tree. This popular garden plant has numerous varieties, ranging in color and size. Shade tolerant, in nearly any soil. Slow growing; avoid heavy pruning. Strong against low temperature, salt air or smokes.

KUROMATSU

Pinus Thunbergii. Black pine. Evergreen tree. Popular as "the king of garden trees", because of its masculine form. Prefers well-drained soil. Fast growing and easy to be pruned. Cut back frequently for small gardens. Rather weak against pests.

SWEET OLIVE
Osmanthus fragrans. Shrub and small tree. Tiny orange flowers with sweet, apricot-like fragrance. Rather slow growing, but tolerates a broad range of soils. Avoid heavy pruning.

MOKKOKU
Ternstroemia japonica. Evergreen shrub or tree. Requires full sun and rich, acid soil. Scarce leaves but well-proportioned naturally in growth. Can be transplanted. Slow growing; avoid heavy pruning. Suitable for larger gardens where the whole form can be viewed.

JAPANESE MAPLE
Acer palmatum. Deciduous shrub or tree. The most airy and delicate of all maples. Soft green in spring, progressing to yellow, orange and red in fall. Fast growing in rich soil. Requires full sun. Avoid pruning to keep the elegant, natural form.

GROUND COVERS

Since *tsuboniwa* and other small gardens are constructed closer to the buildings than spacious gardens, ground covering plants play an important role for the beauty of a small garden. Besides the low growing grasses and lawn grasses, lichens such as mosses and ferns also make good ground covers. The advantage of having mosses in your garden is that unlike lawns, no mowing or trimming is necessary. Mosses are divided into two families, one which clings to the surface of the ground and "creeps" over it, and the other which has roots, stalks and leaves. The latter kind of moss is the one used in gardens. I personally like the green of the type of hair moss in gardens of Kyoto best of all. However, where the soil is not moist enough, or in the urban environments, *tamaryu* or dwarf snake's beard is becoming popular instead.

CAST-IRON PLANT
Aspidistra elatior. Evergreen perennial. Glossy dark green leaf blades with long, sturdy stalks. Spreads widely, and grows 50cm(1.6') tall, in nearly any soil and shade or filtered sun. Planted under trees or added to *tsukubai*. Must be thinned occasionally.

KOKUMAZASA

Sasa albo-marginata. Dwarf, low-growing bamboo grass. Grows no higher than 20cm (8") and the fine leaves are suitable for *tsuboniwa*. Other families which stay low enough to use as a ground cover can be called by this name.

FERNS

Nephrolepis corifolia Presl. Perennial plants favored for their interesting foliage. Because of the long history since ancient times, there are numerous species. Grow well in filtered sun since native ferns grew in shades of forests.

SUGIGOKE

Polytrichum commune. Cedar moss or hair moss. The delicate, star-like leaves are most suitable for *tsuboniwa* and other small gardens, as, "the king of mosses". *O-sugigoke* is most common although other varieties such as *Uma-sugigoke* is also used. Not suited for dry regions.

TAMARYU

Liliacear. Dwarf snake's beard. Perennial. Glossy, dark green leaves resemble beard, hence the name. Great as ground cover. Extremely shade tolerant, suitable where mosses cannot be used because of the climate.

DICHONDRA

Dichondra micrantha. Convolvulaceae. Perennial ground cover plant. Tiny, round leaves resemble miniature water lily pads. Grows well in sun or shade by rooting surface runners. Evergreen in warm climates.

TSUWABUKI

Ligularia tussilaginea. Compositae. Evergreen perennial plant. Leathery, glossy leaves, somewhat kidney shaped. Few yellow flowers on long stalks look graceful. Grows in any sun-filtered place. Speckled or blotched variety is often added to *tsukubai.*

FUKKISO

Buxaceae. Evergreen shrub. Grows 30cm(1') tall, with 5cm(2") long, serrated leaves. Makes fine ground cover when planted in mass. Grows anywhere, often found in hilly regions. Shade tolerant, but needs humidity.

MANRYO

Ardisia japonica. Myrsinaceae. Coralberry. Evergreen low shrub. Grows 60cm(2') high when mature. Beautiful bright red berries throughout winter. Leathery leaves in clusters on top of single, vertical stalk. Requires ample water but needs no pruning since it stays well proportioned naturally. Choice plant for *tsuboniwa* and other small gardens.

STONES AND GRAVEL

One of the most distinctive features of Japanese garden history is the emergence of *keresansui* gardens. *Karesansui*, or dry landscape garden, uses stones and gravel in place of water to represent waterfalls, streams, or the sea. These spiritual gardens suit any place, large or small, sunny or shady. The natural successor to the *karesansui* technique is *tsuboniwa.*
Japan geographically stretches north and south with a number of mountains and rivers that attract us with scenic beauty. Nature provides various kinds of stones and gravels we can enjoy in gardens. Even though quarrying is being limited for the sake of conservation, natural stones, gravels and sands stay popular. If you have to use processed materials, try to select quality products.

STONES

Among all the components of the Japanese garden, stone arrangements have always been the most beloved. Stones used for this purpose are divided into granites, andesites, and blue stones. Granites are most common, produced all over the country. As they weather rather fast, patina is often produced on the surface, which give subtle refinement to garden stones. However, the shapes are usually suitable for level or low base stones and not perfect for three dimensional arrangements. Andesites are weather-resistant, therefore natural angular corners can be kept as they are. But because of the angular sides, they require some experience to be arranged nicely. In comparison with these two kinds, blue stones are easiest to use for arrangements with their well-shaped forms and finely ridged surface. Blue stones can even be cut into long slabs to use as a bridge. For all these reasons, people have loved blue stones since the Medieval period. When selecting stones, consider the usefulness of the whole shape, whichever type of stone you choose. Some say the stones should be set deep in the ground, but this is a superstition.

Granite
Quality granite is named *mikage-ishi* after Mikage, the quarry town, of Kobe. This name became so popular that granite from other districts was named with the suffix-*mikage*. Today, real *mikage-ishi* has to be called *hon-mikage-ishi* (genuine *mikage-ishi*), but products are limited.

Andesites
A kind of volcanic rock. Andesites have been formed by changing the quality of lava. Used for both garden rocks and monuments, they are as popular as granites, especially in *Kanto* region. Quality andesites include *Komatsu-ishi* and *Nebugawa-ishi.*

Blue stones
This is a general name of blue colored stones which belongs to chlorite schist or crystalline schist. The beautiful lines and ridges make these stones suitable for arrangements that resemble Indian ink paintings. There are ranges of rock deposits consisting these stones all over Japan. Typical stones include *Awa* blue stone, *Iyo* blue stone, *Kishu* blue stone, *Sanba* blue stone, *Chichibu* blues stone,etc.

Kiso-ishi

This kind of granite granitite, produced in Gifu, has recently been developed as garden stones. The rugged surface resembles *Tsukuba-ishi* from Ibaragi. Used in arrangements not only as level or flat stones but, covering slabs, piled stones, or shoe stones where shoes can be removed before stepping into the house. Especially favored in the Kansai region.

Awa-ishi

Garden stones produced in Shikoku. Also called *Awa* blue stones because blue colored stones are the most popular of all *Awa-ishi*. Treasured as "the king of blue stones" along with the *Iyo* blue stones produced in the neighboring prefecture. The beautiful colors and contrasing lines of this stone are distinctive. One of the kinds which can be sliced off in slab form is best for making quality bridge stones.

Sanba-ishi

Crystalline schist from the *Sanba* River area in Gunma. Stones in blue shades are especially known by the name of *Sanba* blue stones, the quality blue stone from Kanto region. Today, natural *Sanba* stones quarried from the mountains around Oniishi town are processed by rounding off the sharp corners using machines, to serve for garden use.

Samegawa-ishi

Blue stones quarried at upper stream of *Samegawa* River, *Fukushima*, the northernmost blue stones for gardens. Natural *Samegawa-ishi* have fine shapes and impressive, beautiful ridges, but in rather dark blue hues. It is hard to find natural stones, except for the rounded type.

Koka-seki

A well-known stone material produced in the southern island belonging to *Tokyo*. It is pumice of quartz dolerite brought by eruptions. One that floats on water is said to be of good quality. It is only recently that this stone is favored as garden stones, in the need of lightweight stones to use for inner gardens, terraces, or roof-top gardens. Resists fire.

COBBLE STONES AND PEBBLES

Cobble stones or pebbles used to line the ground have various names according to the size and shape, such as *kuri-ishi*, *gorota-ishi*, and *tama-ishi*. Choose the most appropriate size for the space, e.g., take *kuri-ishi*, the smallest, for smaller *tsuboniwa*. Since natural cobble stones are becoming scarce in Japan, larger stones are crushed and rounded by machine to unify the size. These products have scars on their surfaces, which turn to whitish color when they are dry. Therefore, as for this type of stone, it is suggestible to carefully select from natural materials from China or Korea.

Kuro-Nachi-ishi

Natchi-ishi, naturally jet black round stones found on the seashore of Mie, have long been treasured for making sophisticated pavements and walking grounds. However, shiny black *Nachi-ishi* are hard to find any more, they are being replaced by processed stones. The author has discovered similarly beautiful, black stones in China and began importing them.

Ao-Nachi-ishi

Since *Nachi-ishi* has become so popular as cobbles, traders have taken its name for any other shiny round stones at their convenience. Thus the genuine *Nachi-ishi* had to be called *Kuro-Nachi-ishi* to be recognized. *Ao-Nachi-ishi* is the name for natural small cobbles of pale blue, produced in Taiwan. The supply is not abundant.

Shiro-Nachi-ishi

These also has nothing to do with the *Nachi* of Mie. *Shiro-Nachi-ishi* is a general name for all natural cobbles which are shiny white. Also from Taiwan, these similar stones are produced in Mainland China. Whiter cobbles suit inner gardens whereas brownish ones are for gardens in place of *Shirakawa* sand, because pure white pebbles are too dazzling to the eye.

Awaji-kuri-ishi

Granite cobbles originally produced on Awaji island, Hyogo, are favored for their interesting, rustic appearance. They are almost impossible to purchase today, except for processed ones, which are rather harder and whitish.

Ise-gorota-ishi

Granite cobbles produced in Mie, especially favored for their rough surfaces and rustic hues. They are widely used for edging stones, bamboo fence bases , paving stones, or front stones for *tsukubai*.

The term *gorota* stands for 5cm(2") to 20cm(8") large cobbles, larger than *kuri-ishi* and smaller than *tama-ishi*. Produced in many regions.

Kuri-ishi

Traditional name for *kuri* or chestnut size stones, which are larger than gravel and smaller than *gorota*, the medium size so to speak. They are very widely used for covering the grounds, symbolizing the streambed for *tsukubai*. Place names make prefixes, such as *Awaji-kuri-ishi*. Some gardeners call them *guri-ishi*.

OTHER STONES

Tanba-ishi

A general name for stones produced in Kameoka, Kyoto, *Tanba-Kurama-ishi, Tanba-teppei-seki*, and *Tanba-tama-ishi. Tanba-Kurama-ishi* have a thick, dignified appearance, and make quality pavements, stepping stones, or shoe stones. *Tanba-teppei-seki* are used for pavements and wall coverings. *Tanba-tama-ishi* are used as monument stones or tomb stones besides garden stones.

Roppo-seki

Rock crystals which naturally form hexagonal prisms, when "peeled" from the rock bed. As a stone material, they belong to the basalt family, and are produced in Shizuoka and Yamagata. Widely used for retaining walls, stakes, fences or stairways. Easy to shape by breaking lengthwise.

GRAVEL

Gravel started to be used in the *Heian* period, and the use spread when *karesansui* gardens became popular in the late *Muromachi* Period. The first gravel practically used was *Shirakawa* gravel, produced in Kita-shirakawa, Kyoto. In *karesansui* gardens, water was depicted by laying white gravel. Therefore, whitish gravel was most favored, although pure white stones like *kansuiseki* or white Japanese marble were not suitable for their dazzling brightness. Gravel laid on the ground is usually raked into various patterns called *samon*. The patterns last longer than you expect, since the grains are large enough to stay in shape. Make sharp ridges, and light rains will not spoil the pattern.

Nowadays as the designs continue to develop, gravel in various other colors such as brown or blue are also used. An extreme example is a *karesansui* garden with red and black gravel.

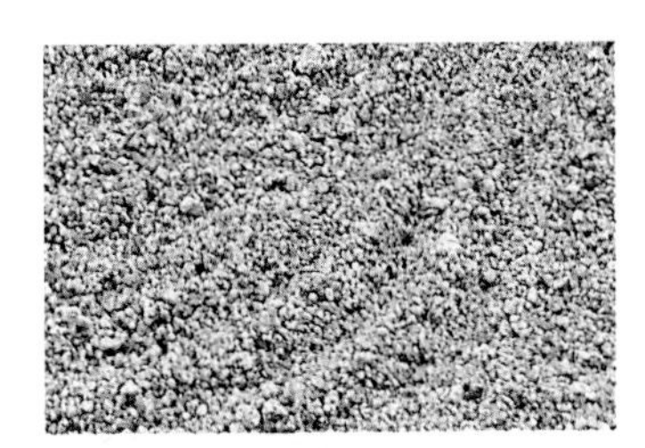

Shirakawa-suna

This name originally meant soft granite from the Shirakawa district weathered to form fine gravel. Today since quarrying is limited to preserve the environment, machine-crushed granite is on the market. Favored for its soft whitish color dotted with black grains which is peculiar to granite stones.

Mikawa-shirakawa-suna

Also granite gravel from Mikawa, the old name for Aichi. Although the product is becoming limited, the author would like to recommend this type of gravel for gardens, rather than processed *Shirakawa-suna*. Raked patterns appear very soft and pleasing to the eye.

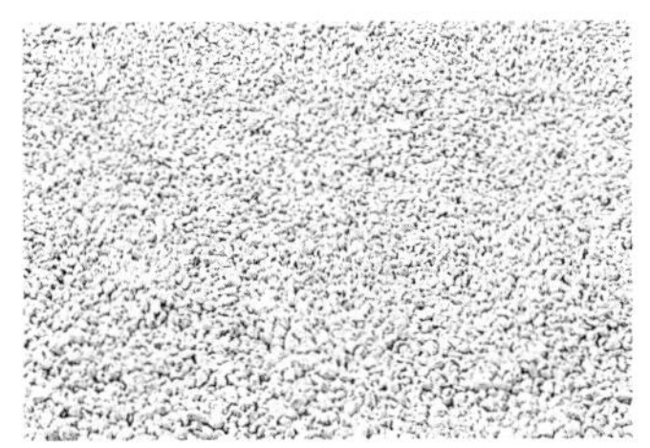

Ise-jari

Special granite from Mie, crushed into gravel. Rather soft and brownish, it turns dark when wet. It is an abundant product available in a variety of sizes and popular for use in modern gardens.

Naruto-ao-jari

Fine, blue gravel processed from the previously mentioned *Awa* blue stones. Like other gravels, this one was favored so much that other quarries "hire" the name for any gravel made from blue stones. When selecting, check for its dark blue when dry.

CONSTRUCTING *KINKAKUJI-GAKI*

Now let's make a bamboo fence. A single bamboo fence will give your garden an entirely different look. Among all the fence designs, I recommend *Kinkakuji-gaki* for your first project. This fence is a simple, low structure(approximately 50cm/1.6' in height), used as a divider or a handrail as well as a decoration.

Blueprint

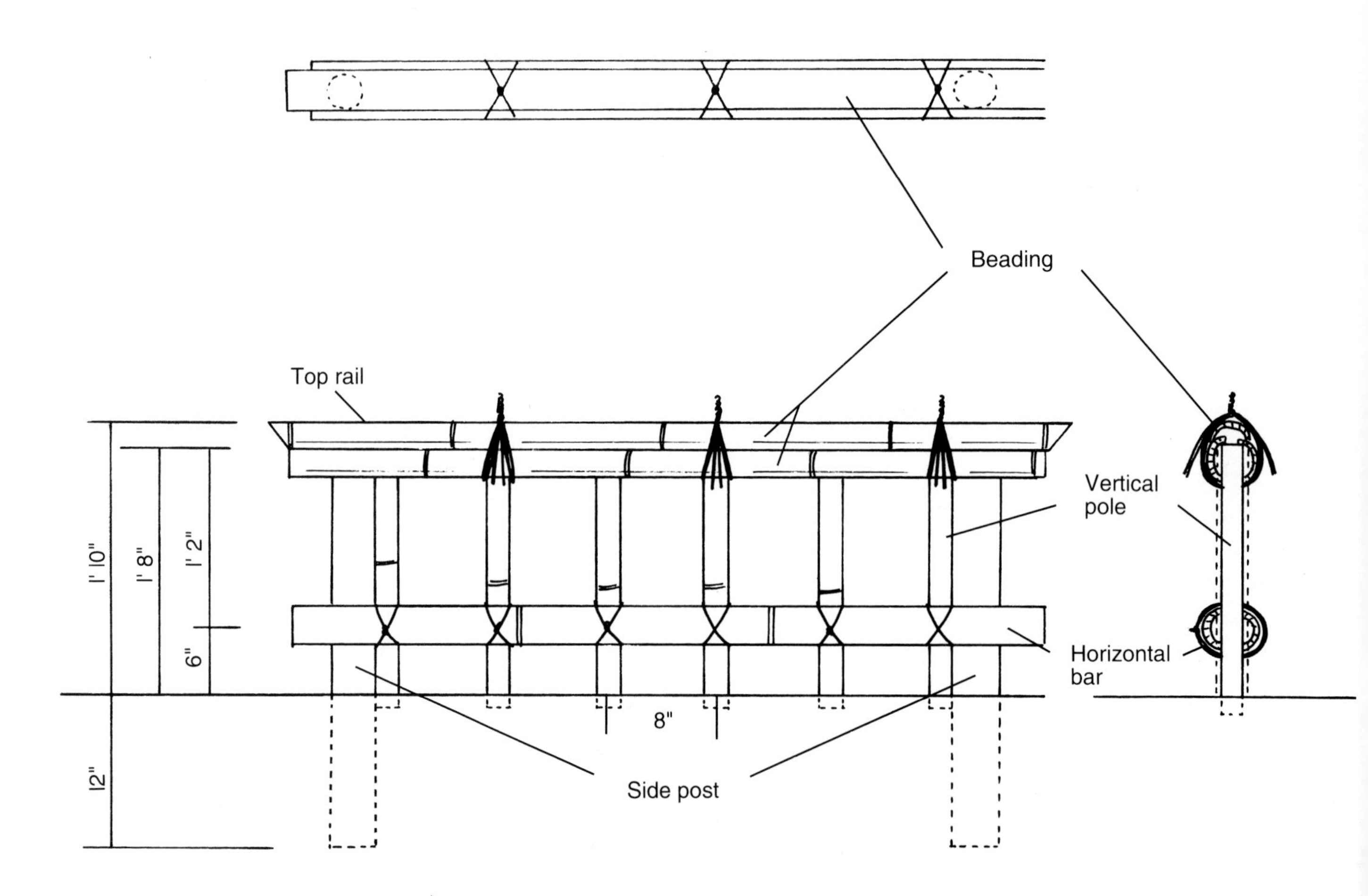

You will need:

1 x 5-6cm (2"-2$\frac{1}{2}$") diam, 70-80cm(27"-31") long scorched log

5 x 3-4cm (1$\frac{1}{4}$"-1$\frac{1}{2}$") diam, 50-60cm(20"-24") long bamboo for vertical poles

2 x 5-6cm(2"-2$\frac{1}{2}$") diam, 180cm(6') long bamboo for horizontal bar

1 x 5-6cm(2"-2$\frac{1}{2}$") diam, 180cm(6') long bamboo for top rail

Black hemp rope

Bucket, Scouring brush, Saw, Post-hole digger, Level, Red marker, Brass brush, Saw for bamboo, Hammer, Wooden mallet, Hatchet, Lineman's pliers, Wire, Ataritori, Chisel, Nail, Bevel grind knife, Drill

1 Clean shop-bought scorched logs: Soak a brush in water and wash off the soot on the surface. This way the carbonized outer surface will be removed.

2 From the cleaned log, make 2 side posts of 90cm(3') length each. When cutting, hold the saw at right angle to the log surface.

3 Dig a hole using a post-hole digger . Work vertically to make approximately 50cm (20") deep hole.

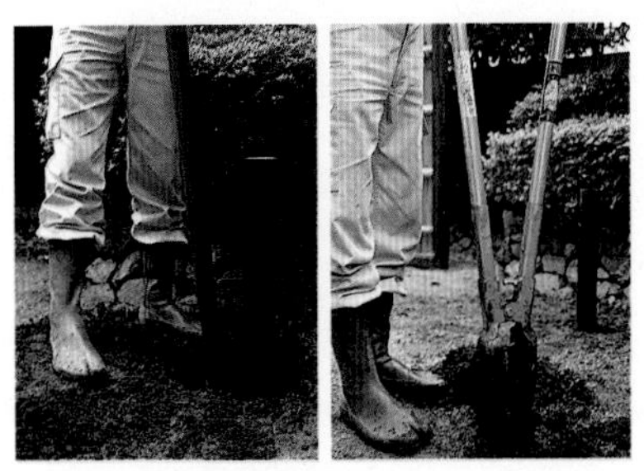

4 Check the hole by putting a side post about 30cm(12") deep from the ground, and by filling the bottom with pebbles or soil. If the post is stable, make another hole the same.

5 Lay a long board on the posts. Using a level, check that the heights of both posts are the same. If not, hammer down to adjust.

6 Place the board between two posts, and mark at every 20cm(8") . These marks will serve as a guide when standing vertical bamboo poles.

7 Choose narrow bamboo stalks to use as vertical poles. Since bought bamboo stalks have dust, wash with water.

8 Wet bamboo thoroughly, and wash with brass brush. Do not put too much pressure as it may damage the surface.

9 Cut the cleaned bamboo into 55cm(22") length.

10 When cutting the upper end of the pole, cut just above the joint. This will prevent rainwater which will gradually spoil the bamboo. Make 6 poles in the same manner.

11 Set poles starting at sides. Stand one each next to the side posts. Using a wooden mallet, gently drive them down.

12 Stand remaining poles according to the marks.

13 Adjust the heights by topping a board and driving down gently to align with the board.

14 Six poles are set. Check the balance again before adding horizontal bars.

15 Next, prepare the top cover. Choose a thick bamboo stalk and wash by wetting with water and scrub gently with a brass brush.

16 Cut the bamboo stalk in two. Be sure to hold a saw for bamboo at right angle to the bamboo.

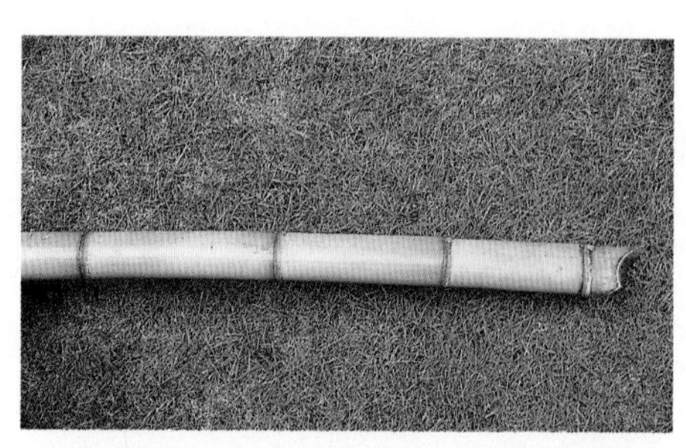

17 Bamboo stalks do not look straight from every angle. Place with the sprouting side above. This way you have the most straight line.

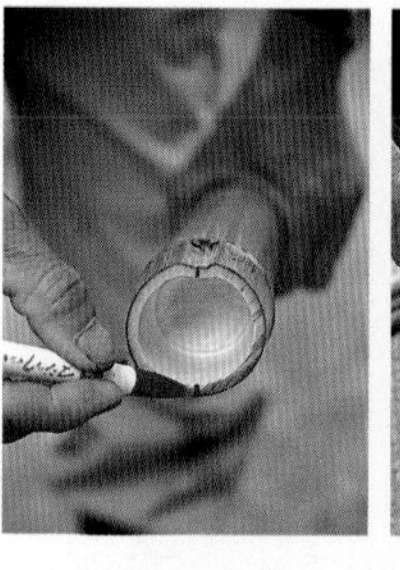

18 Split the stalk: Bamboo stalks can be easily split if cut at the sprouting points. Mark the points near the joints. Place a hatchet across the marks and drive it using a wooden mallet.

19 Precisely split bamboo stalk. The inside is very clean. Make three split stalks; one for the top rail and two for supporting bars.

20 Sandwich vertical poles with two split stalks. Cut ends, leaving the joints, in a slightly longer length than the post.

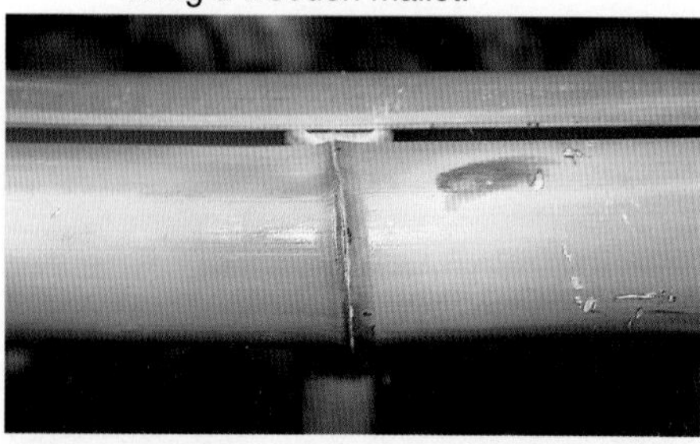

21 If the joints meet the pole, the poles cannot be covered completely. In this case, remove joints.

22 Hammer away the joints that hinder.

23 Wrap the top ends of vertical poles with bamboo halves and secure with wire. This temporary wire will be removed later.

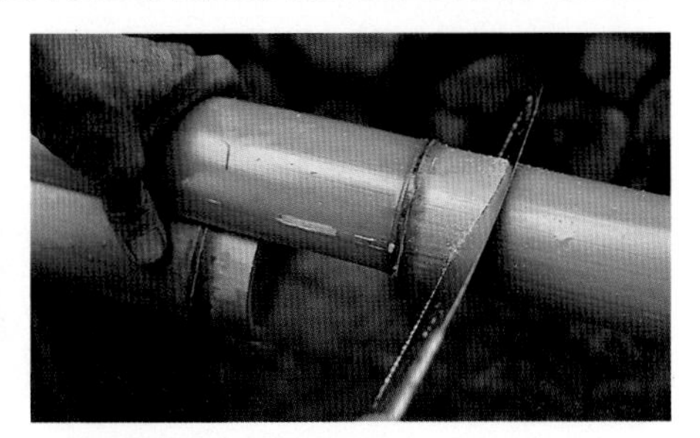

24 Place the topping half on the supporting bars, and cut ends diagonally as shown.

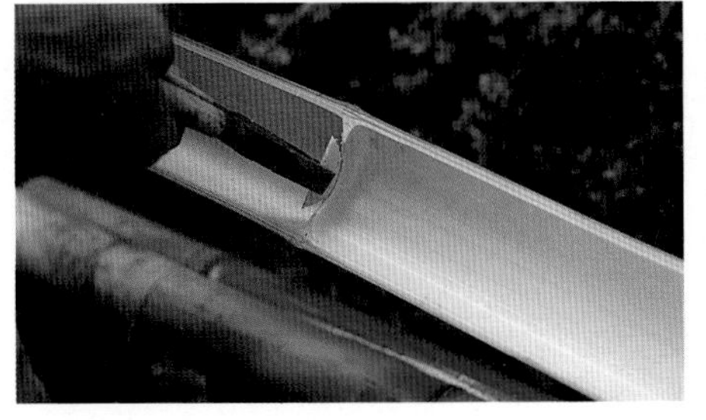

25 Using a plier, remove all the joints.

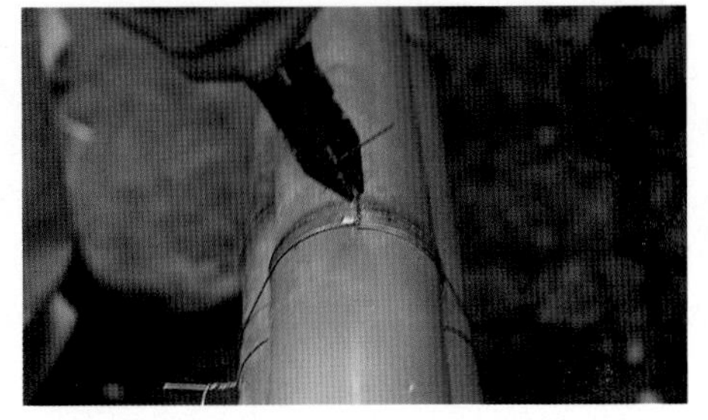

26 Bind the top rail tightly with wire, temporarily.

27 The whole top rail is temporarily set. This rail is called "*tamabuchi*" or beading.

28 Next, make the lower bar. Choose a thick stalk and split in two. Be sure to make halves from one stalk so that the joints meet neatly when put together.

29 Hold the hatchet at right angle to the bamboo, and hammer down with the wooden mallet.

30 When partially split, pull the halves apart using your foot and hands. Check that the halves are of same thickness, turning occasionally.

31 When split, trim the ends to match the upper set.

32 Remember to cut just outside the joints. Check the length.

33 If the posts are too thick, the crossbars may not touch the bamboo poles. In this case, cut out bamboo using *ataritori*, a curve copying ruler.

34 Put the ruler horizontally to the post. Transfer the curve, one spot at a time.

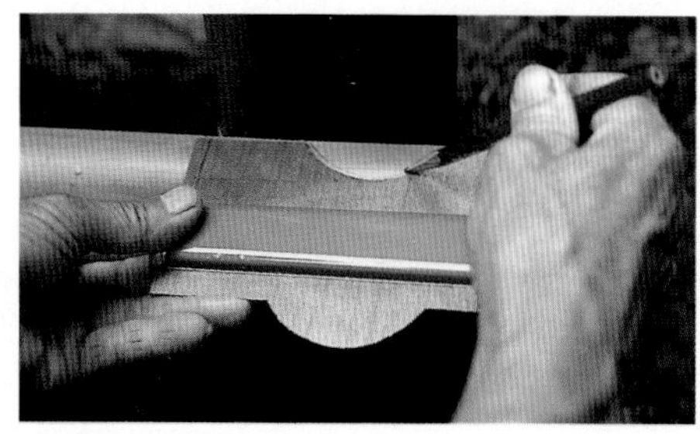

35 With the guide of the ruler, mark the curvy line on bamboo. Mark the underside as well.

36 Start shaving the bamboo by hitting a chisel with a hammer.

37 Shave with a knife to make a smooth curve.

38 Both sides are cut out.

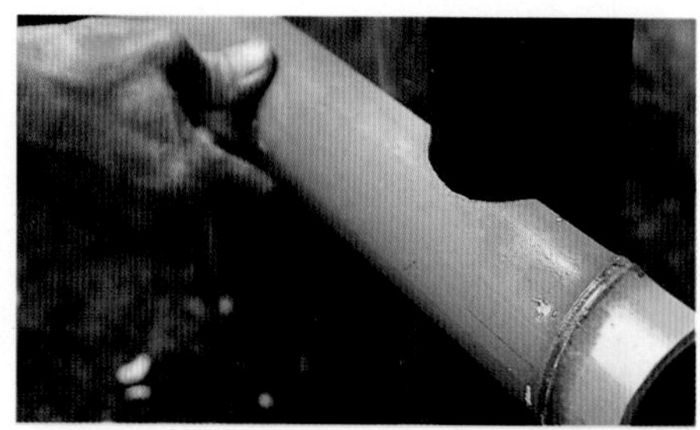

39 Check the curve by holding the bamboo against the posts. If the straight sides touch the vertical poles, cut out the other end in the same manner.

40 When two halves are prepared, bind one to the poles using wire, temporarily, but tightly.

41 Bind the other half as well.

42 Now cross bars are set from both sides, temporarily.

43 Secure the upper bars. Remove the top rail to pierce the halves. Using a drill, make one hole at the end of each half.

44 Set nails and hit just until the halves are stable.

45 Hammer the nails carefully. Excess strength may split the bamboo.

46 Next, pierce a hole at each end of the top rail.

47 Nail the rail down to the wooden posts.

48 Now the top rail is secured.

49 Using a drill, make holes in the lower bars.

50 Nail the bamboo on the wooden posts.

51 When all four corners are secured with nails, remove the wire.

52 Using hemp rope, bind the vertical and horizontal bamboo stalks; start at the second pole, and bind every other pole in *ibo-musubi* knot. See page 34 for *ibo-musubi.*

53 Bind the remaining poles from the other side, so that the knots show on every other pole.

54 Check if the knots are all in the same position.

55 Now the lower bars are finished.

56 Finish the top with decorative knots. Use triple rope together for a neat look. See page 35 for decorative knot.

57 When all the knots are done, wipe off dirt with damp cloth to finish.

IBO-MUSUBI KNOT

This knot is also called *otoko-musubi* (male knot) or *yuibo.*

In order to show the procedures clearly, a special rope is used here. The right half of the white rope is dyed red to show the contrast.

1 Pass the left-hand end(white) under the bar, upwards.

2 Pull down the end across the pole.

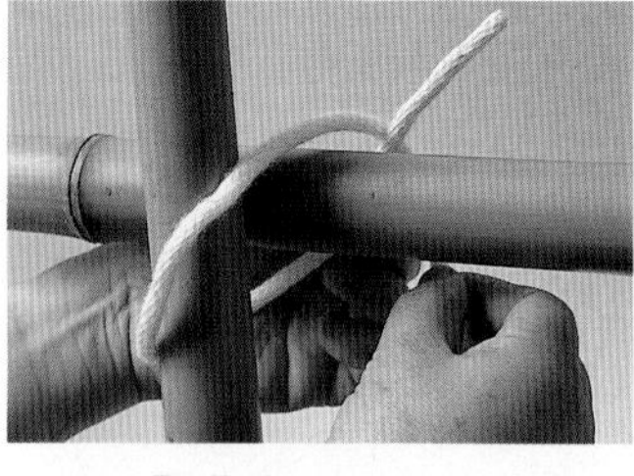

3 Pull the end up to the right so as to make a cross behind.

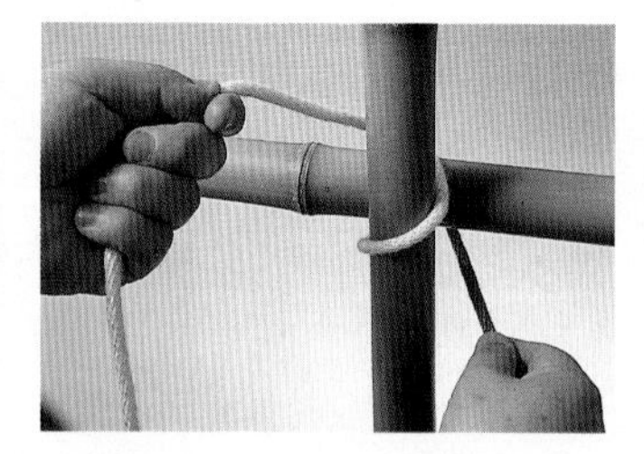

4 Tighten by pulling both ends.

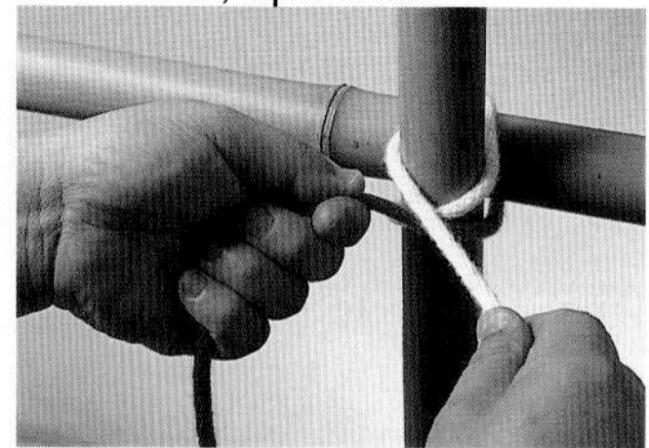

5 Bring both ends to the front and cross each other, white over red.

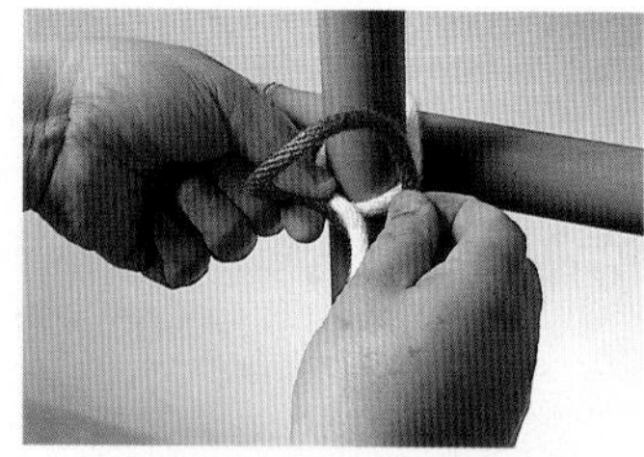

6 Holding the crossing point with your left fingers, loop right-hand (red) rope.

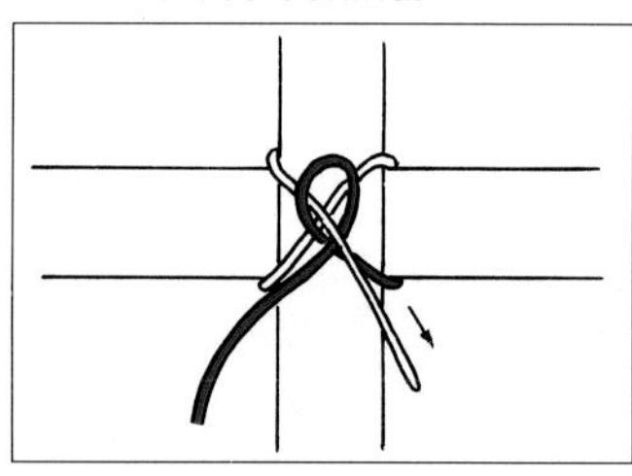

7 Pull down the white end through the loop.

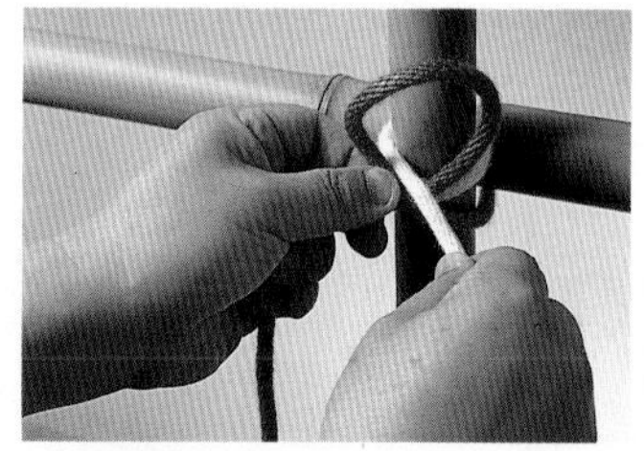

8 When pulling the white end, be sure to hold the cross of red loop with your left thumb.

9 Pull the white end tightly backwards, covering the cross.

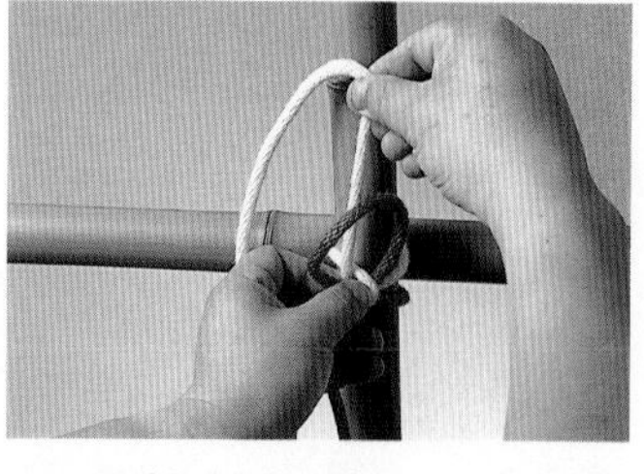

10 Holding the cross with your left fingers, change your grip and pull up the white end.

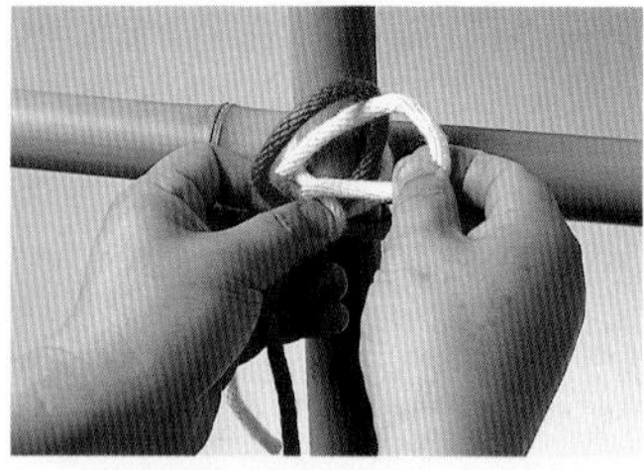

11 Bring the white end through the loop towards you.

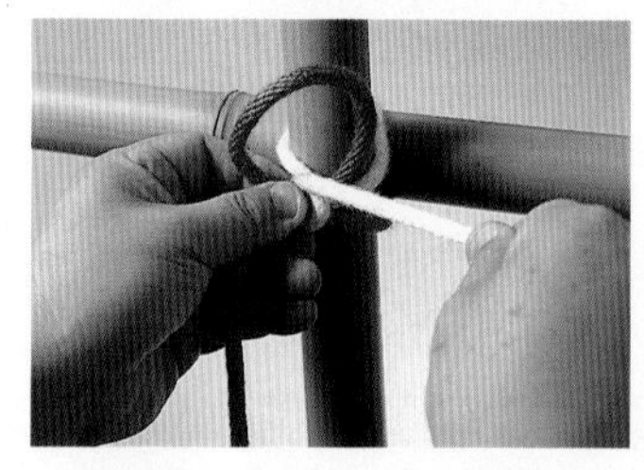

12 Pull the end tightly.

13 With your left thumb and forefinger, press the crossing point.

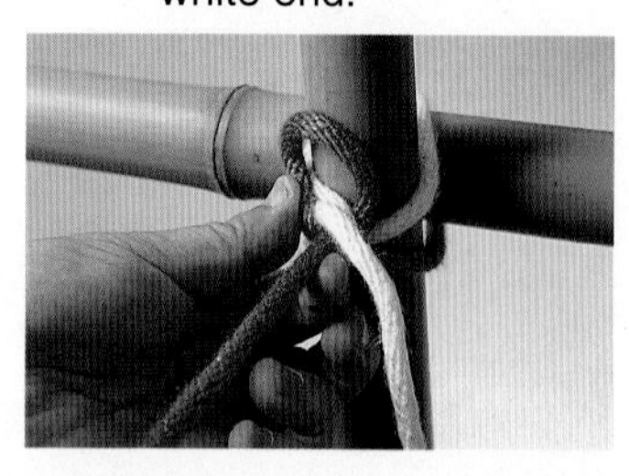

14 Pull the red end towards you.

15 A knot is made as you pull the red end.

16 Cut away excess rope.

17 Completed *ibo-musubi* knot seen from the front.

18 Completed *ibo-musubi* knot seen from the back.

DECORATIVE KNOT

In order to show the procedures clearly, a special rope is used here. The right half of the white rope is dyed red to show the contrast.

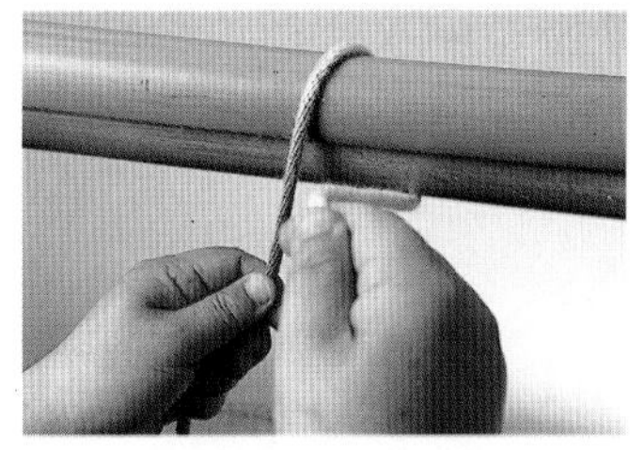

1 Pass the rope under the rail, with the red end up.

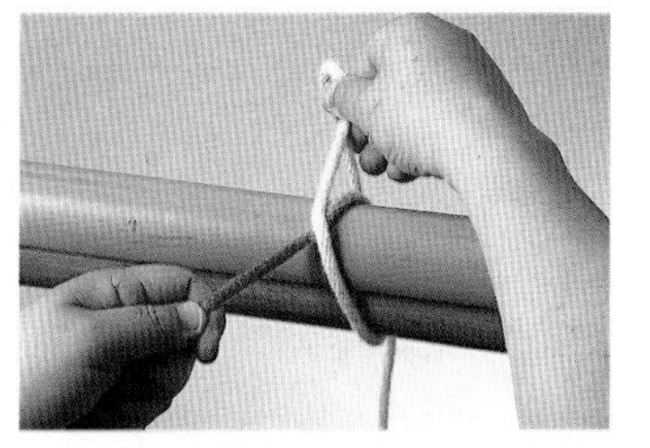

2 Make a white-over-red cross.

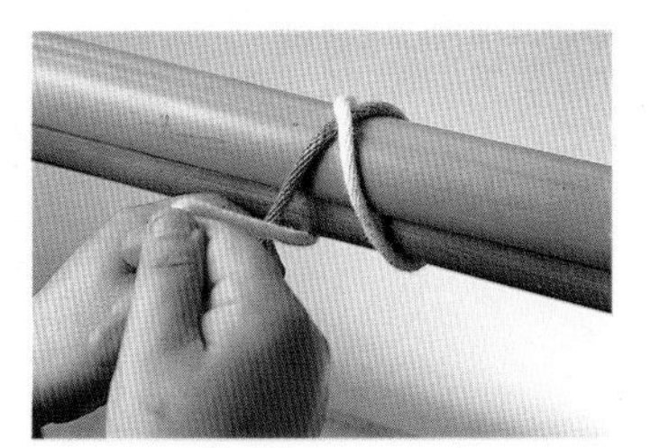

3 Bring the white end over and under the rail.

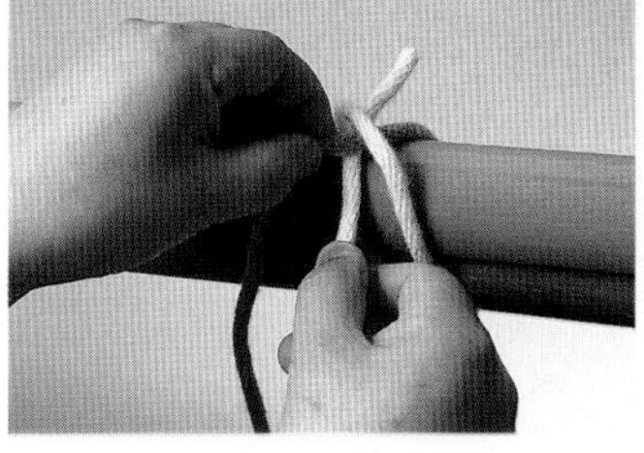

4 Pass the white end under the cross, away from you.

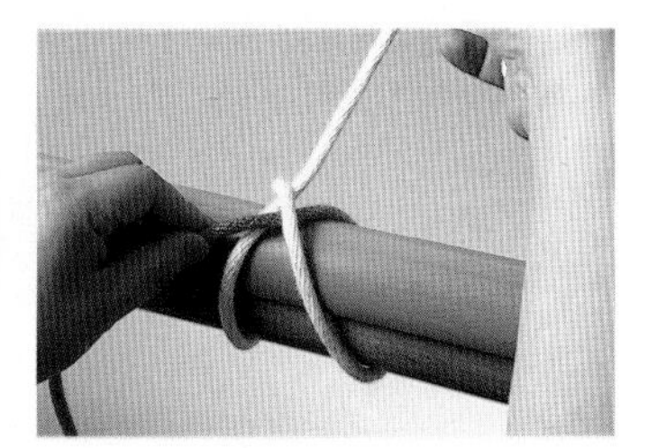

5 Now the white end is passed through.

6 Tighten the cross by pulling both ends.

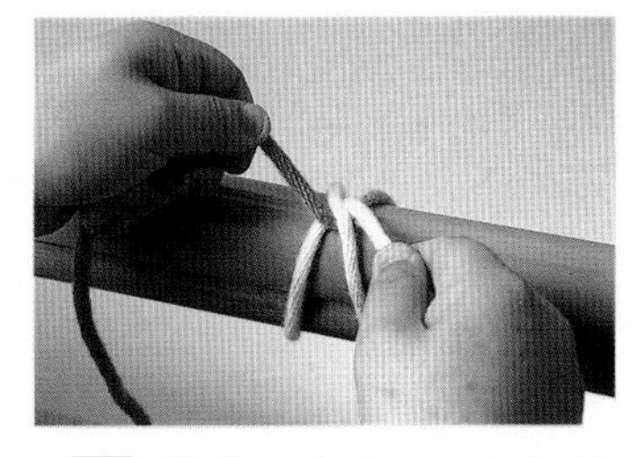

7 Pull ends towards both sides to make a "*tokkuri-musubi*" tie.

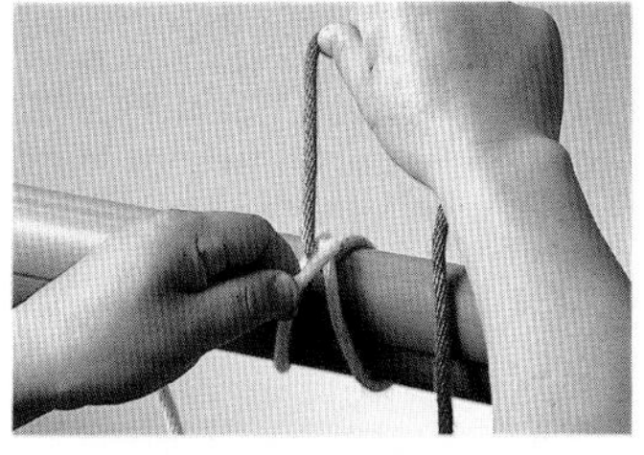

8 Hold the white with your left hand, the red with your right hand. Pull the red upwards.

9 Make a loop, ending underneath the white.

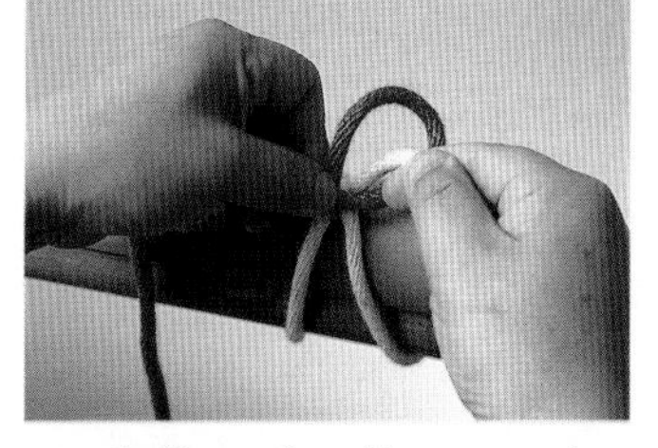

10 Pressing the crossing point with your left fingers, pull the white end tightly.

11 Then pull the white end downwards to the left.

12 Pass it under the red and then upwards, tightly.

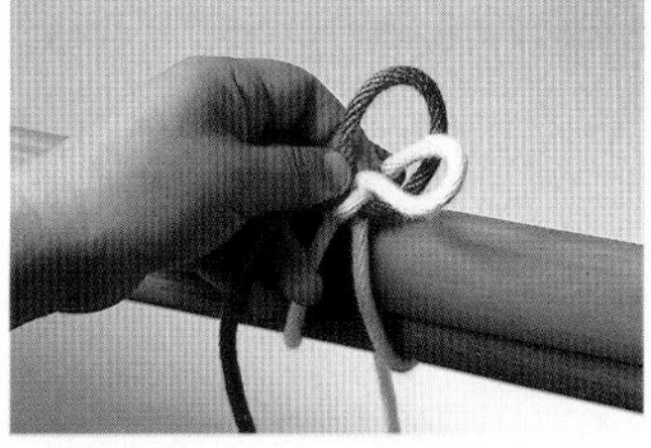

13 Pull out a loop of the white through the red loop.

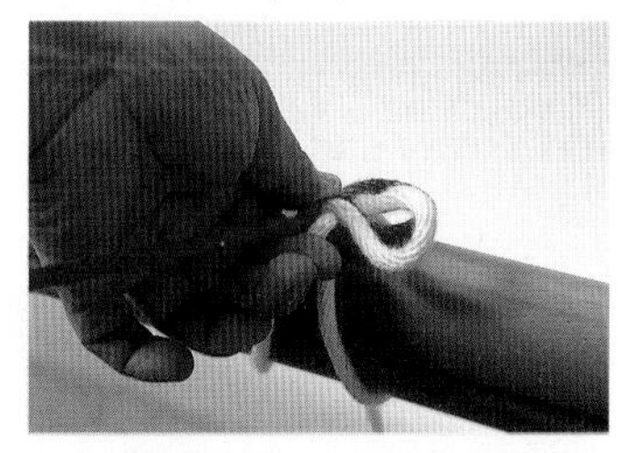

14 Holding the crossing point with your left fingers, pull the red end.

15 Tighten until only the white loop remains.

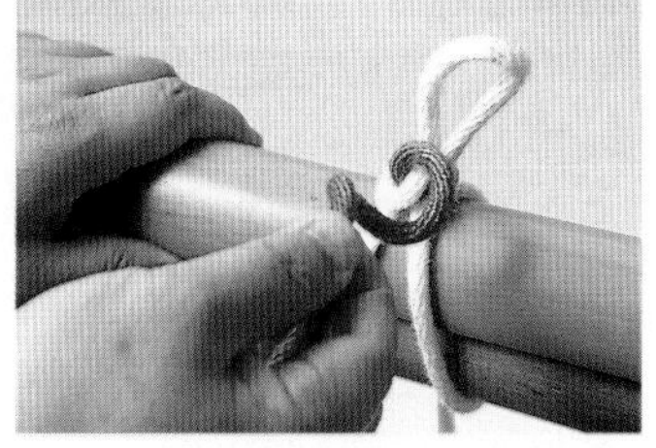

16 Twist the red near the knot, tightening the twine.

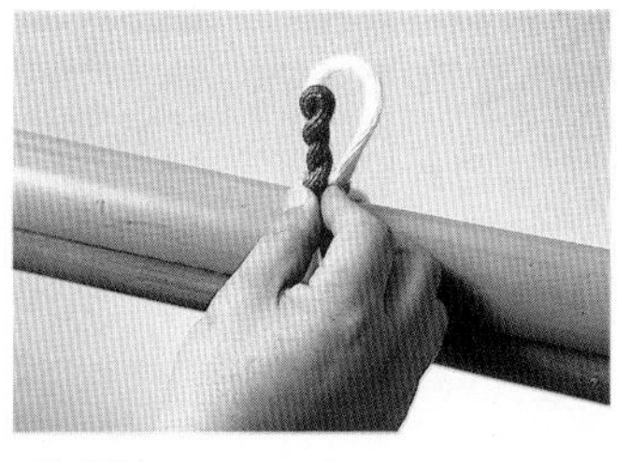

17 Hold the twisted red as shown.

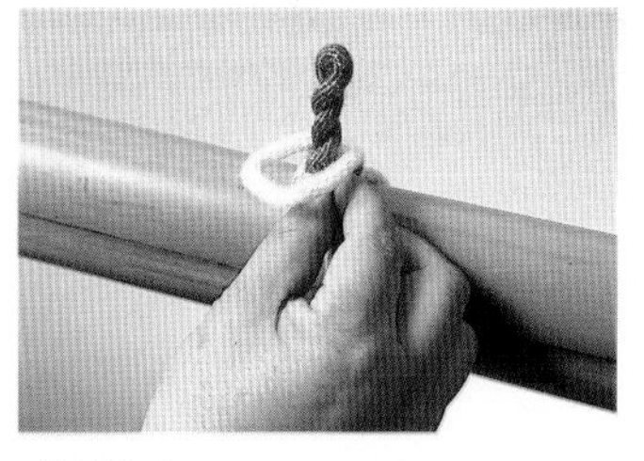

18 Bring the white loop over the twist.

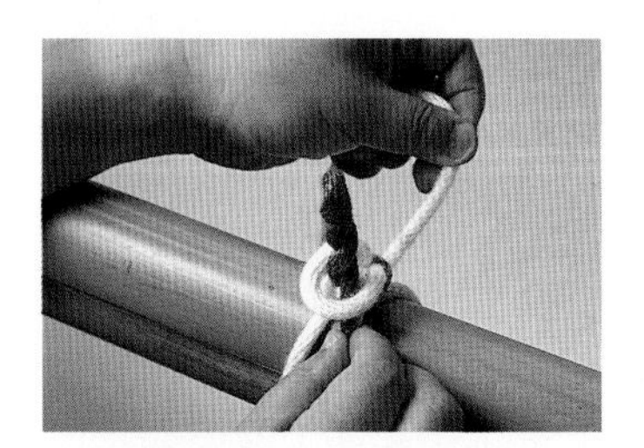

19 Pull the white end away from you.

20 With the red end, make a loop.

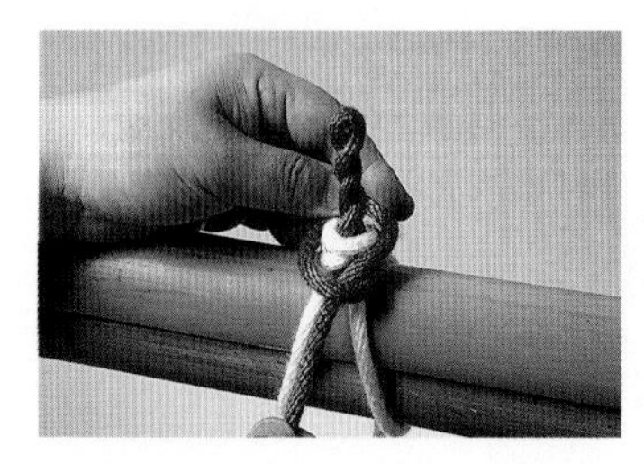

21 Pass the red loop over the twist.

22 Tighten the base by pulling the red end down.

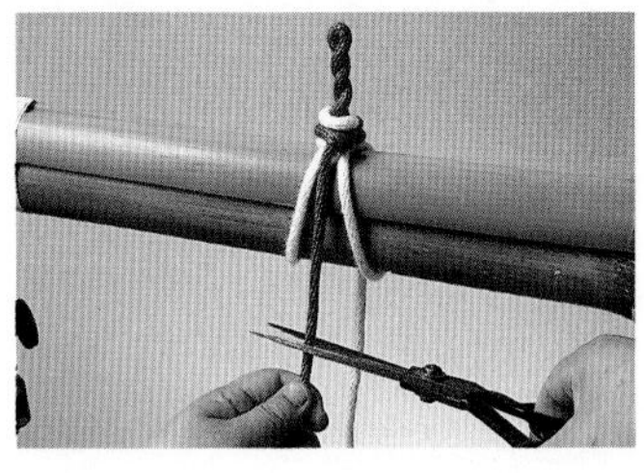

23 Trim away excess rope.

24 Finished knot.

Practice the knots using a cotton rope as above, then try with the black hemp rope. It is unusual to work with a single strand. Use two or three strands together so that it looks nice and also stay secure and durable.

1 Hemp rope is sold in two styles: hanks and "balls".

2 Soak hemp rope in water thoroughly. The fibers of hemp will be softened by this process and easy to handle. Besides, the ties are secured when dry.

3 Take out the rope from water. Now it is ready to use.

Points of Reference

No matter how large or how small the garden is, the principles of gardening stay the same. However, a small scale garden would require more ideas and techniques than a larger one, because of the limited space. Generally speaking, a garden can be divided into several sections according to the location of the building: main garden, front garden, courtyard garden, alleyway garden, and kitchen garden. *Tsuboniwa* and other small gardens used to be found only in minor locations such as alleyway gardens or kitchen gardens. Since it is becoming more and more difficult today to allocate space to gardens, small gardens, if they exist at all, often end up being occupied by cars or bicycles. Thus it is the trend of the modern times that even the main gardens are constructed as small gardens. Actually some houses have no larger gardens than the front ones, which may seem unbelievable in comparison to some spacious Western gardens, but at the same time it must be agreed that the Japanese style of garden making has turned the smallest gardens into grand, refined landscapes.

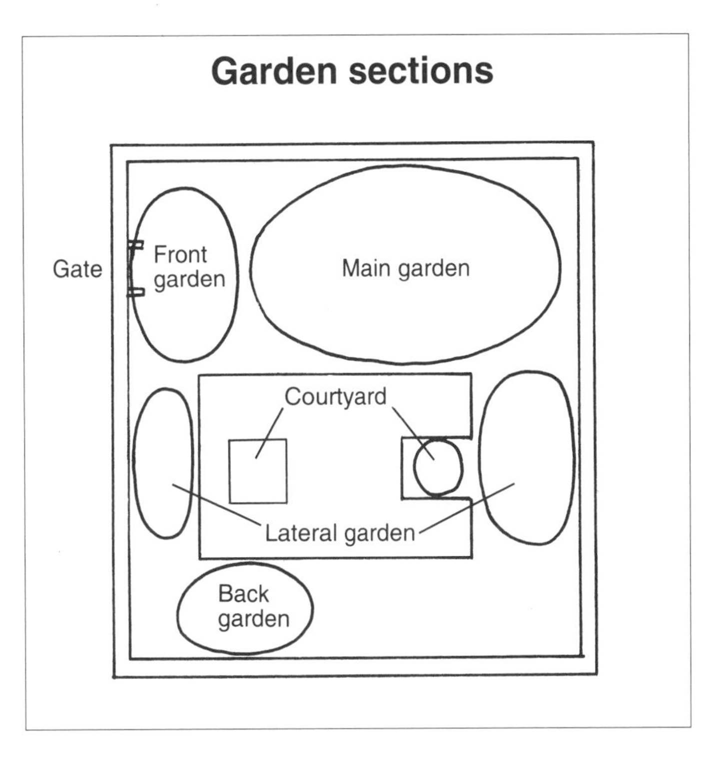

In garden construction, it is important to design each section in consideration of its function. If you are making a new front garden, the walkway from the gate to the front door should be designed for function rather than for scenic beauty, whereas the main garden should be designed as an artistic landscape or a reflection of nature. In other words, do not lay stepping stones in the front garden because it is dangerous to step on them on a rainy day or in the dark. On the contrary, conceive other gardens to be the framed pictures you choose for your rooms. The more hectic our life becomes, the more peaceful moments we need. For example, it is becoming popular these days to make a small garden to gaze at from the bathroom. Whatever garden you are making, it should reflect your own taste. Decide your own goal before you move.

History of *Tsuboniwa*

You might have heard of "*The Tale of Genji*" or "*The Pillow Book*", the ancient Japanese literature written in the *Heian* Period when *Kyoto* was the seat of Government. These texts introduce the term "*tsuboniwa*" with examples of "*Fuji-tsubo*", "*Kiri-tsubo*" and so forth, meaning " courtyard planted with wisteria" and "courtyard planted with paulownia trees". These small quadrangles were viewed with pleasure by the women who lived next to them. This type of *tsuboniwa* can still be found in such places as the Kyoto Imperial Palace.
Later, in the *Muromachi* Period, a new style of garden appeared from among the *Zen* sect temple gardens. It is called *karesansui*, which use stone arrangements and white sand to symbolize their spirit in a limited space. Eventually, the *tsuboniwa* and *karesansui* adopted each other, and later, the concept of the tea garden was added to complete its distinctive style. Now, attention is being focused on the old private *tsuboniwa* left in Kyoto and other old districts, as the ideal gardens of today.

Designs of *Tsuboniwa*

Japanese gardens have created their own aesthetics by displaying natural materials in subdued colors, which could be related to the sense of *wabi* or *sabi.* However, Japanese gardens are not just copying nature or minimizing it. They see a heart-warming, spiritual beauty that surpasses nature.
The biggest influence on Japanese gardens was brought by the tea ceremony starting in the *Momoyama* Period. Tea gardens were practically used to give ceremonies and as a matter of course, the gardens were equipped with stone lanterns, water basins, paving and stepping stones. The use of stone lanterns and stone basins was epoch-making because items of artificial beauty had never before been placed among the natural materials. These stone-made components are essential to *tsuboniwa* and other small gardens, and success depends on the effective use of them.

Enjoying *Tsuboniwa*

Once you make your own *tsuboniwa*, you will feel very close to it. It will be a joy for you to take care of it by removing fallen leaves or changing the water of the basin. The more work you put into it, the more you will love it just as with any other garden lovers. A garden, even a small one, will make you feel the season. As a matter of fact, in winter you will have to take out water from the basin to prevent from being frozen, which can be another pleasure to welcome the season.

Lighting is also important for *tsuboniwa*. Be sure to install a candle or electric bulb in your stone lantern. The whole garden can be lit up in many ways. Illuminate your garden from above, or from behind a stone arrangement, to enhance the silhouette and the textures of stones.

Design Tips

-Everything starts with the ground plan. Do not be preoccupied with 3D objects, and be sure to put enough time into planning the beauty of ground division.
-Keep in mind that *tsuboniwa* is basically suitable to *karesansui* with stone arrangements.
-Decide the best viewing point in the building.
-Take the space in consideration as a whole whether on ground or 3D plan.
-Harmony with the background is very important. Consider a bamboo fence or other devices to set off the arrangement.
-Do not use too many objects. Never try to make many landscapes in one garden.
-Be sure to have one main landscape in focus.
-Let the sun come into the garden, as much as possible.
-Try to design an easy care garden on the whole.
-Do not compromise with cheap substitutes. A good stone lantern or stone water basin will give you viewing pleasure for a long time.
-Consider sun, shade and water requirements before planting.
-Select trees that do not grow lower branches. Choose evergreen trees as main plants.
-Select shade-tolerant trees since *tsuboniwa* are often made in the shade.
-Avoid fast-growing trees and trees that grow too large.
-Use ground cover effectively.
-If water is desired, use a stone water basin.
-A pond is not appropriate for *tsuboniwa*, except in special cases.
-Consider draining devices carefully, as they must be dug in ahead of any other garden features.
-Avoid displaying animal-shaped objects which may spoil the mood.
-Look at your garden as an art work such as drawing or sculpture.

TOOLS FOR MAKING *TSUBONIWA*

Most technical experts say that their tools do all the work. This is true because fine workmanship requires fine tools to heighten the efficiency. For this reason experts try to obtain tools in good quality at any cost. Although amateurs need not purchase expensive tools, cutting tools such as knives, scissors, saws and chisels should be selected carefully. Blades of good quality will last longer and stay sharp. Besides, sharp tools make the work easier and prevent injuries caused by overexertion.

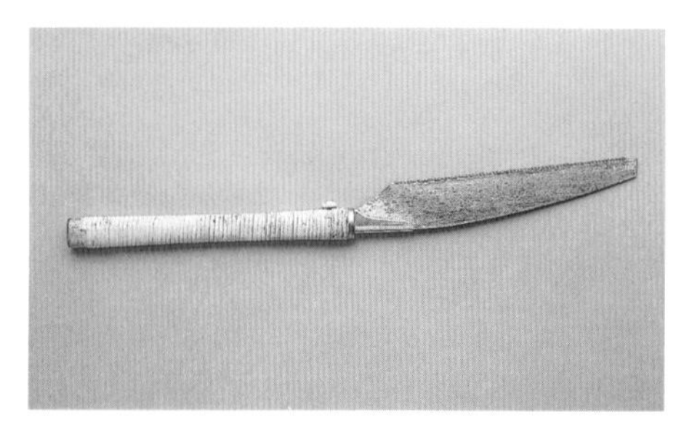

Saw for bamboo

Special saw for cutting the tough fibers of bamboo with its fine teeth.

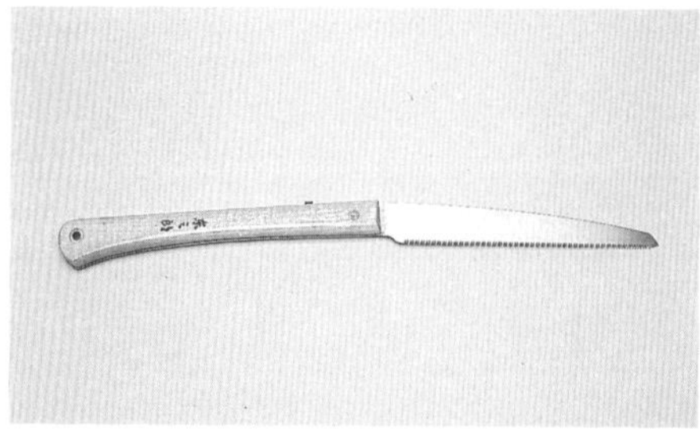

Folding saw

A handy saw which can be carried in your pocket. Some have all sorts of interchangeable blades.

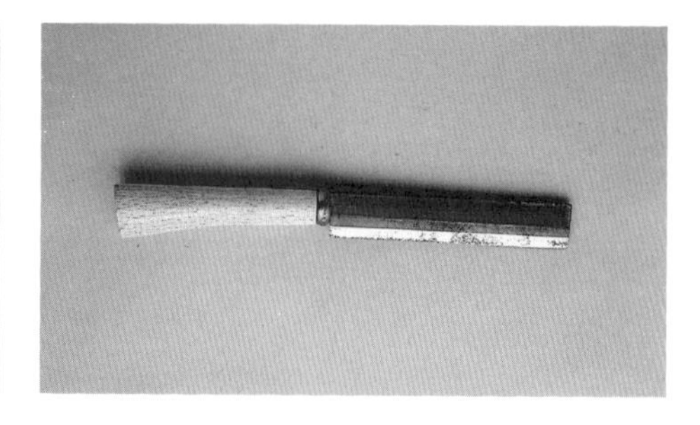

Hatchet for bamboo

Also a special cutter for bamboo. The thin blade makes a precise cut with its V-grind blade.

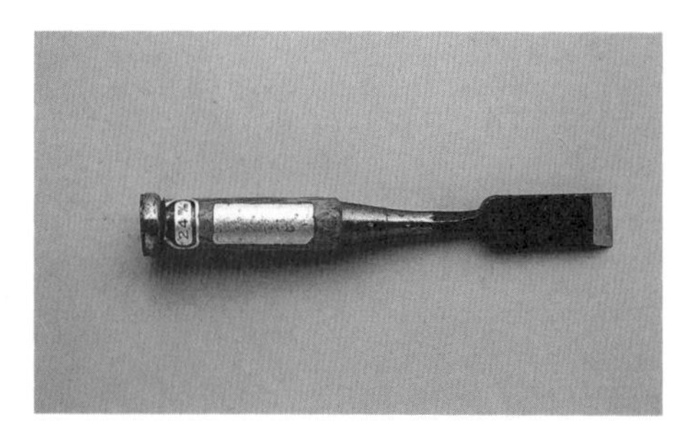

Flat chisel

Carpenter's common tool. Flat bladed chisels come in many sizes and are mainly used to make vertical grooves along the poles of bamboo fence.

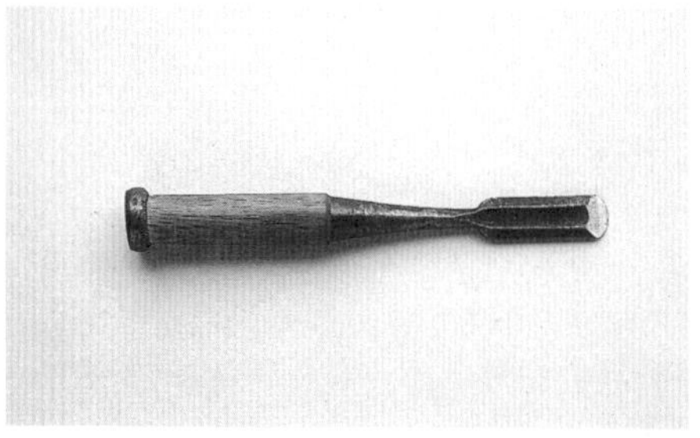

Round-nose chisel

Chisel which has rounded blade, mainly used to make round tenon holes.

Pointed knife

Small sized knife used mainly for bamboo crafts. Its long, sharp pointed blade works well when shaving or piercing bamboo.

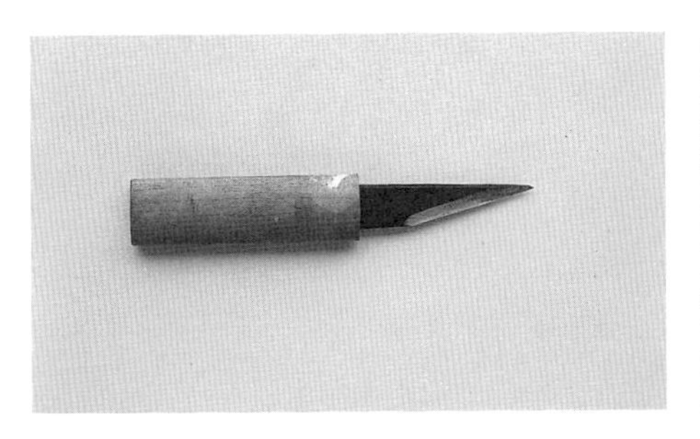

Bevel grind knife

A multi-purpose knife which is ideal for shaving bamboo. Choose the one which is not tempered too hard.

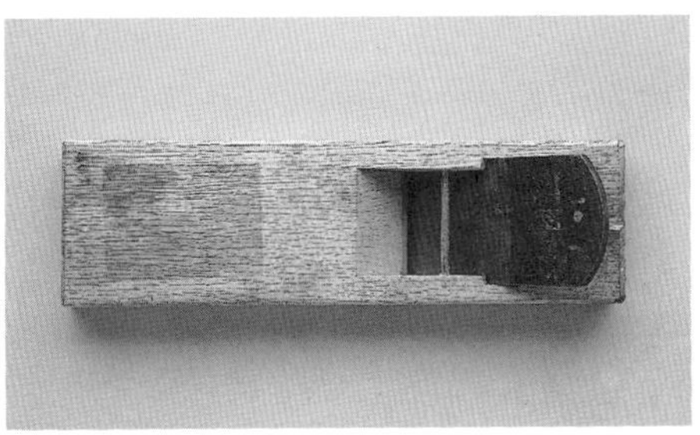

Plane

Carpenter's common plane comes in two types: single bladed and double bladed. Always use a single bladed plane for shaving bamboo.

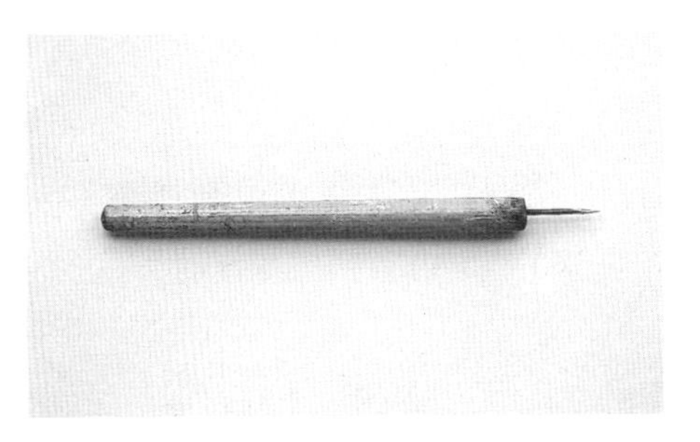

Gimlet

Comes in a variety of blades, such as four-sided or three-sided. A three-sided one is best suited for driving holes in bamboo to be nailed.

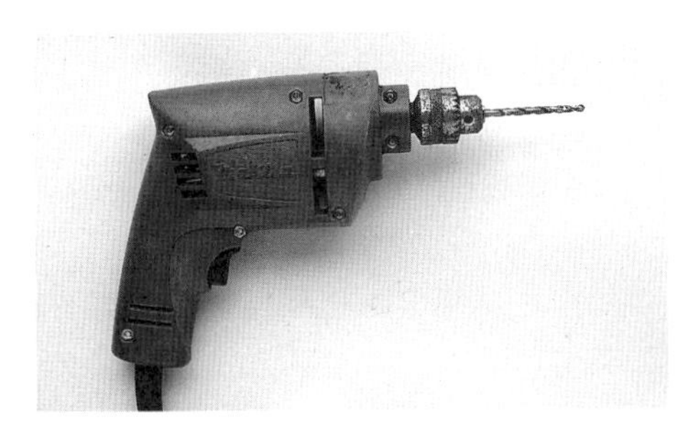

Drill

Versatile power tool used in place of gimlet. Bits are interchangeable. Some drills are rechargeable.

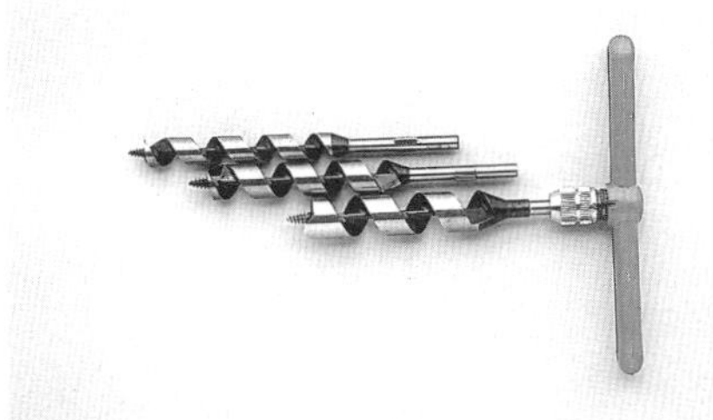

Hand drill

Can bore a larger hole in wooden posts. Portability is another feature of this hand tool.

Hammer

Comes in a variety of shapes and sizes depending on the purpose. A common carpenter's hammer is good enough for gardening.

Mallet

Wooden mallets protect the surfaces from the hammer. Mainly used when driving bamboo stalks into the ground.

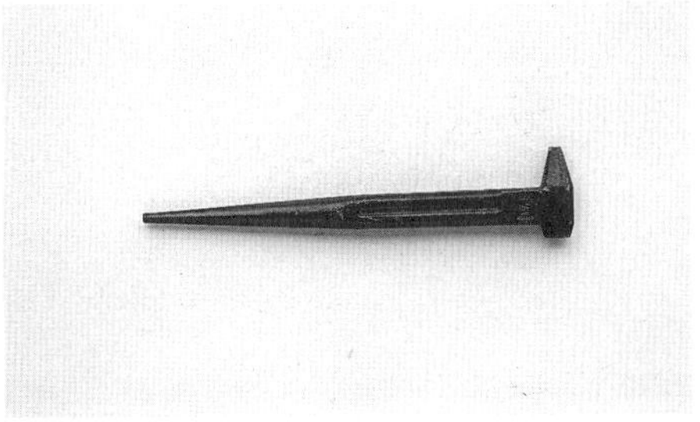

Nail set

When driving a nail deeper than the surface, a nail set is placed on top of the nail.

Ripping claw (or Pincers)

A ripping claw as the one shown above or pincers can be used to remove nails. If using a lever type as shown, be sure to protect the surrounding surface with a piece of wood.

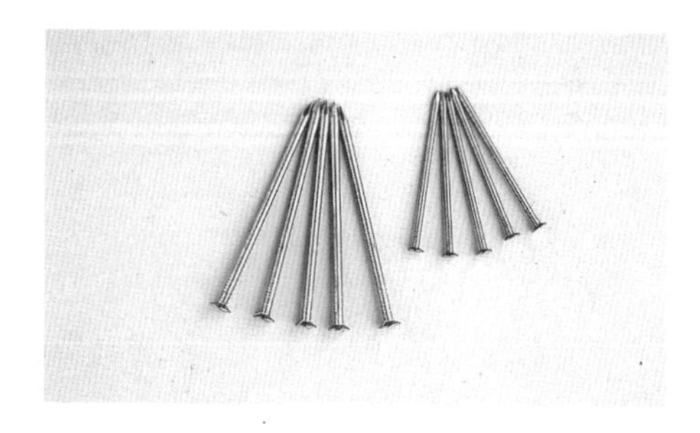

Nail

Nails used for bamboo fences come in many lengths and materials. Iron nails are the most common, but copper, brass and stainless steel nails can also be found.

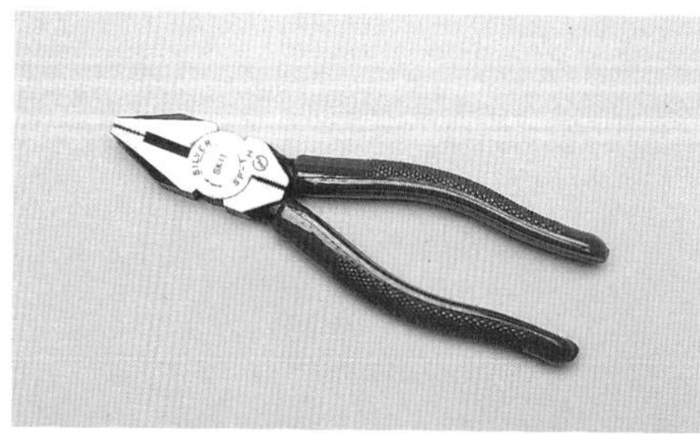

Lineman's pliers

Used to cut and twist wire. When twisting wire to secure the bamboo fence, do not twist too hard.

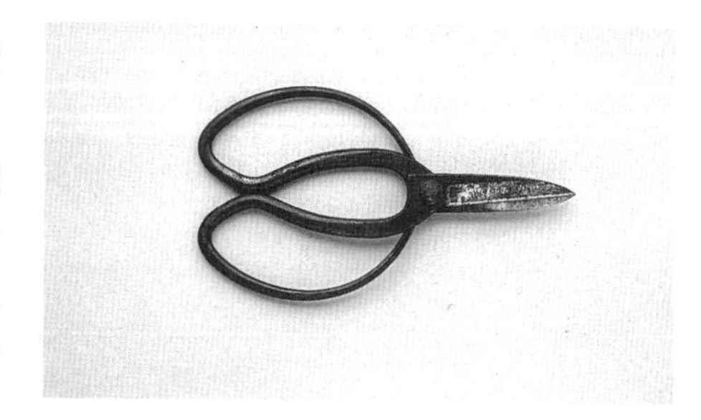

Gardening scissors

Versatile, heavy-duty scissors made specially for cutting branches and stems.

Hooked needle

An essential device for making bamboo fences by yourself. Black hemp rope is threaded through this needle, brought to the back side and tied at front.

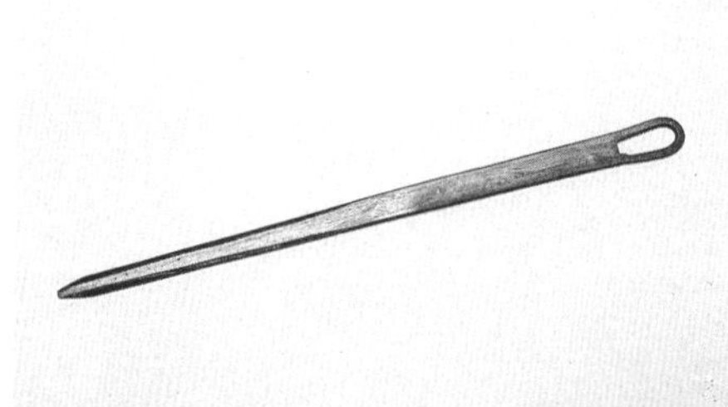

Flat needle

Another special needle for binding bamboo fences. Used when two persons thrust rope through a narrow space back and forth.

Hemp rope

Common rope used to make parcels. The bamboo poles are secured temporarily with this rope in construction bamboo fences and removed when completed.

Scouring sponge

Green bamboo stalks should be washed thoroughly before being used. A sponge for scouring is useful to remove stains on bamboo surface.

Brass brush

Brass brushes are useful for removing dirt in the joints of bamboo. Choose the softest brush to prevent scratches.

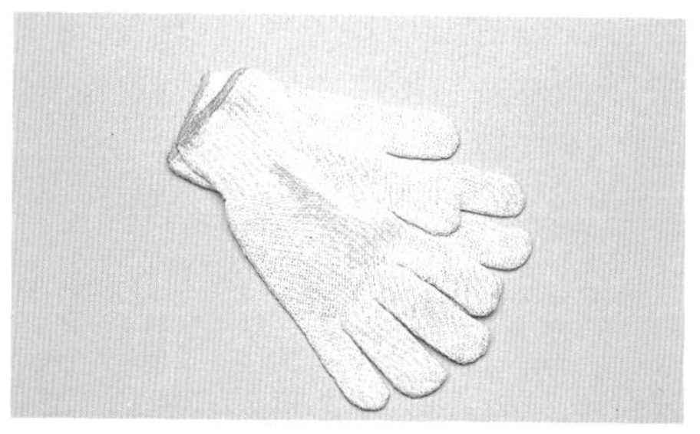

Gardening gloves

The most common gloves for outdoor jobs are cotton. A variety of gloves can be found depending on the job such as rubber-surfaced gloves.

Jikatabi or gardening shoes

Traditional working boots for workmen. Made of cotton, reinforced with rubber for light weight and safety.

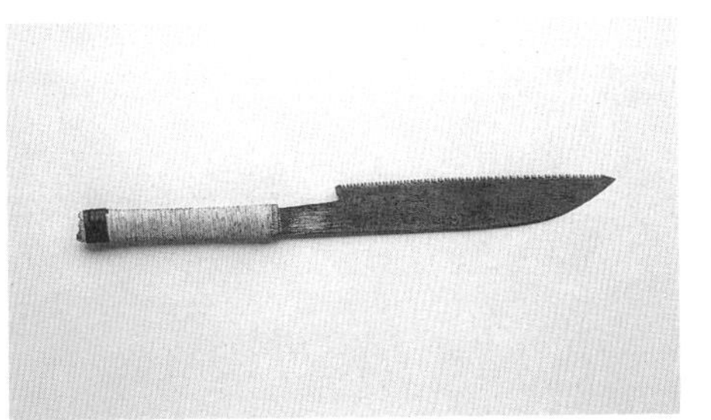

Large hand saw

Larger hand saw to cut thick branches and logs.

Leveling string

Thread or string to mark the horizontal lines. Recently available in several bright colors.

Tape measure

An essential tool for gardening because every work is based on correct measurements. The length of tape should be around 3.5m(11.5') for this purpose.

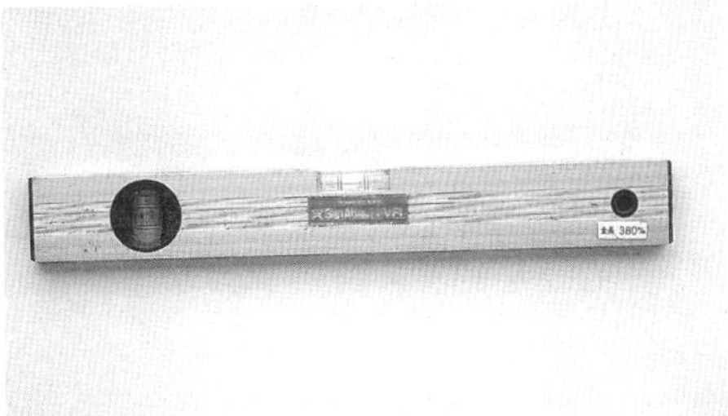

Level

Used to mark horizontal lines with leveling string, checking with bubbles. One 40cm (16") long is easiest to use.

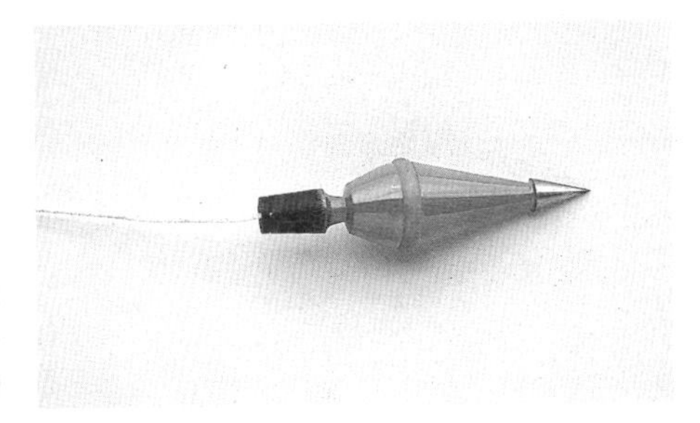

Plumb bob

Simple and the most reliable tool for marking perpendicular lines. A weight is hung with leveling string, which suggests the vertical line for setting poles.

Ataritori (curve marker)

A convenient tool for transferring irregular circular shapes on to different surfaces. Small ones are made of metal, and larger ones of fine bamboo.

Steel trowel

Used by carpenters to apply, spread or smooth mortar. For garden construction, select a trowel that is larger than the usual size. There are also wooden trowels.

Brush

Palm or hemp palm fibers are bundled into an oval shape, so that the brush can be held securely. Most recommendable for washing scorched logs because such brushes are durable.

Wooden pole (left)

A log to press down the soil. Usually cypress or other hard logs are used for this purpose. It is best to have two poles in different thicknesses.

Double shovel or post-hole digger (middle)

This is useful when digging a narrow hole to set posts for bamboo fences, because of its double-headed shovel.

Shovel (right)

Of all the various shapes and sizes, shovels with a pointed tip are most commonly used to dig holes.

Gardening outfit

When selecting clothes for gardening, safety should come first. Do not work semi-naked or with extremities exposed even in summer. Be sure to wear clothes with long sleeves and full-length pants. It is most advisable to wear work clothes , but you can wear something old. In winter, avoid sweaters or thick and heavy clothes for safety because cold weather already dulls your movement. Above all, the most important is the footwear. Comfortable light-weight shoes are essential, as well as water-resistant ones. When working with soil, avoid shallow shoes and wear rubber boots to prevent soil from getting into your shoes.

BASIC TECHNIQUES OF JAPANESE GARDENING

Making a garden yourself may sound like a huge amount of work. However, every garden has been constructed by building up one technique on another. Even a complicated-looking bamboo fence can be made successfully, by following simple instructions. In order to master the necessary techniques, the following chapter explains and guides the novice gardener in planning, preparing, and constructing the garden. There are step-by-step photographs along with detailed directions. I especially gave a generous number of pages to constructing bamboo fences since its construction requires careful attention to proper order. When you actually make your garden, several of these techniques will have to be combined.

Measuring the ground

Drawing your designs

Preparing the ground

Dividing the ground

Making a drainage system

Building a mound

Setting edging stones

Setting *toro*

Making *tsukubai*

Arranging stones

Laying paving stones

Setting stepping stones

Laying gravel

Making *karesansui*

Planting trees and shrubs

Planting grasses

Planting mosses

Constructing *Kenninji-gaki*

Constructing *Tokusa-gaki*

Constructing *Misu-gaki*

Constructing *Koetsu-gaki*

MEASURING THE GROUND

Before beginning to work, check what size of garden is possible. If you have the blueprint of your house when it was built, use this. Otherwise, measure the width and the length of your site and draw a simple ground plan. Include the heights of any walls or fences.

You will need:

Tape measure, Pencil, Set square, Compass, Note pad

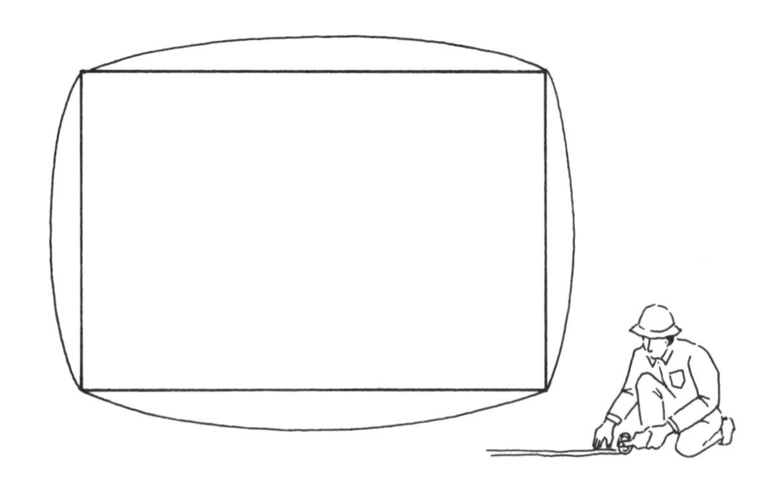

1

If the ground is rectangular, measure each side and take notes. When measuring, ask someone to hold one end of the tape. If measuring by yourself, fix the other end securely.

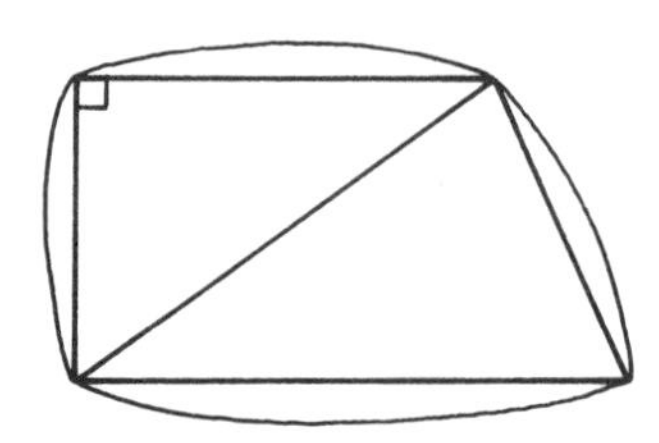

2 If the ground is of any trapezoidal shape, divide it into triangles and measure all sides and any diagonal line.

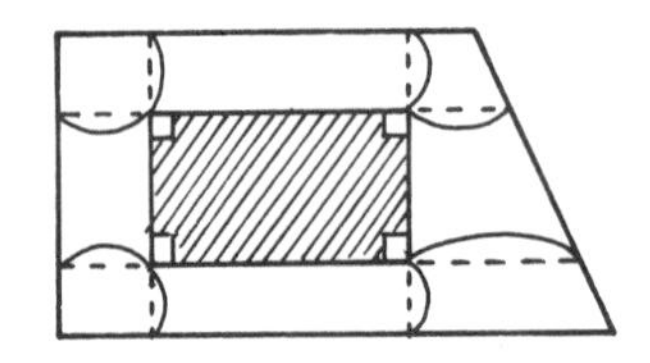

3 If there is a building next to the site, measure the distance from each side of the ground to all four corners of the building.

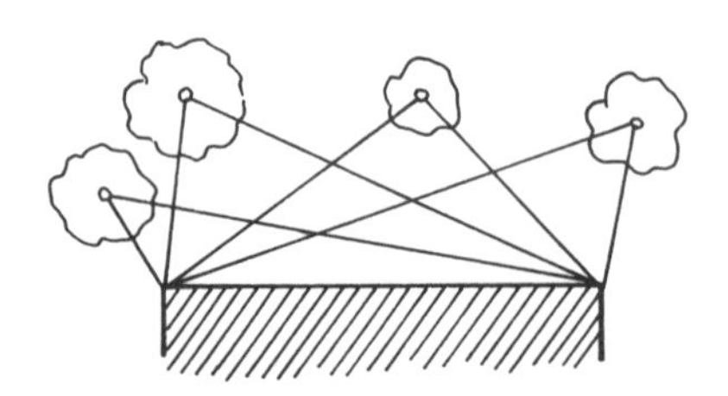

4 If there are any trees or stones and you want to leave them as they are, also measure the distances between them and the building.

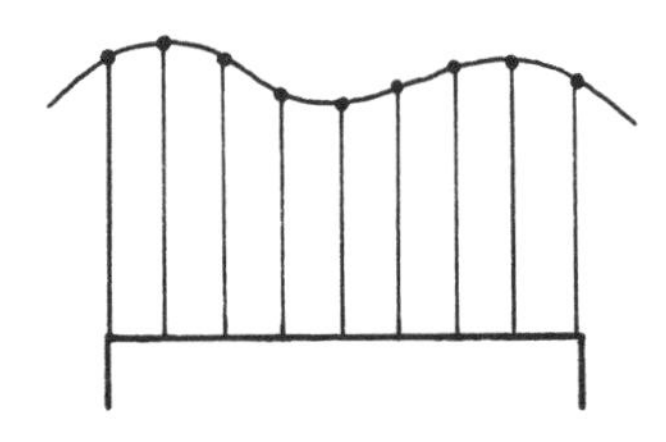

5 If there is a curvy line such as a passageway, measure the distance from the building at a certain interval.

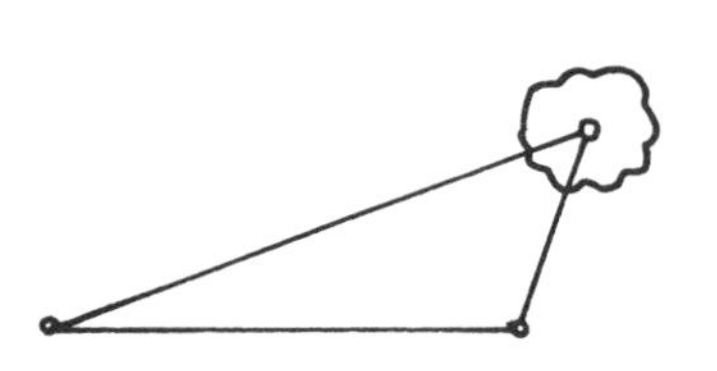

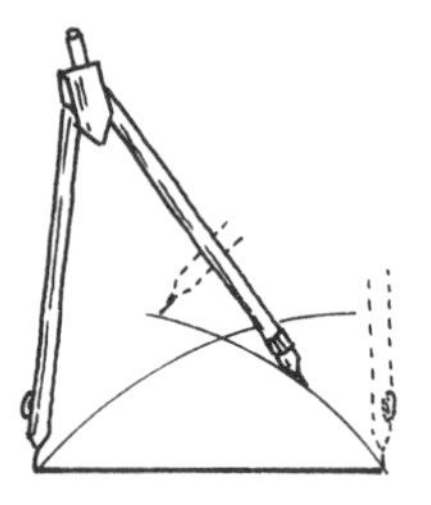

6 When drawing a ground plan, reduce the measured lengths. First, draw lines of the building which will face the garden, then draw each line. To position the trees and stones, use a compass to get an intersection.

DRAWING YOUR DESIGNS

When the ground plan is done with all the measurements, draw your design. You do not have to make an intricate blueprint the garden designers make. Just draw a guide plan for your work. Start with a rough drawing, and add bamboo fences or *toro* according to your image.
Since this plan is for yourself, you can mark with whatever you like, but following symbols might be easy and convenient.

You will need:

Pencil, Set of squares, Compass, Graph paper

- When drawing, position a room facing the garden toward you. This will make the plan easier to draw and see.
- The standard reducing rate would be 1/10 or 1/20 for small gardens, although it can be any size you like.

Gardening Symbols

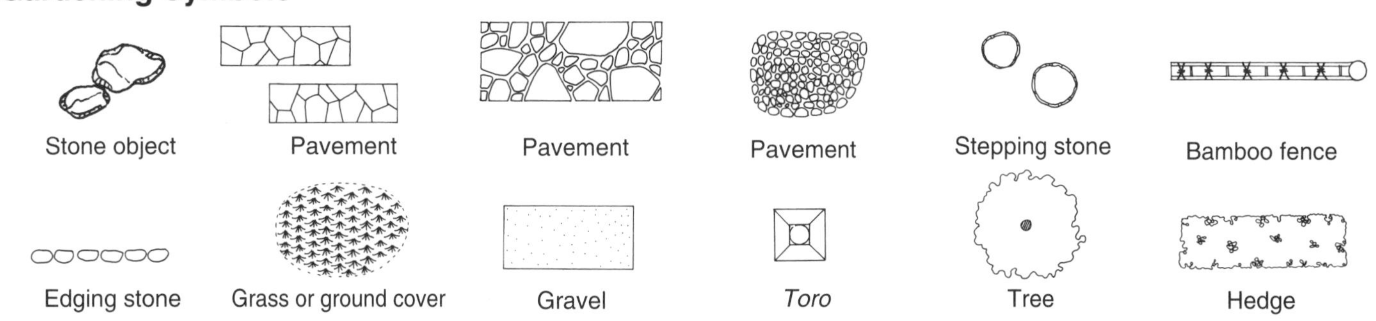

Sample Plan with Gardening Symbols

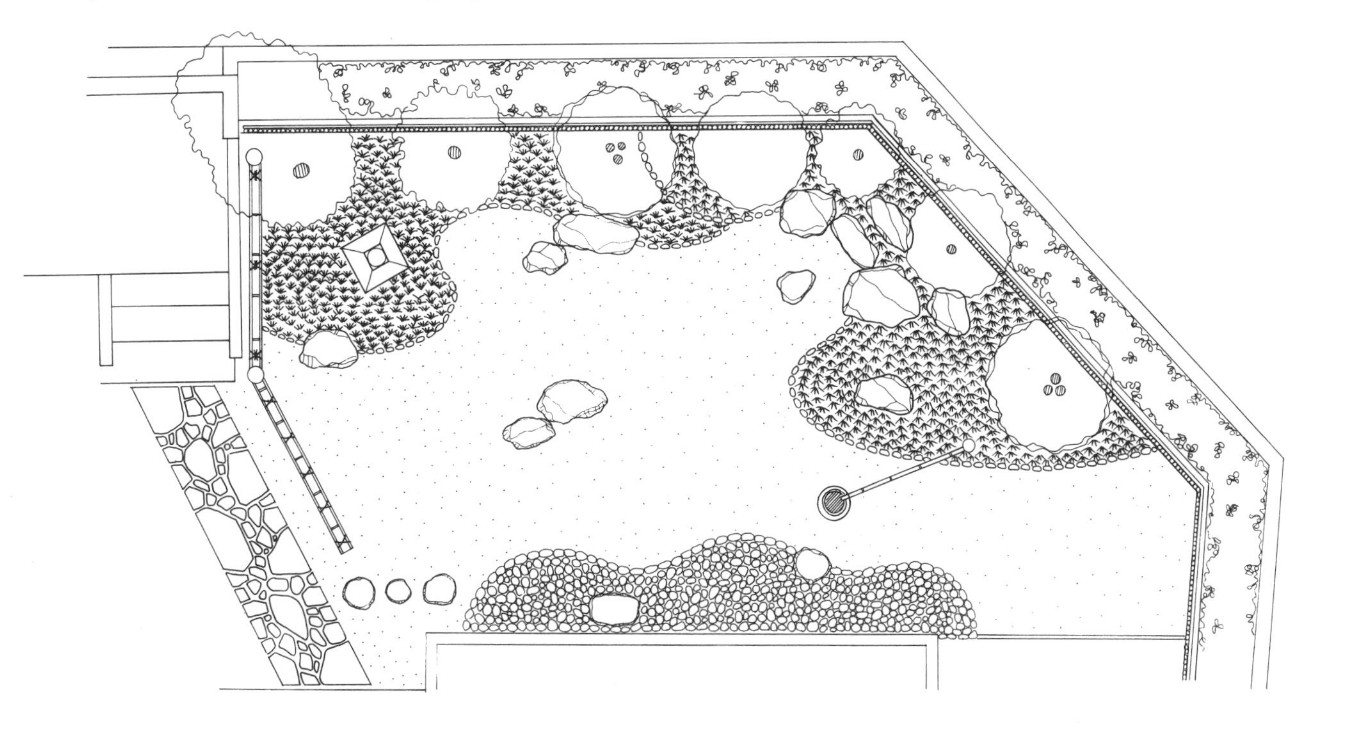

PREPARING THE GROUND

Before the actual garden construction, prepare the ground. Remove unnecessary stones and rubbish, then flatten the surface of the soil so that you can work easily.

You will need:
Shovel, Straw rope,
Hand rammer

1 Check the soil condition. If it has a greasy smell or the surface looks greasy when wet, replace the soil completely.

2 Remove any bits and pieces on the ground. Also search inside the ground since rubble in the ground may disturb the later work.

Replacing the soil
When planting trees or grasses, it may be necessary to replace the soil of the site with the soil in good quality. Generally speaking, good soil for most trees and grasses have appropriate contents of sand and clay, which results a well-draining soil. If the ground is too hard, dig out and fluff the soil.

3 If using a tree of your old garden, prepare the tree for transplanting. Mark a circle around the root, about four times as large as the trunk.

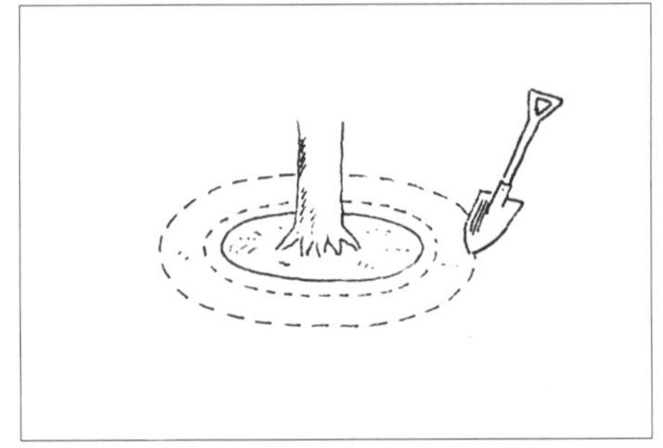

4 Using a shovel, dig a hole around the tree, starting from outside the mark. Be careful not to damage the root by digging or removing the soil that belongs to the root.

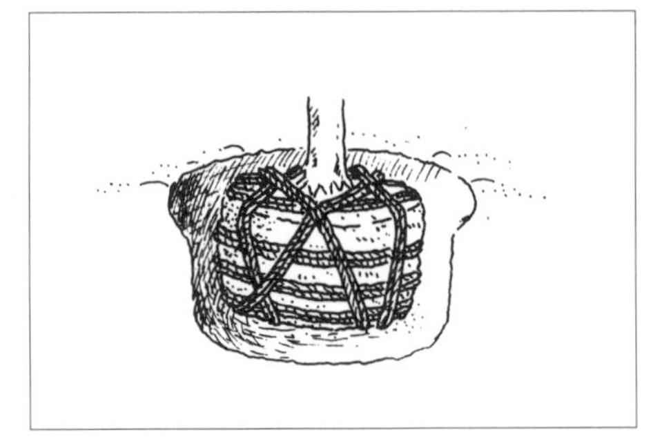

5 When dug deeply enough, cut off excess root ends in the ground. Bind the root and surrounding soil with a straw rope. Plant this in a spare space temporarily until the new garden is ready.

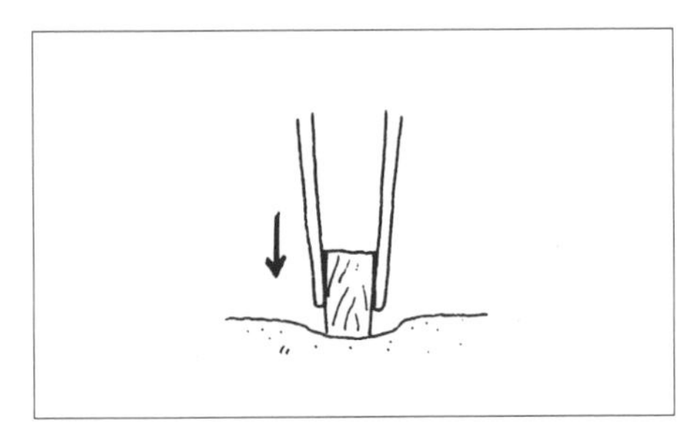

6 Flatten the surface of the ground. You can press down with a shovel, but a hand rammer will pack the soil efficiently.

7 Lift the hand rammer as high as possible.

8 Drive down the hand rammer onto the ground. Be careful not to drop it onto your feet. Continue until the desired firmness is achieved.

DIVIDING THE GROUND

After preparing the ground, mark lines to divide the ground. You can draw lines directly on the ground, but these lines may be erased during work. I suggest the insertion of bamboo stakes along the line.

You will need:

Bamboo stakes, Axe, Straw rope

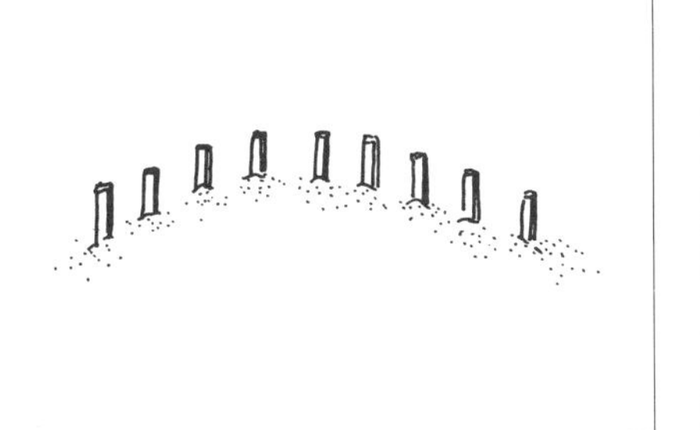

1 According to your plan, insert bamboo stakes checking the measurement. Take a look from a distance once in a while to see that the shape is balanced.

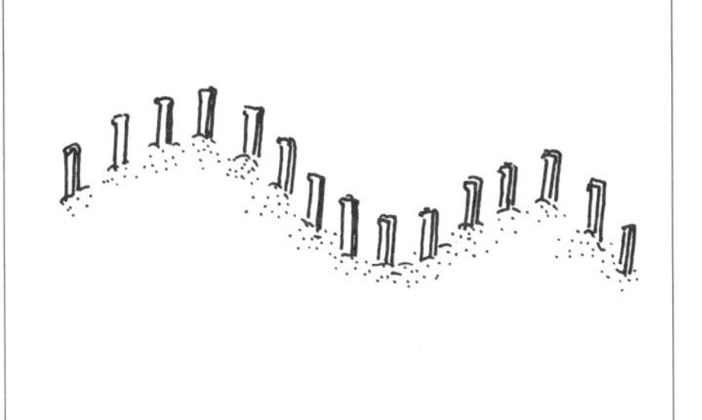

2 Bamboo stakes arranged in a curvy line. You can trace the line almost perfectly if you place the bamboo stakes at intervals of 10-20cm (4"-8").

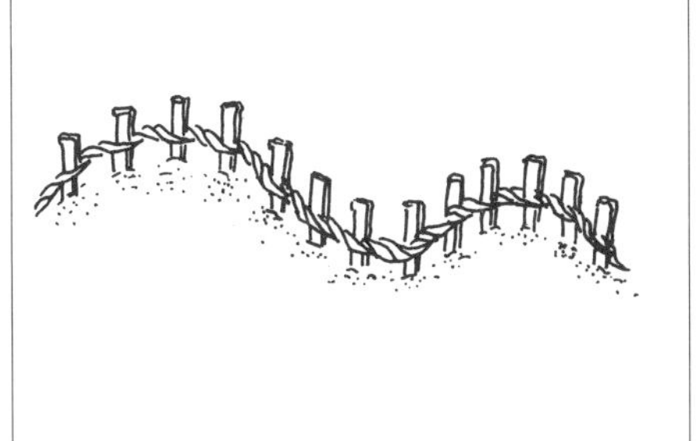

3 Link the stakes using a rope, by thrusting the stakes between the twists of the rope.

HOW TO MAKE BAMBOO STAKES

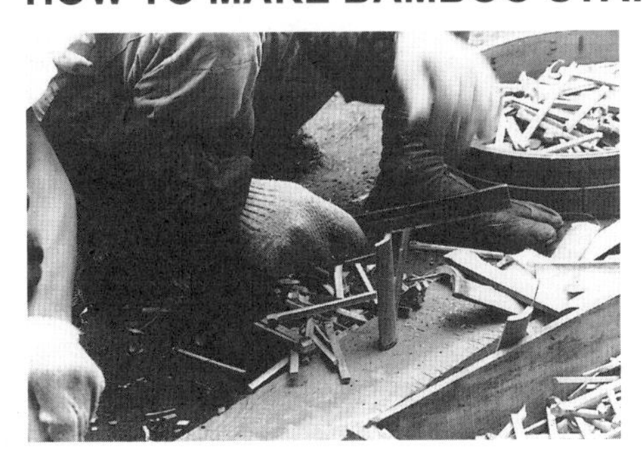

1 Using a hatchet, split bamboo into pieces.

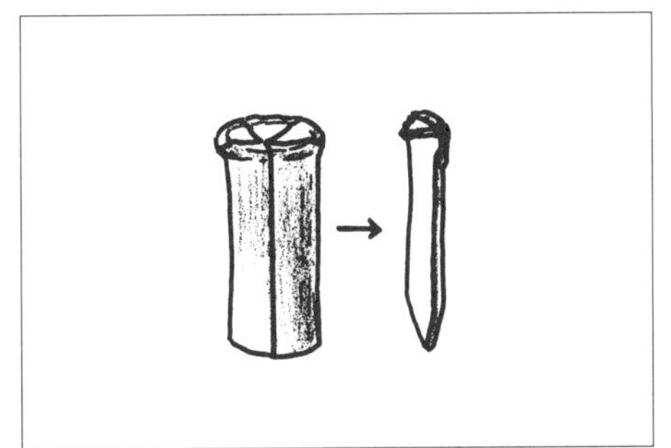

2 Make approximately 1.5cm($\frac{5}{8}$") wide stakes. Leave the joints; they will keep the rope in place.

3 Make as many stakes as you can.

MAKING A DRAINAGE SYSTEM

Drainage system for the garden is not a must. However, graveled ground may look muddy after heavy rainfall because the soil underneath will splash over the stones. If you make *tsukubai* where water flows all the time, it is essential to make a drainage.

You will need:
Drain tank, Pipe, Shovel
Wire net, Mortar

Drainage System

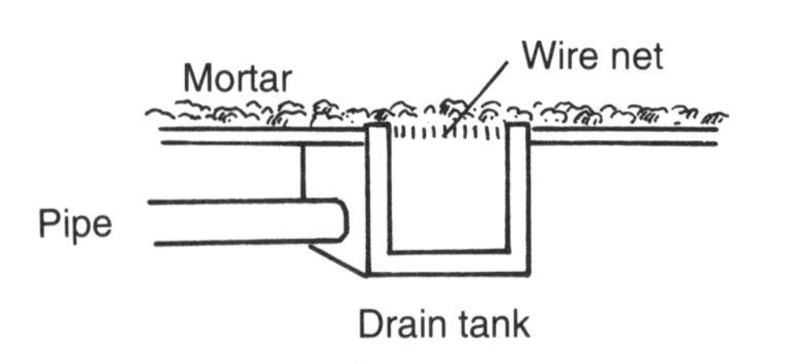

Procedure

1 Dig a hole to bury the drain tank. If the ground has a slope, dig at the lower side. If the ground is flat, take the spot where you can easily connect to the outer drainage.

2 Place the tank in the hole. Bury it deeper than the surface of the ground so that the water flows in.

3 Dig another hole to insert the pipe.

4 Set the pipe at an angle so the water flows smoothly.

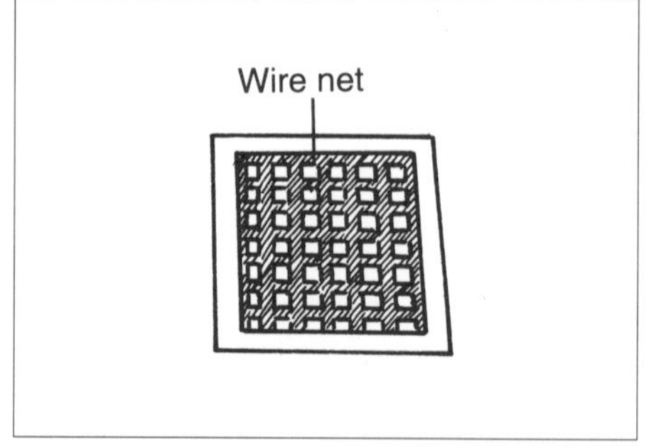

5 Cover with wire net and you are finished. Lay pebbles or gravel to conceal the tank.

APPLYING MORTAR

If you want to make a perfect drainage system, apply mortar over the ground. Mortar is a mixture of cement, sand and water. Since it takes some time to dry, plan the working time well ahead. Prepare the mixture of mortar, and apply several coats after drying each layer.

If the ground is covered with mortar, the gravel will always look clean, especially when white gravel is used. Set the draining tank as above.

You will need:
Cement, River sand, Metal or wooden trowel, Drain tank, Drain pipe, Shovel

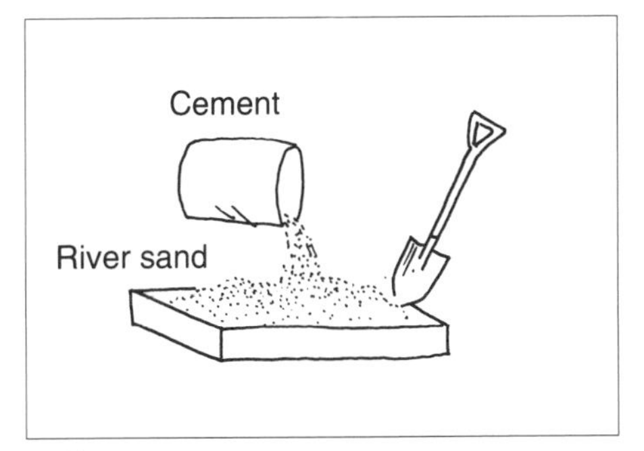

1 Prepare mortar. Mix cement and river sand, 1 part of cement with 2 parts of river sand.

2 Blend well using a shovel on a large sheet of plywood. If blending a small amount, a metal bucket can be used.

3 Gradually add water as you knead the mixture. When the mixture become smooth and soft, the mortar is ready. Do not add too much water.

4 Check that the ground is tamped well and flat. Soft and uneven ground will cause cracks in the mortar.

5 Sprinkle water over the site. This will help the mortar stick to the ground well.

6 Using a metal trowel, spread mortar over the surface of the ground.

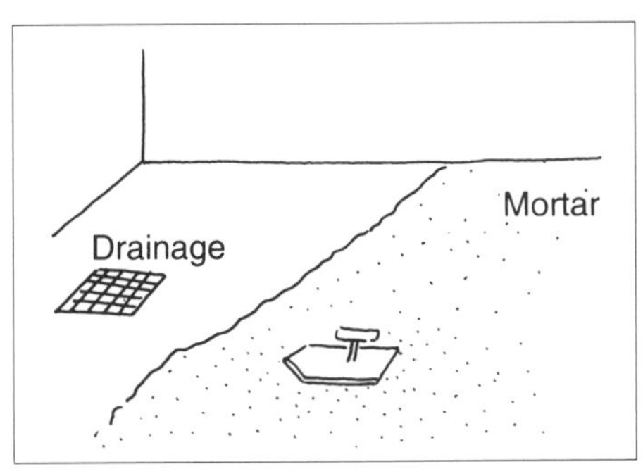

7 When applying mortar, start from one edge and step back as you proceed. Make a gentle slope towards the drain tank.

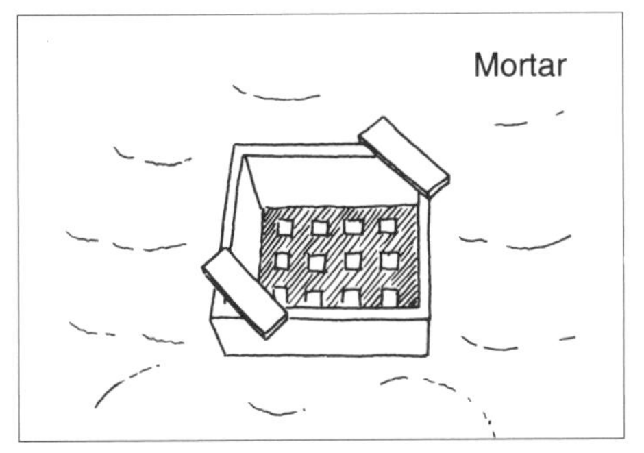

8 Make a "frame" around the tank with pieces of wood in order to keep the mortar in place. When the mortar is completely dry, spread pebbles or gravel over it.

BUILDING A MOUND

Since a flat-grounded garden looks dull, a small mound is often perferred. A mound can be covered with grass to give a soft atmosphere to your garden. Mounds are usually made at the farthest point from where the garden is viewed.

You will need:
Shovel, Wooden pole

Procedures

1 Dig a hole about 30cm(12") deep from the spot where you will make the mound.

2 Tamp the soil in the bottom of the hole using a shovel. Fill up the hole with soil and tamp down again. Tamp firmly to prevent possible sinking later. Next, decide the height of the mound.

3 Stand a stick to mark the height.

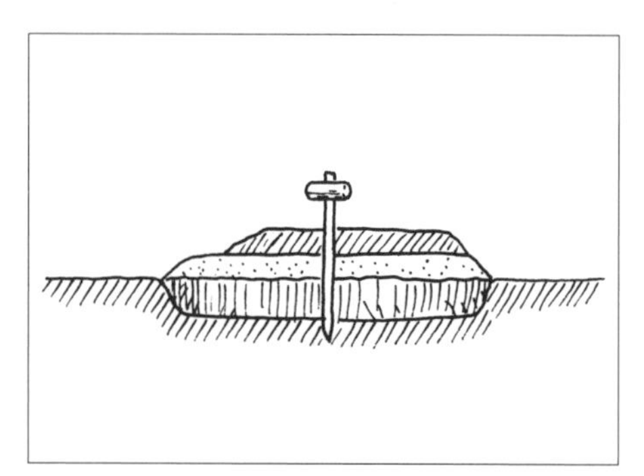

4 Pile up the soil as high as 20-30cm(8"-12"), tamp down and pile again the same. Repeat this procedure.

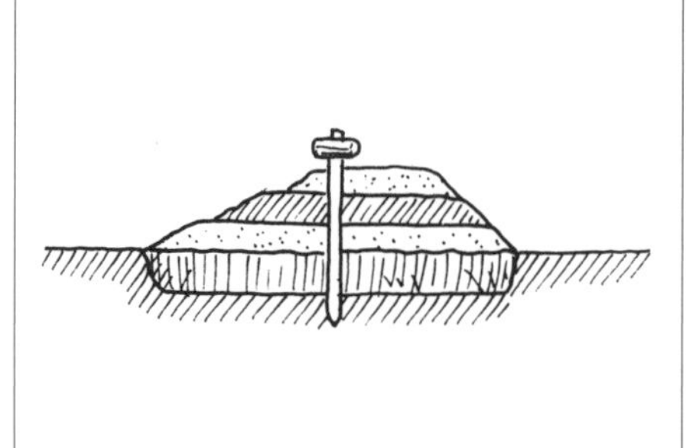

5 It is recommendable to make a gently sloped mound rather than a steep one. When piled to the intended height, pull the pole out.

6 Tamp the slope all around the mound using a trowel or a flat board.

SETTING EDGING STONES

Set cobbles along both sides of walkways or along the border of a mound and graveled ground. For edging stones, use large size cobbles of 15-20cm(6"-8") length, preferably in angular shapes.

You will need:
Cobblestones, Shovel, Wooden mallet, Trowel, Mortar, Wooden pole.

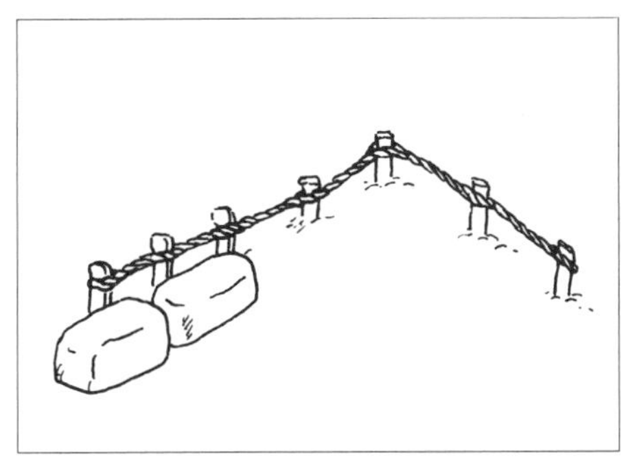

1 Place edging stones along the border marked with bamboo stakes and rope. Check the whole balance.

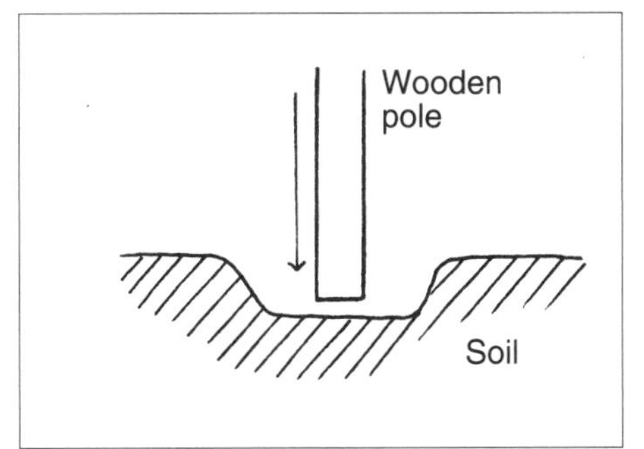

2 Dig a hole for the first stone. Dig until it is as deep as 1/3 of the stone height.

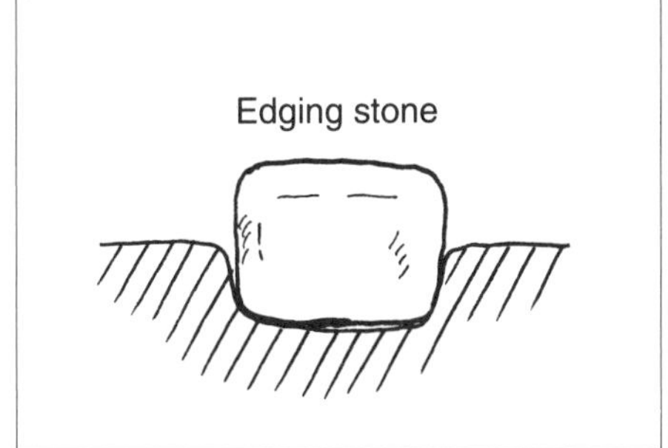

3 Place a cobblestone.

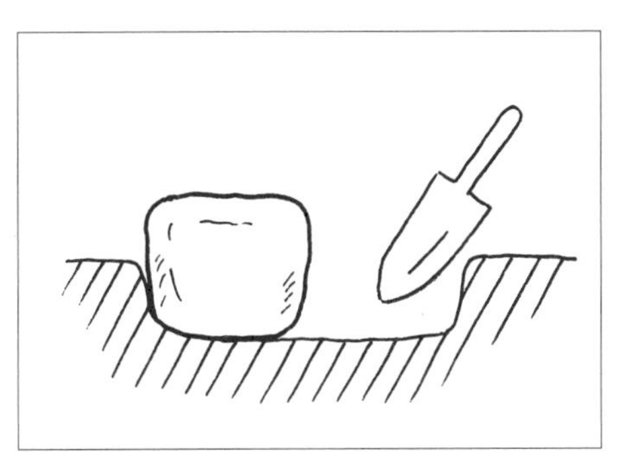

4 Dig a hole for the second stone.

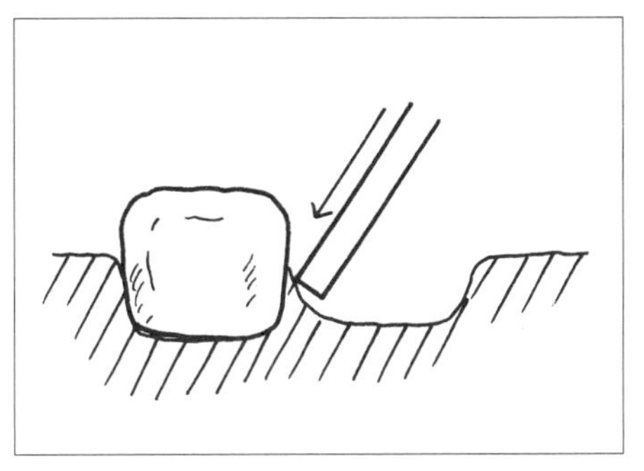

5 Press the soil around the first stone.

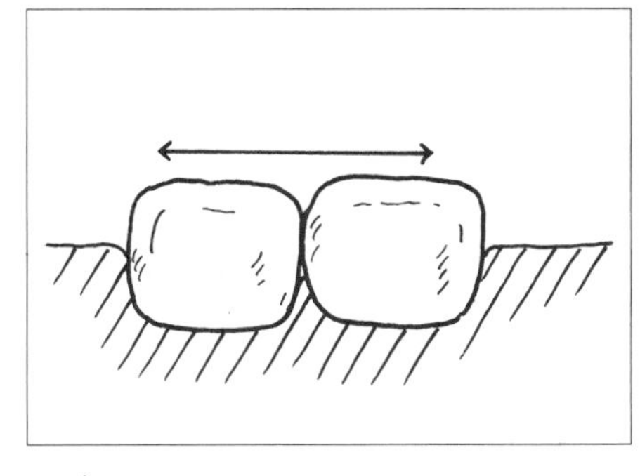

6 Level off the height of stones.

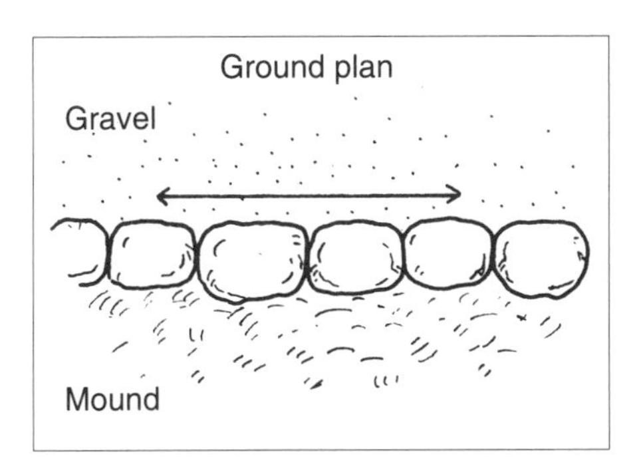

7 As you proceed, check that the surfaces are leveled.

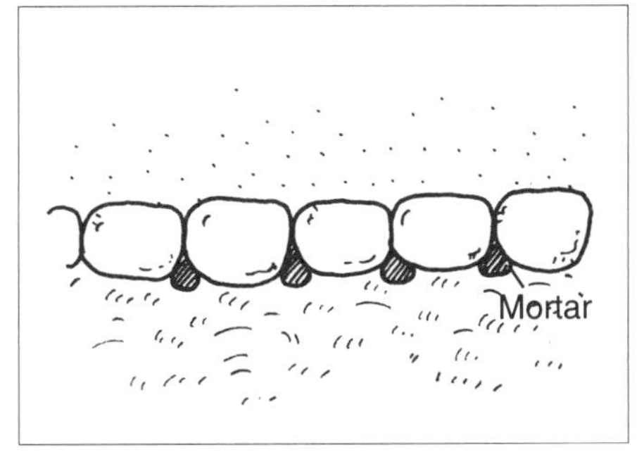

8 Fill the lower gaps between the stones with mortar.

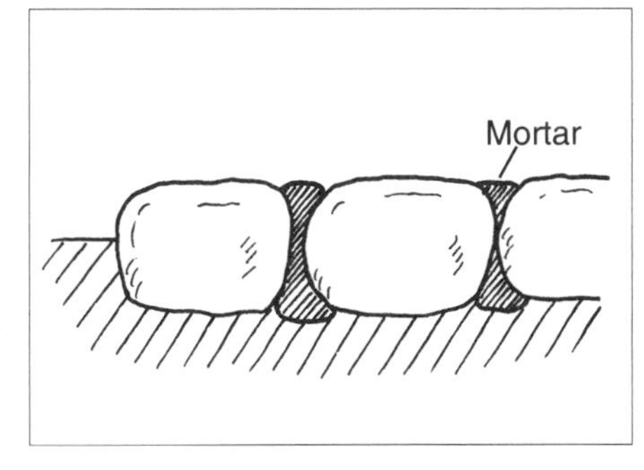

9 Fill the upper gaps and between the stones with mortar to finish.

SETTING *TORO*

How to set a traditional type

Large stone lanterns need special professional tools to carry. The following procedures are only for smaller lanterns that you can handle yourself.

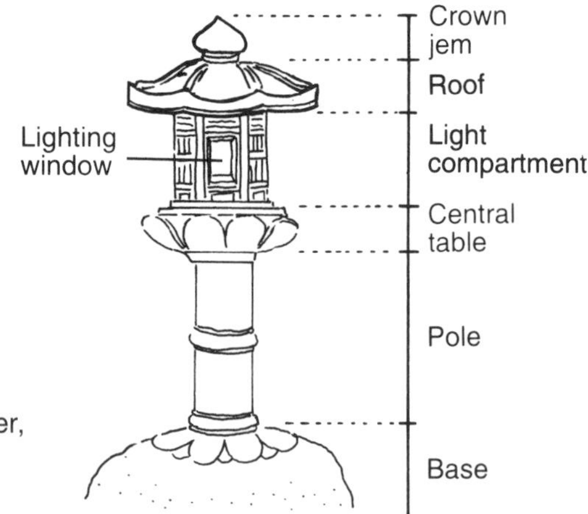

HOW TO SELECT A GOOD *TORO*

Upon purchasing a *toro*, there are some points you should keep in mind. Select your favorite design with the following conditions:

- *Toro* should be solid and durable.
- *Toro* should be nicely proportioned.
- The surface should be clean, without moss or dirt.

You will need:
Cart, Chalk, Shovel, Hand rammer, Level

1 When carrying a *toro* on a cart, take it apart. Be sure to place marks where to join the pieces using a piece of chalk.

2 Dig a hole in the place to set the *toro*, about 10-20cm(4"-8") deep. Keep in mind that the window side is the front of the *toro*.

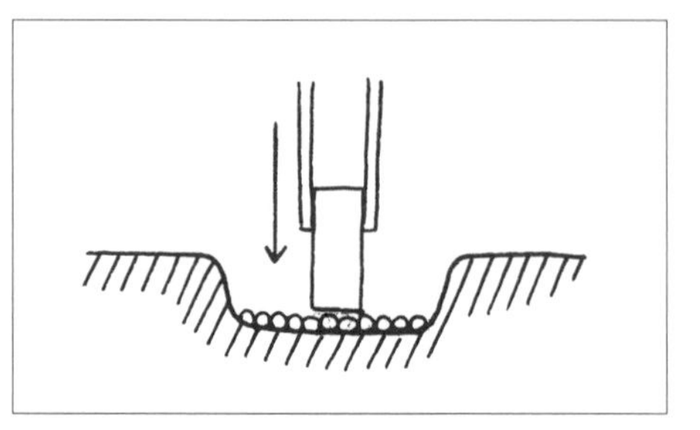

3 Tamp down the bottom of the hole. Line with gravel or pebbles for a secure base.

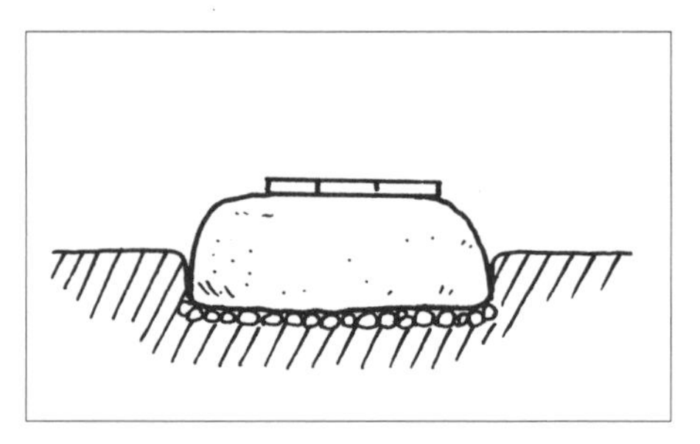

4 Using a level, set the base stone. Carefully, without upsetting the balance.

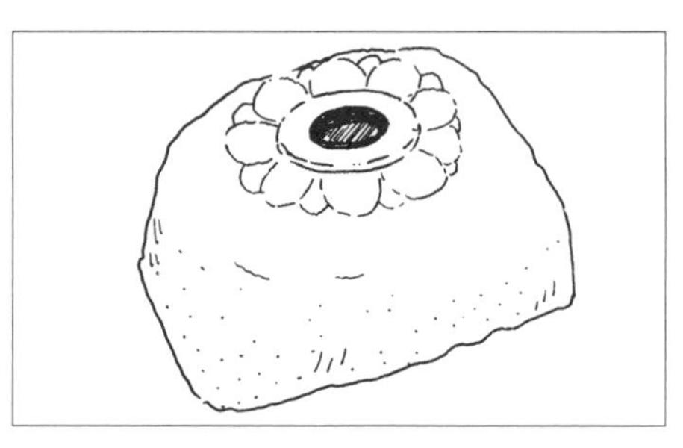

5 The base stone has a hole on top, slightly larger than the pole.

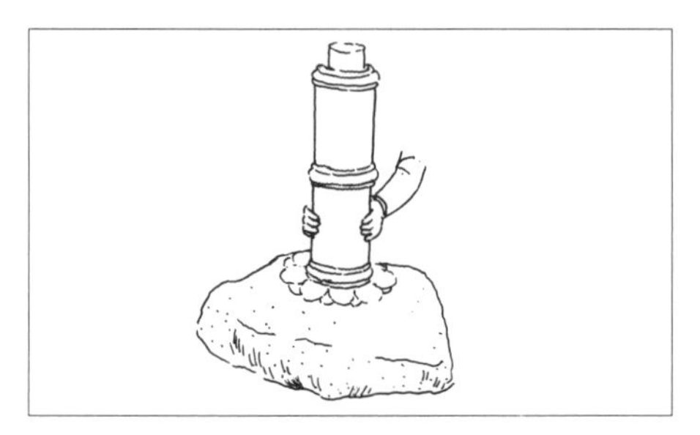

6 Put the pole in the hole. Stand slowly and carefully until the bottom part is inserted completely.

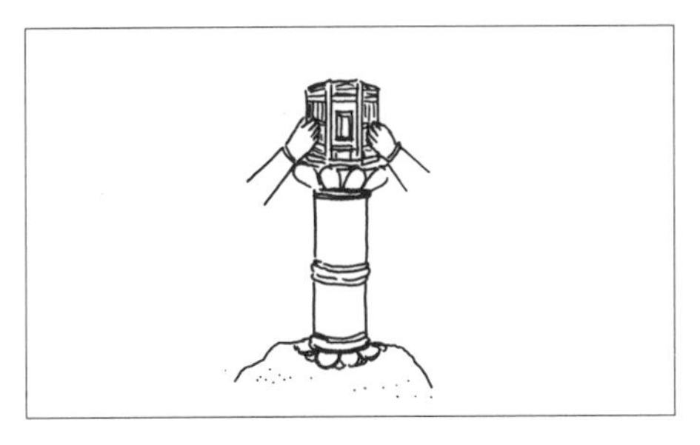

7 Layer the supporting table and the lantern in order.

8 Set the roof, taking care not to loose the balance.

9 Place the crown jem on top and you are finished. Wash off chalk stains or dirt.

Implanted *toro*

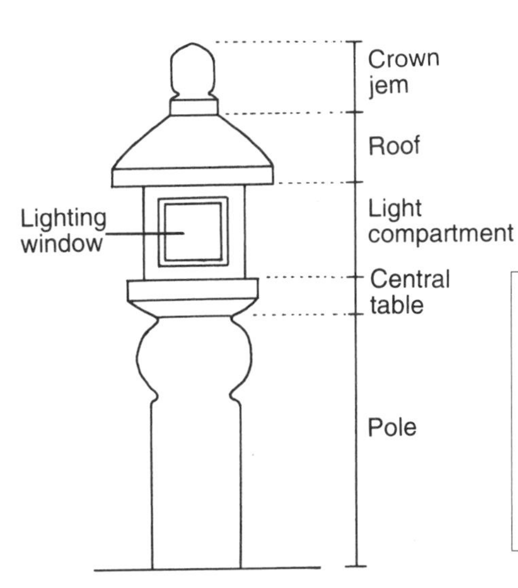

1 Dig a hole for setting the *toro*, deep enough to implant to the indicated depth.

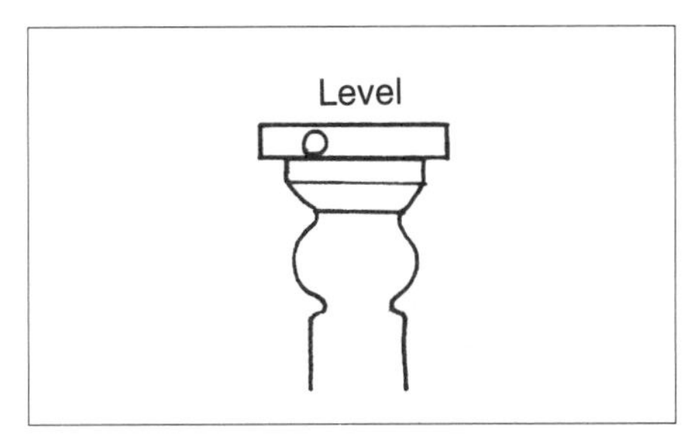

2 Make sure the pole stands vertically. Use a level to check on each side of the pole, and then tamp down the soil around it.

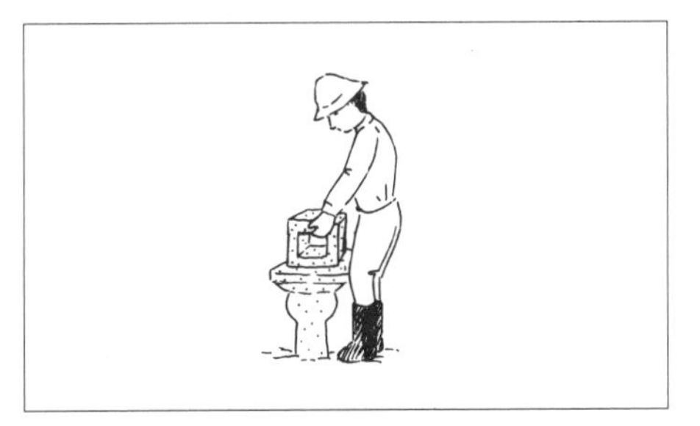

3 Lay the supporting table and the lantern in order.

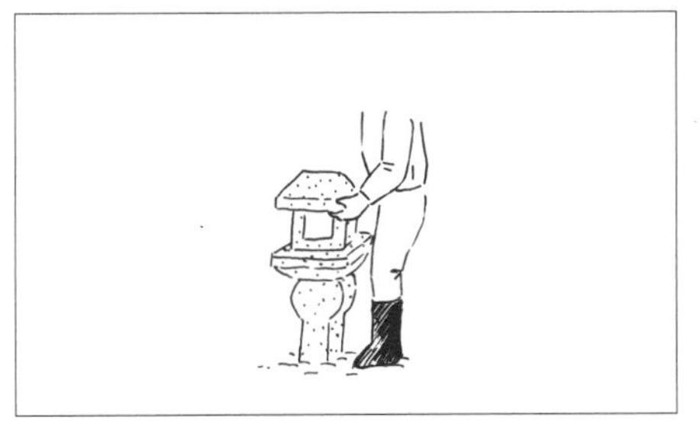

4 Place the shade, trying not to lose the balance.

5 Top with the crown jem and you are finished. Wash off the chalk stains or dirt.

MAKING *TSUKUBAI*

Tsukubai **is consisted of water basin and accessory stones. Usually, a drainage system is constructed before setting them.** ***Tsukubai*** **has two styles:** ***mukaibachi*** **style and** ***nakabachi*** **style. The following procedures are for** ***mukaibachi*** **style basin front.**

You will need:
Stones, Gravel, Drain tank, Drain pipe, Cement
Shovel, Wooden pole.

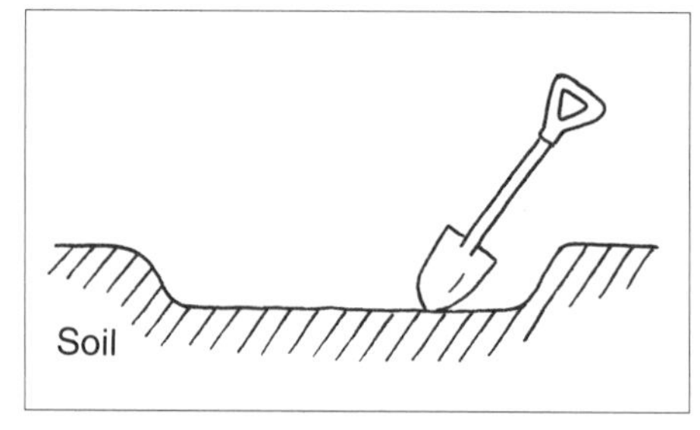

1 Dig a hole in the position according to the plan, 20-30cm(8"-12") deep.

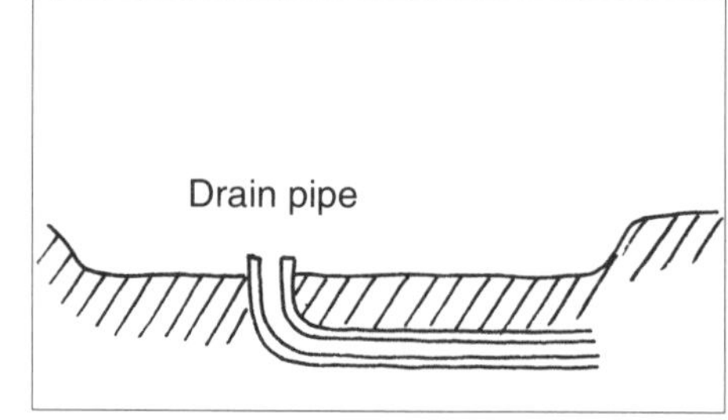

2 Dig another hole for drainage underneath. Install a drain tank and drain pipe.

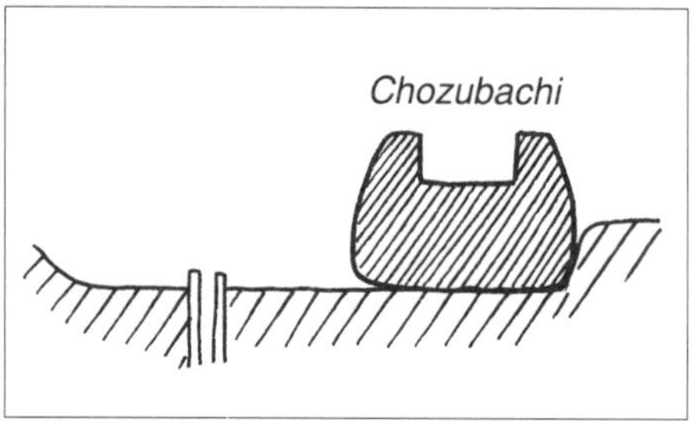

3 Decide the position of the basin. Set the basin horizontally; fill with water and see if it flows over the front.

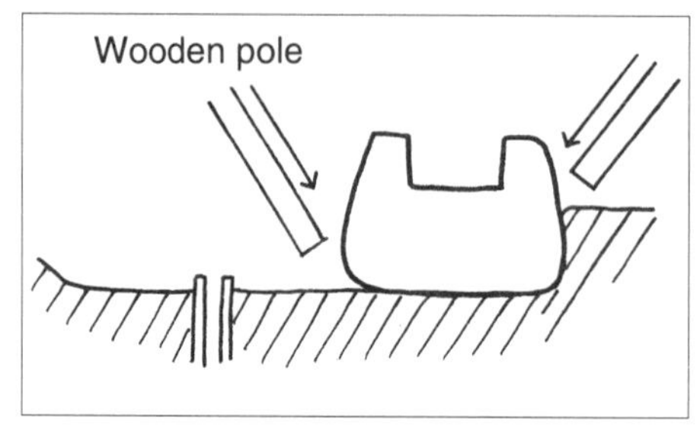

4 To set the basin securely, thrust pebbles or gravel between the ground and the basin, using a wooden pole.

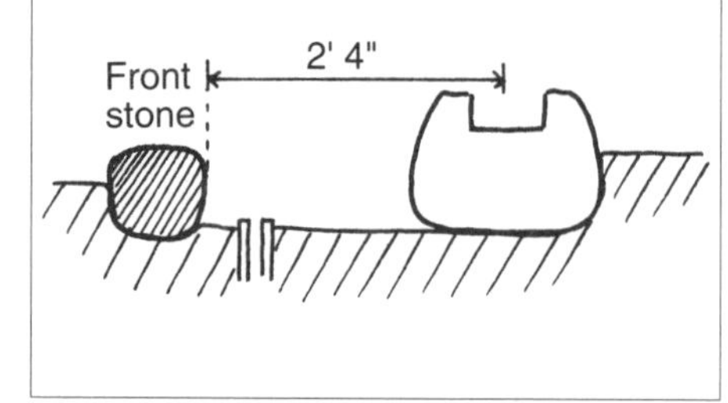

5 Set the front stone. Secure the front stone 70cm(2'4") apart from the basin.

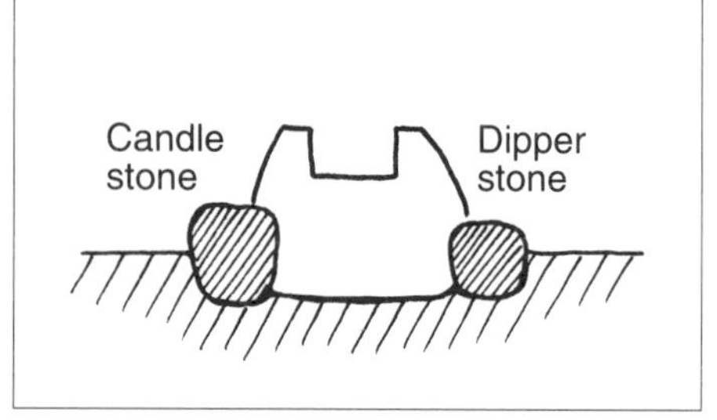

6 Cross section seen from the front. Set a candle stone on the left of the basin, a dipper stone on the right. set the candle stone higher than the dipper stone.

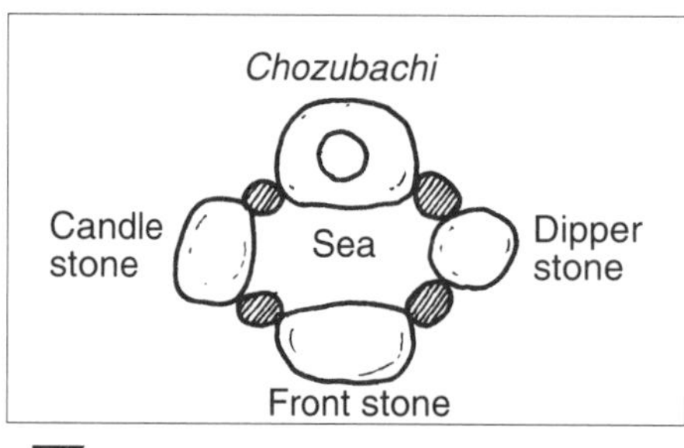

7 Fill the space between each stone with cobbles, to prevent the soil to come into the drain.

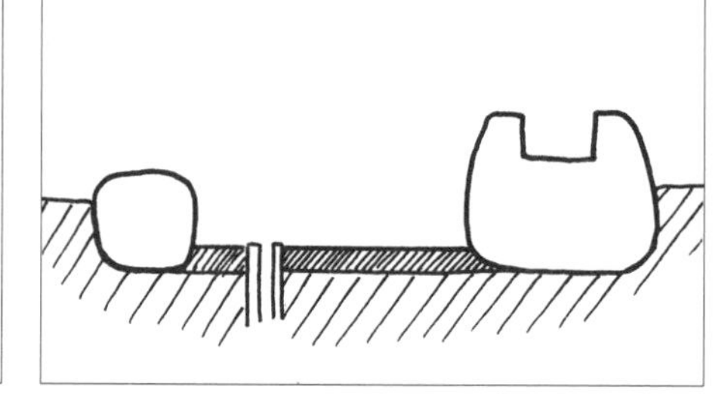

8 Place mortar over the drain. Make a slope towards the drainage hole so that water flows in.

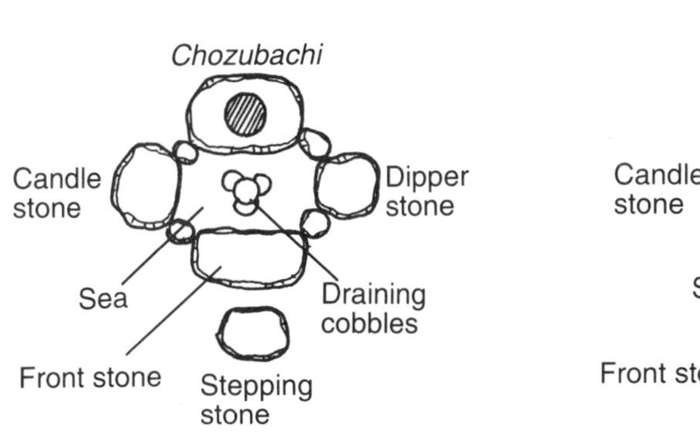

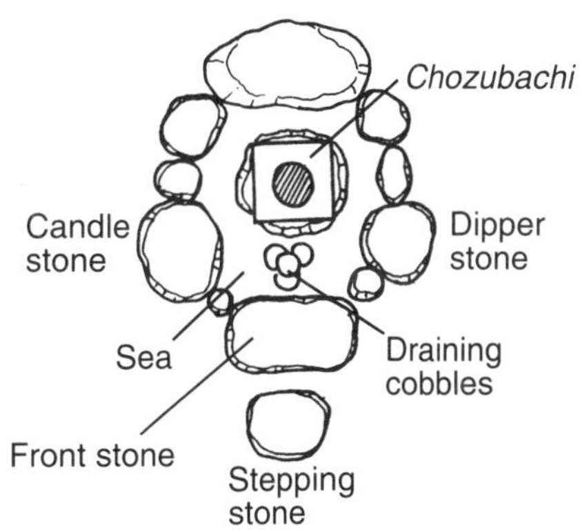

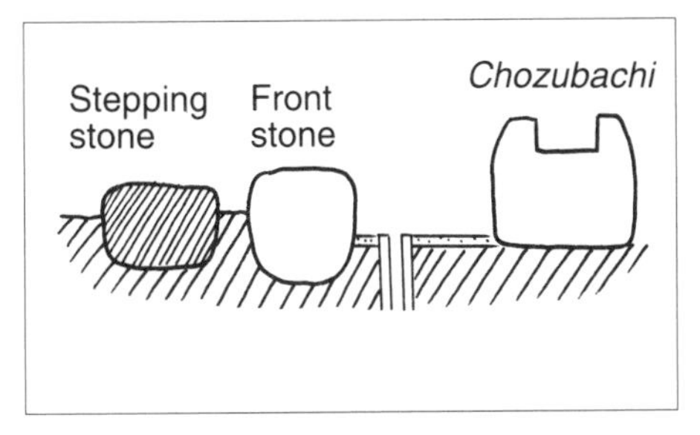

9 Set a stepping stone in front of the front stone. Be sure to set it slightly lower than the front stone.

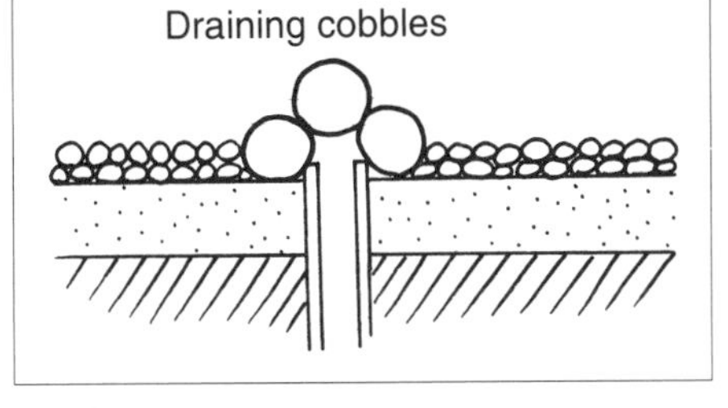

10 Pile up four large cobbles over the drain pipe in the center of drain. These are called drain stones.

11 Fill the drain with *kuri-ishi* pebbles, and wash off dirt to finish.

KAKEHI SYSTEM AND HOW TO SET IT

The water in the basin should be changed occasionally. The water can be added automatically when necessary, if you set *kakehi*, the tap-water supplying system. *Kakehi* is usually made of bamboo stalk. Cross section of *kakehi* is shown on the right.

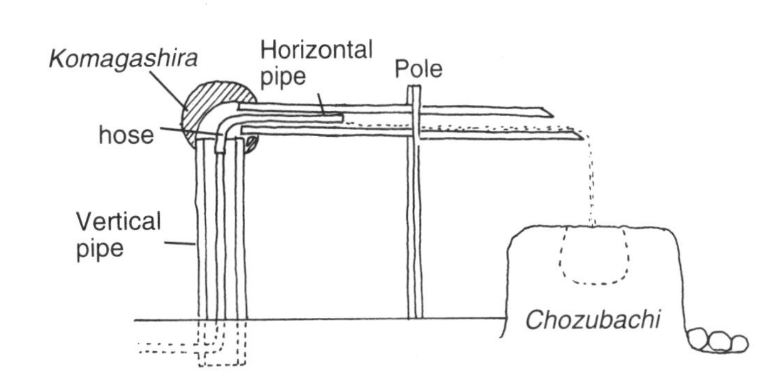

Shapes of *kakehi* spout

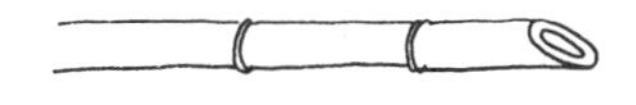

Diagonal cut

Gutter cut

Vertical cut

ARRANGING STONES

It is dangerous to carry large and heavy rocks yourself. Therefore the following guide is for smaller rocks a person can carry himself. Select the stones to set and lay them out according to the plan. You can lay them out to your liking, but there are several patterns that give a well-balanced impression. Stones are not just placed on the ground but are secured to it using a special technique. Once you have figured out a plan, try to arrange some variations until you are really satisfied.

Tips for selecting stones

- Select one particular quarry or location and stick to the same product.
- Do not use stones in various colors.
- Round and smooth stones can be difficult to balance with each other. Choose stones with some convex and concave features.
- Select while the stones are dry because the colors change when they are wet.

Names of stones according to the setting

Stones can be called differently depending on how they are set: standing stone, horizontal stone and diagonal stone. The setting style is decided by the shape and the direction of ridges.

Standing stone

Horizontal stone

Diagonal stone

Basic patterns of stone arrangement

Stone arrangement is based on a one-stone, two-stone, or a three-stone unit. Increase the number of stones by adding proportionally to each unit: five-stone, seven-stone, fifteen-stone unit.

One-stone arrangement

Simple arrangement setting a well-shaped stone as a focal point. Good for house entrances but not very popular otherwise.

Two-stone arrangement

Two stones are positioned in a good proportion. Do not use stones of the same size; pair up large and small stones to create a balance.

Three-stone arrangement

A group of three stones in different sizes: one main stone and two flanking stones. Form a triangle with the three. Do not place the three in a line.

HOW TO SET STONE ARRANGEMENTS

Standing stone

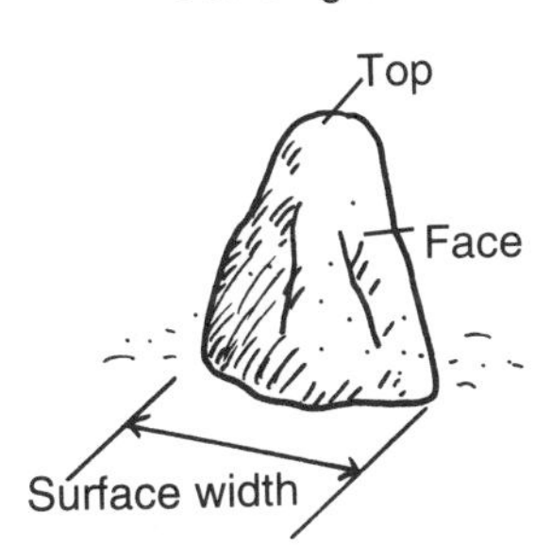

Horizontal stone

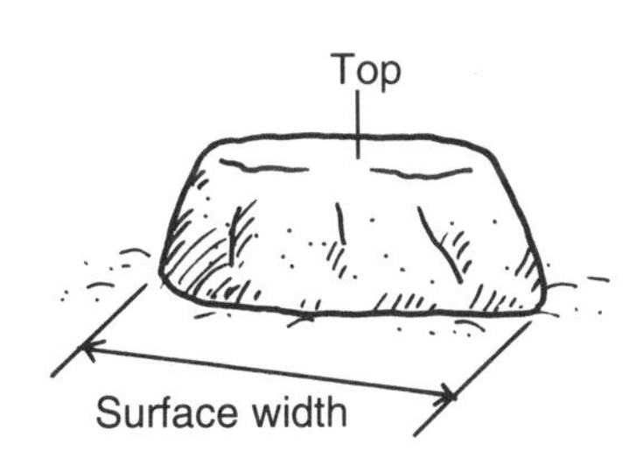

You will need:
Stones, Shovel, Wood pole, Gravel, Small stones

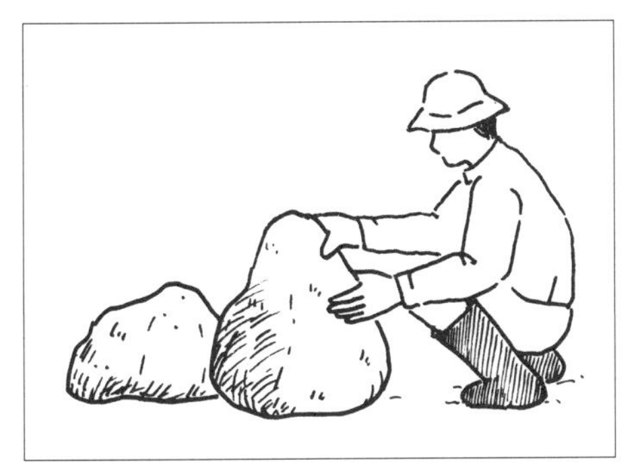

1 Place stones according to the plan and check the balance. Place the main stone first, them add the flanking stones for a good result. If the stone is unstable, support with small stones or a piece of wood.

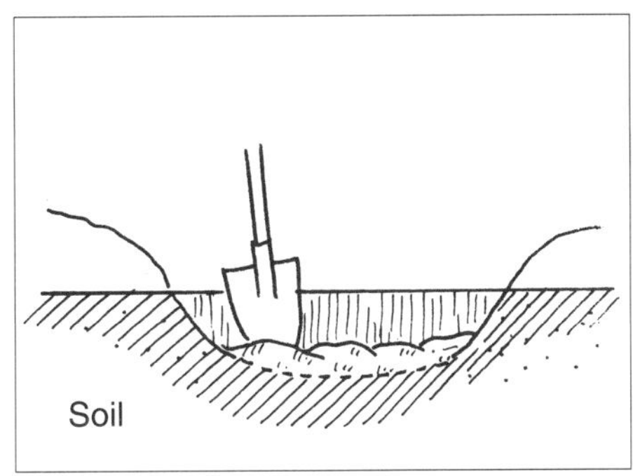

2 When the location is determined, start digging a hole for the main stone. The bottom space should be large enough to hold the base of the stone.

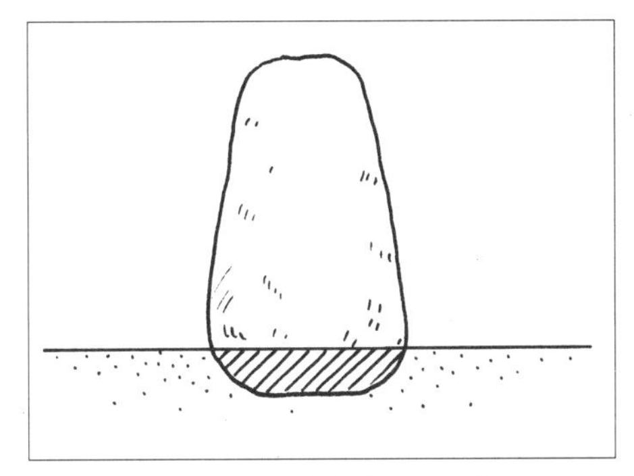

3 To give a stable impression, try to set the stone so that it looks as if rooted deeply and widely. If unstable, the stone may fall in time. Be sure not to bury the stones too deeply, so you can rearrange them later on.

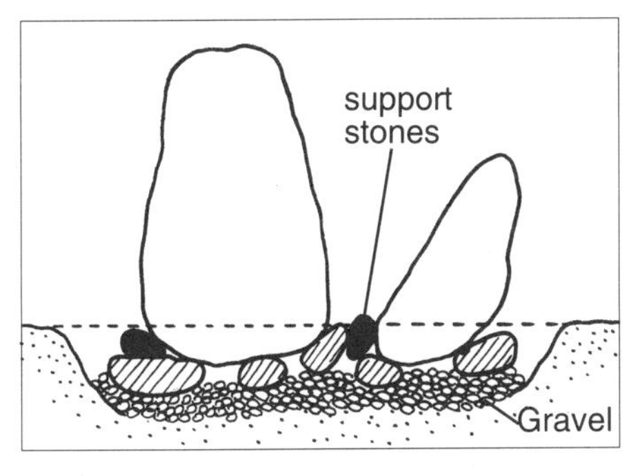

4 Lay gravel on the bottom and place small stones as support stones. For this purpose, avoid concrete pieces or fragile stone, opting instead for hard stones such as granite.

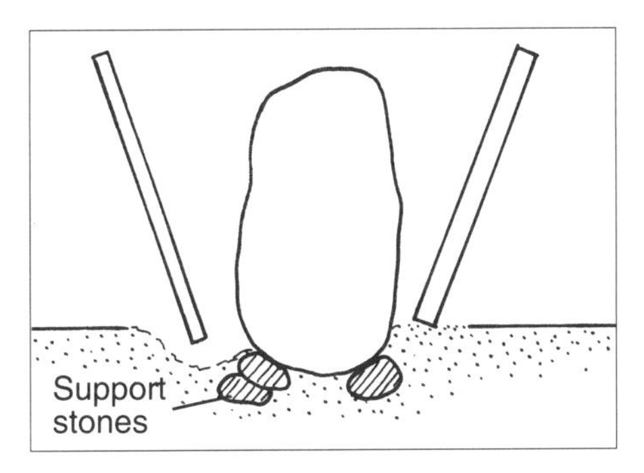

5 Put some soil into the space between stones and supporting stones and tamp down using a thin pole. Add soil little by little, tamping down after each filling. For the last tamping, use a thick pole. Be sure to pack soil firmly at each layer.

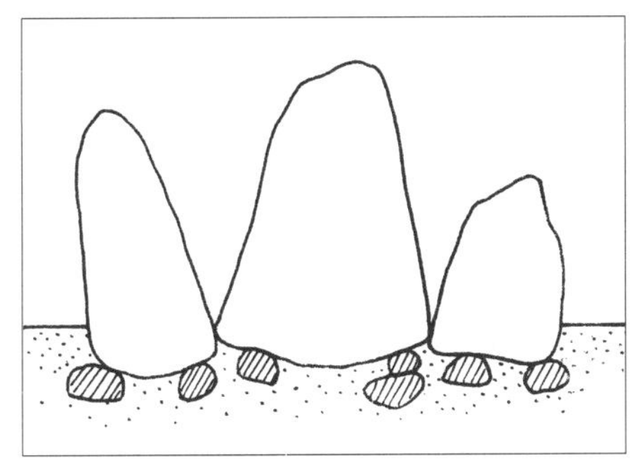

6 If arranging multiple stones, lean them against each other for stability. When the stones are set, smooth out the surrounding ground.

LAYING PAVING STONES

Paving stones are used for a passage leading to the front door or a pathway to the ceremonial tearoom. Beautiful appearance is important, but even more importantly, the paved surface should be easy and safe to walk on. For this reason, avoid smooth-surfaced stones that are slippery, allow appropriate width for the walking, and fix the paving stones firmly in place.

Kinds of Stone Pavements

Stone pavements are classified into three types depending on the stone materials used.

Natural stone pavement:
Pavement using only natural stones.

Cut stone pavement:
Paving with processed or cut stones.

Mixed stone paving:
Combination of natural and cut stones.

Stones for Paving

Generally, paving stones are sorted into two kinds: natural-shaped stones and processed stones such as cut stones.

Natural-shaped stones:
Iyo-aokoban-ishi, Ise cobbles, *Tsukuba* cobbles, *Awaji* cobbles

Cut stones:
Tamba-Kurama-ishi, Tamba-teppei-seki, Teppei-seki, Chichibu-aoita ishi, Light green andesite

Paving Designs

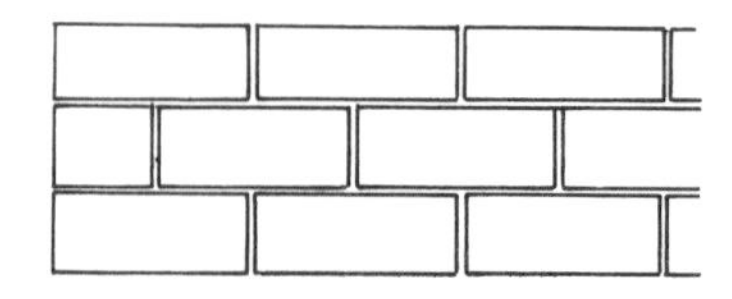

***Shin*-style**
(basic pattern)
Cut stone paving

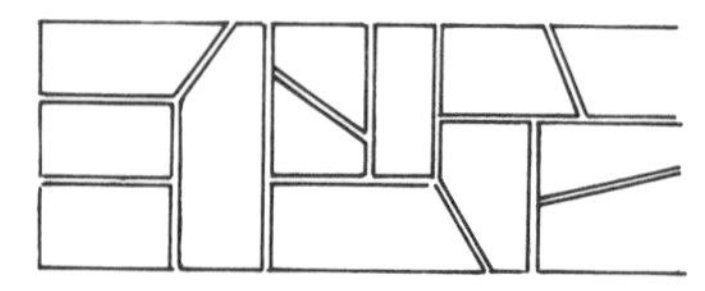

***Gyo*-style**
(semi-basic pattern)
Cut stone paving

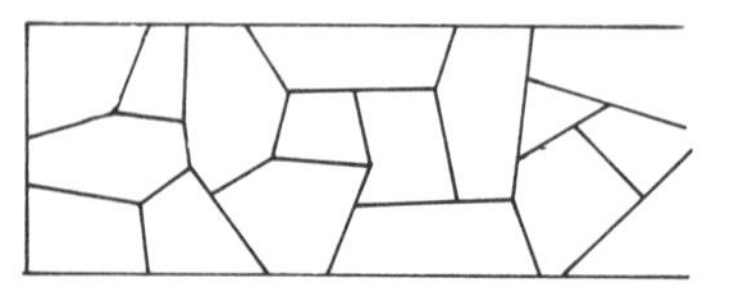

***So*-style**
(abstract pattern)
Cut stone paving

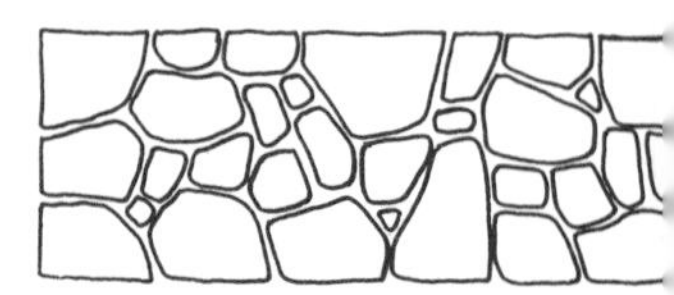

***Gyo*-style**
(round abstract pattern)
Processed stone paving

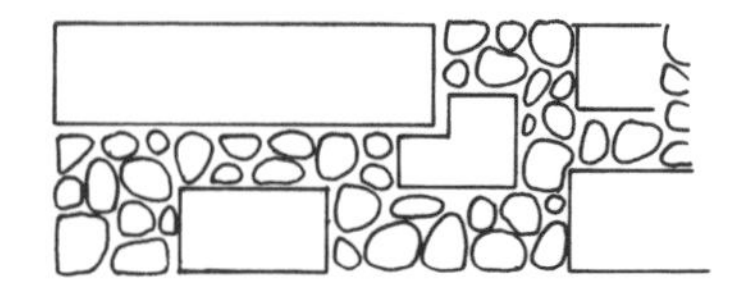

***Gyo*-style**
(semi-abstract pattern)
Combination paving

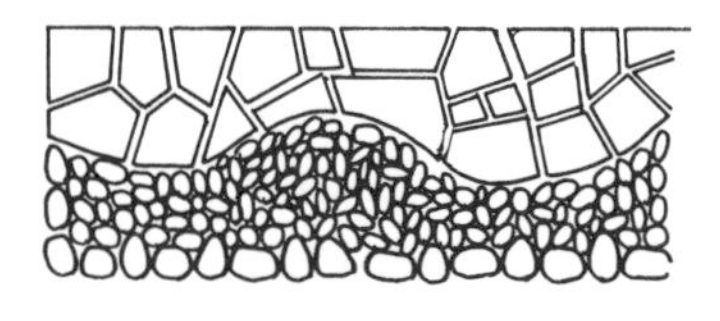

Modern
Combination paving

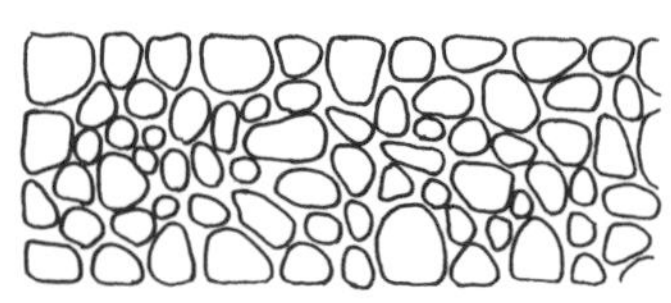

***So*-style**
(abstract pattern)
Natural stone paving

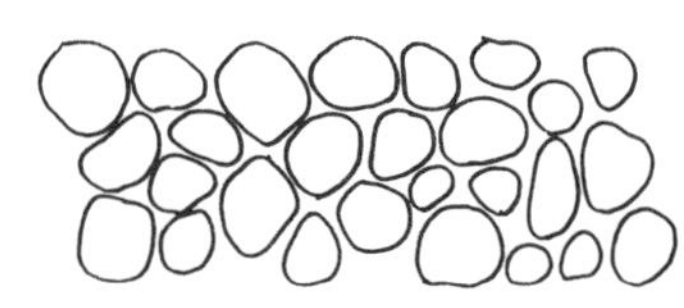

***So*-style**
(abstract pattern)
Natural stone paving

Paving Hints

- Place paving stones starting from a corner.
- If using stones of different sizes, set larger stones first, then fill with smaller ones.
- Use larger stones for the edges, and smaller stones for inside.

You will need:
Shovel, Hand rammer, Hammer, Steel trowel

Instructions

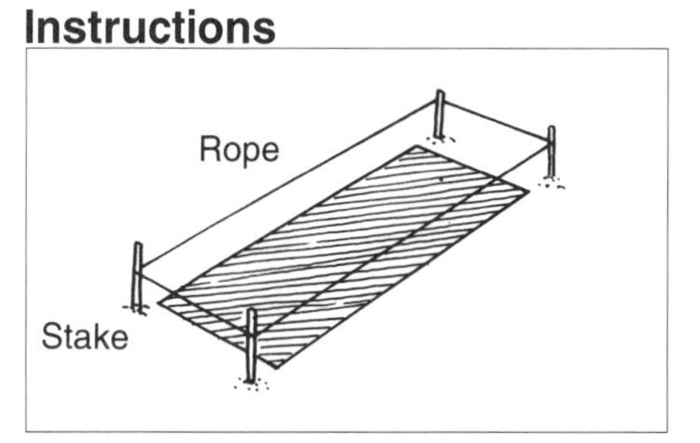

1 Following the plan, rope off the site using stakes and rope. If your have some extra space, try doing a practice paving to see how the design will look.

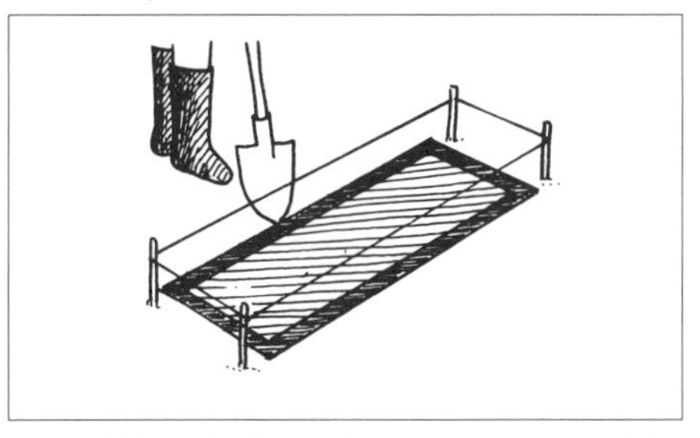

2 Dig a hole at the paving area, 20-30cm(8"-12") deep. Make the hole slightly larger than the pavement (usually 45-180cm/1.5'-6' wide).

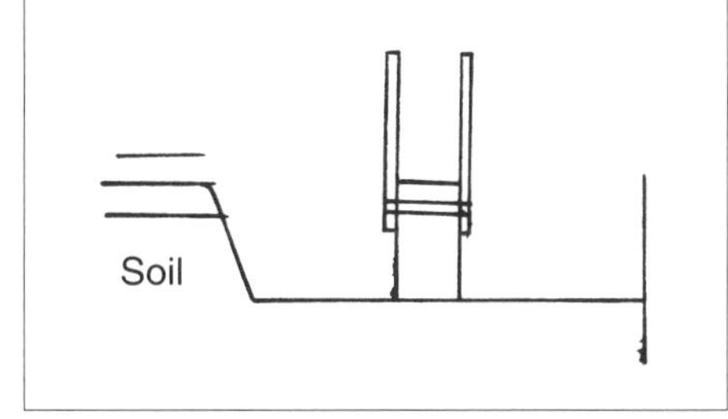

3 Using a shovel or a hand rammer, tamp the bottom of the hole. Be sure to pack down the soil firmly or the paved surface will become uneven in time.

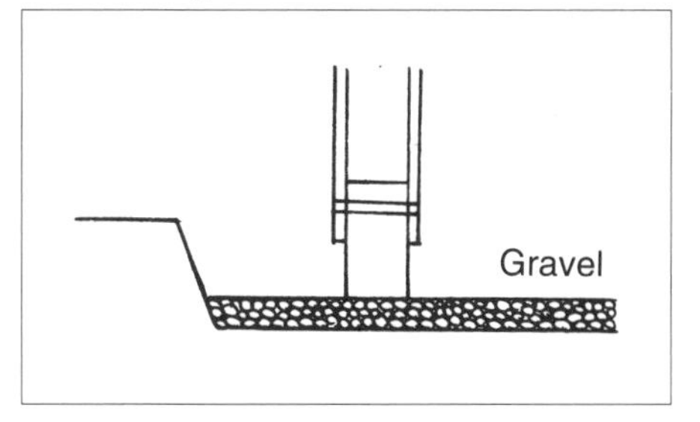

4 Cover the bottom with gravel or pebbles, about 5cm(2") thick.

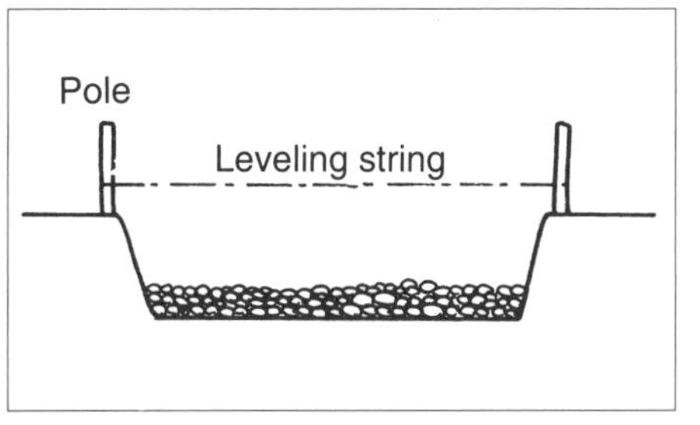

5 Set the leveling string to mark the planned height. This will serve as a guide for making the surface flat.

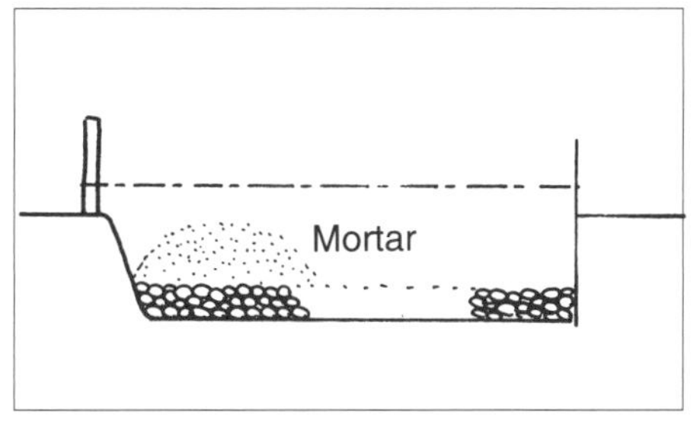

6 Place a slightly hard mix of mortar, about 10cm(4") thick. See page 50 for mixing mortar.

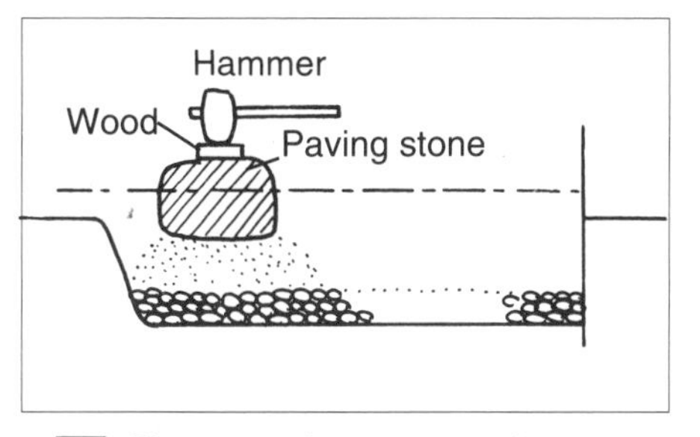

7 Place a paving stone on the mortar. Cover with a piece of wood and hammer down, until the stone surface is level with the string.

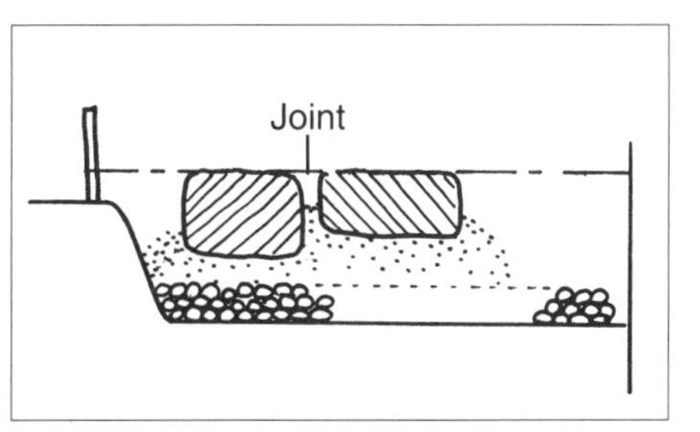

8 In the same manner, continue setting the paving stones, with 1-3cm($\frac{1}{2}$"~$\frac{1}{4}$") spaces in between.

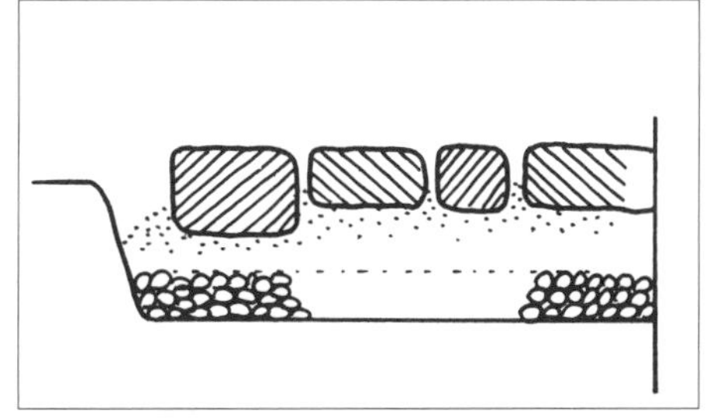

9 Check if all the joints are of the same height. Adjust by scraping off the extra mortar or adding where necessary.

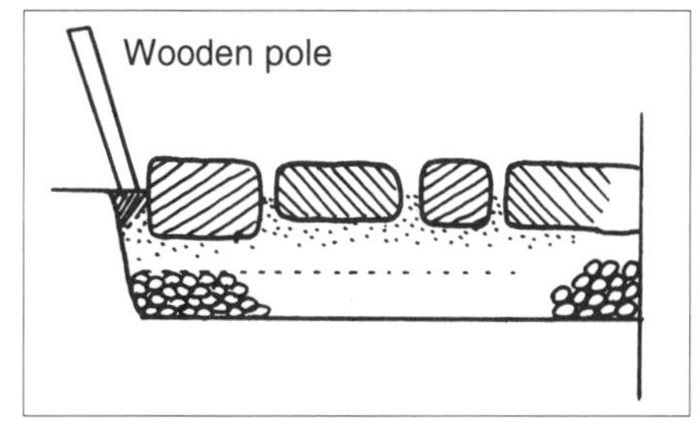

10 Lastly tamp down the soil on both sides.

SETTING STEPPING STONES

Stepping stones are used to make freer, informal walkways, while paving stones are for proper spaces. A stepping stone path is a must for a tea house and gives the walkers a "private" feeling. Although it is important to consider the aesthetic effect of the stone shapes and layout, walking safety should come first of all.

Materials for Stepping Stones

–Stepping stones can be sorted into four types according to the processing conditions:

Natural stone type: Naturally shaped stones. Typical examples are *Kurama-ishi, Tanba-ishi, Koshu-Kurama-ishi, Iyo-ishi, Kishu-ishi* and *Chichibu-ishi* stones.

Semi-natural type : Natural stones with rounded corner

Processed type : Stones cut into rounds

Cut type : Stones cut into angular shapes

Sizes of Stepping Stones

–Stepping stones can be sorted into two types according to the sizes:

One-foot size:30-40cm(1'-1'4") in diameter, large enough for one foot

Two-foot size:50-60cm(1'8"-2') in diameter, large enough for both feet

Setting patterns

Select whichever pattern that suits your taste. Just remember that curvy line steps are easier to walk on than straight line steps.

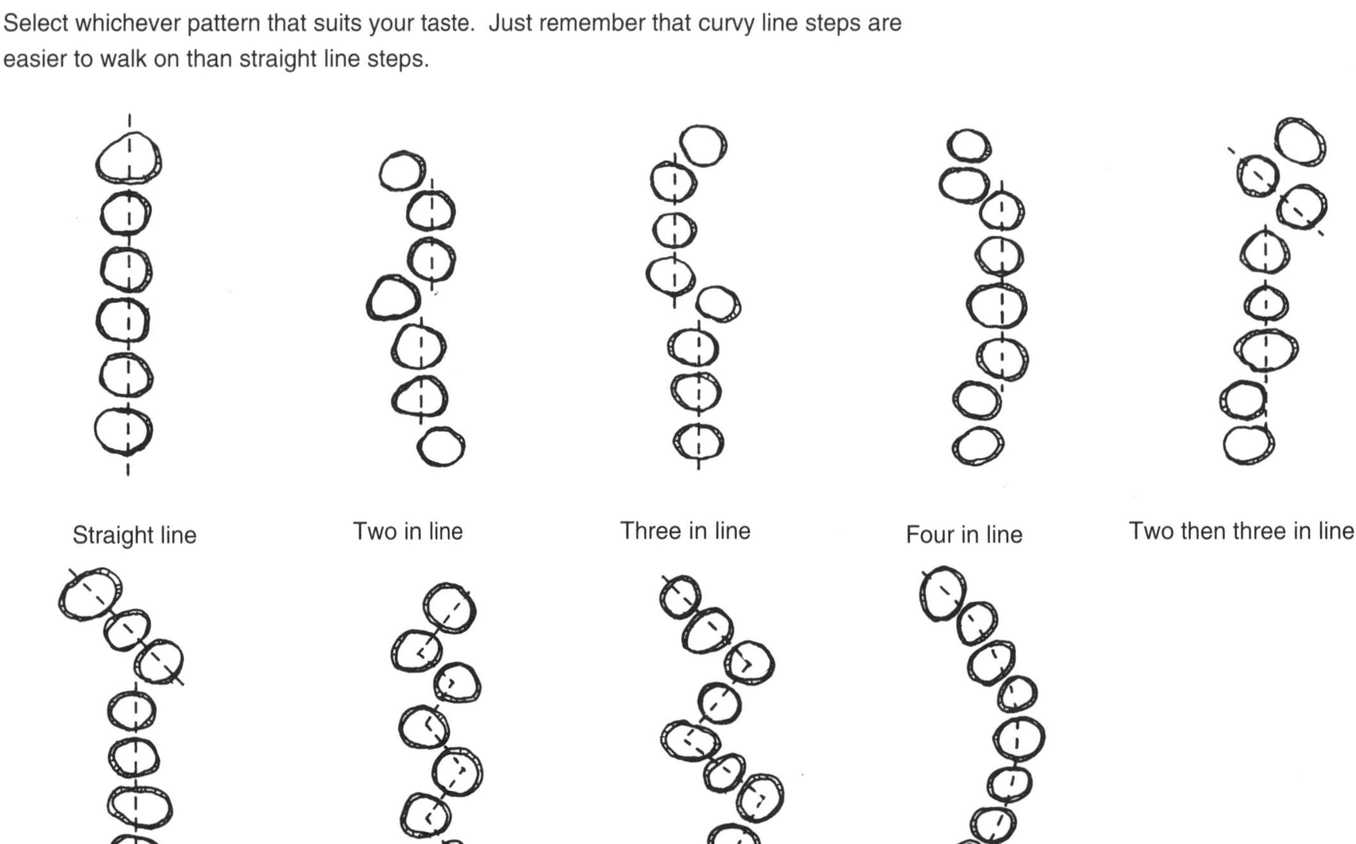

How to Select Stepping Stones

You can be selective regarding the colors of the stones, but there are some points to keep in mind as to the shapes.

- **The surface should be flat. If the surface is uneven, it is difficult to walk on.**
- **Each stone has higher center. If the center is hollow, then rainwater will collect, form puddles, and make for difficult walking.**
- **Stepping stones should be 10cm(4") thick or more. Thinner stones will sink into the ground.**

You will need:
Shovel, Hand rammer, Wooden pole, Hammer, Crowbar

Instructions

1 Measure the length of the pathway where the stepping stones are to be laid, then decide how many stepping stones to lay. Aim for 10cm(4") spaces between each steeping stone. You can practice by laying pieces of paper in place of stones.

2 Place the stepping stones on the walkway and check how they look. Adjust the placement of the stepping stones so that it is approximately 40-50cm (16"-20") from the center of one stone to the center of the next.

3 Once you have decided the positions of the stepping stones, place the stone beside the position where it is to be laid and dig a hole. The hole should be deep enough so that the stepping stone protrudes 5cm(2") above the ground.

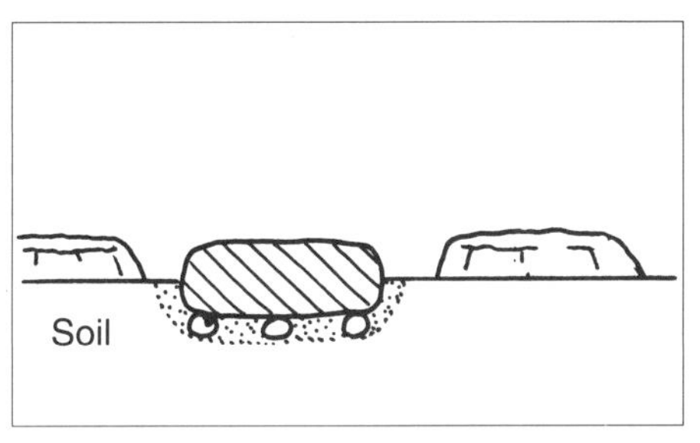

4 Place the stepping stone in the hole and adjust it so that the surface is level. Match the height to the height of the other stepping stones by using a level.

5 Use a pole to pack the soil around each stepping stone. If the surrounding earth is not firm, use gravel or pebbles around the stepping stone to make it sit firmly.

6 Actually stand atop the stepping stone and check to see if it is wobbly.

7 Level the earth around the stepping stones with a small board, then you are finished.

Some Tips for Placing Stepping Stones

- If the stepping stones are shaped rectangularly, arrange them so that they are wider rather than long and narrow.
- Do not lay same sized stones next to each other. Combinations of large and small stones will look beautiful.
- Lay a large stone for the junction. This is called *fumiwake-ishi*.
- Adjust the height of stepping stones, by hammering down or elevating by prying with a crowbar.

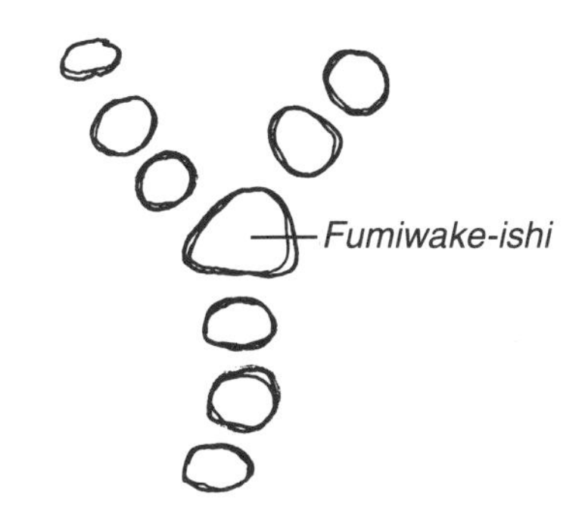

LAYING GRAVEL

Since Japan has much rain, the earth of our yards and gardens have often been covered with gravel to prevent us from soiling. Gravel also prevents the weed to grow and therefore makes gardening easier. It can be used in terraces or rooftop gardens of the condominiums because of the weight which is lighter than you would expect. The sound when you step on the gravel will ease your feeling. Graveling is an easy work. The only thing you should consider is drainage.

Types of Gravel

Gravel has various colors, shapes and sizes depending on the quarry, hence the name. Common examples are: *Ise* cobbles, *Shirakawa* granite sand, *Mikawa* granite sand, *Naruto* blue gravel, *Chichibu* blue gravel.

Hints for Selecting Gravel

- Aim for the gravel that does not show dirt easily.
- Select gravel in equal size for an ordered look.
- Avoid gravel that breaks easily.

Procedure

There are two ways for laying gravel. You can gravel the ground directly, or you can make a drainage before graveling. If the earth is firm and drains well, you can just lay gravel directly over the earth, but to completely conceal the earth, you would need to lay 6-8cm($2\frac{1}{2}$"~3") thick gravel, which may cost a lot. If the earth does not drain well, it is best to install a drainage and cover with mortar before graveling.

You will need:
Gravel, Shovel, Hand rammer
Drain tank, Drain pipe
Mortar, Metal trowel

Direct Graveling

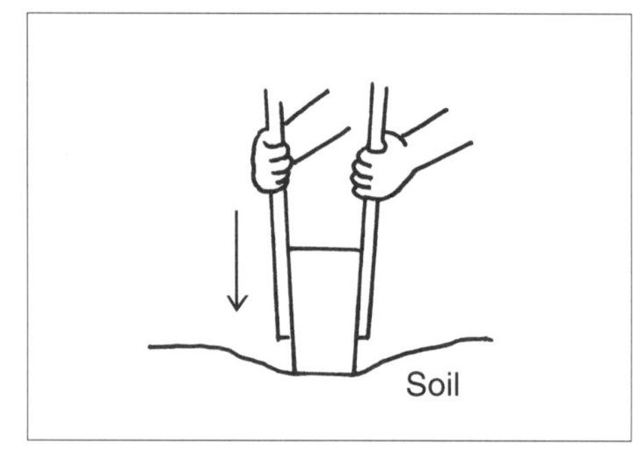

1 Using a shovel or hand rammer, tamp down the soil where the gravel is to be laid. Press firmly because the soft soil will sink in time, causing uneven surface of gravel.

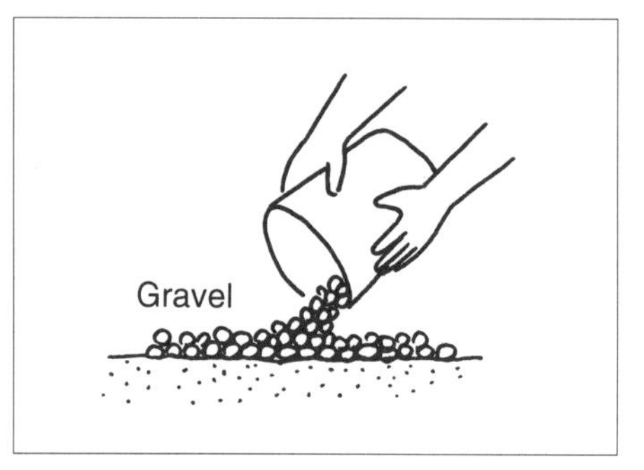

2 When the ground is pressed enough, lay gravel, 6-8cm($2\frac{1}{2}$"~3") thick. Level the surface and wash off dirt with water, then you are finished.

How to Make a Drainage before Graveling

1 Dig a hole to bury the tank. If the ground has a slope, bury the tank in the lower level. If burying in flat ground, choose a place where you can easily connect to the outer drainage.

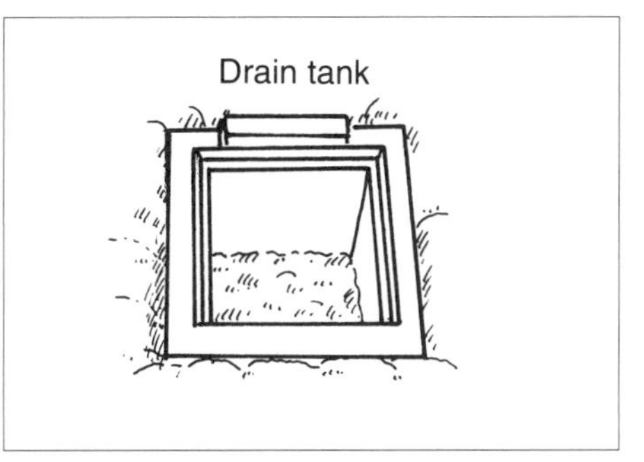

2 Place the tank in the hole, deeper than the ground so that the water pours smoothly into the basin.

3 Install the drainage pipe at a slant. If you set it horizontally, the water will not flow.

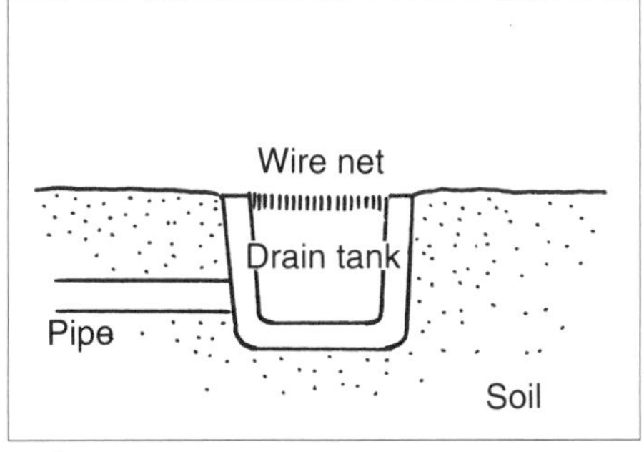

4 Cover the tank with wire screen, then the basin is completed. If you want to hide the basin, cover with cobbles or gravel.

5 Mix mortar : Combine cement and river sand, adding a small amount of water at a time. Mix until very soft, and the mortar is ready to be spread.

6 Wet the ground where the mortar is to be applied. The moisture will help the mortar stick to the ground.

7 Using a steel trowel, spread mortar evenly over the ground.

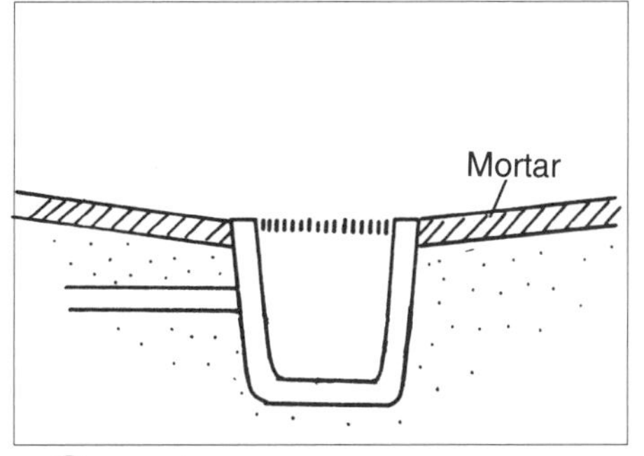

8 Make a gentle slope towards the drainage tank so that the water flows in.

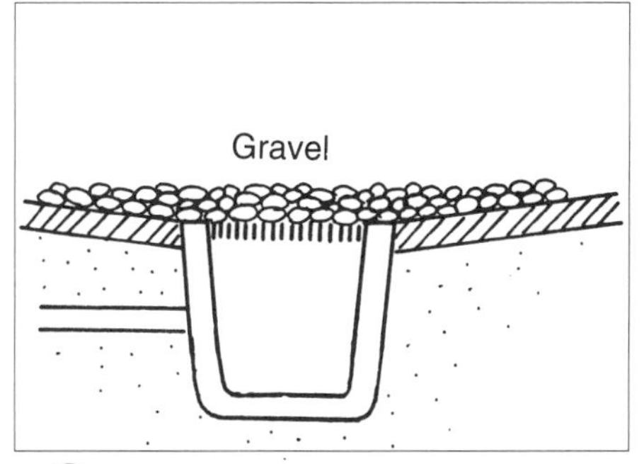

9 Lay a 3cm($1\frac{1}{4}$") layer of gravel over the mortar. Level the surface and wash off dirt to finish.

MAKING *KARESANSUI*

***Karesansui*, or dry streams, are often seen in Japanese gardens in place of real waterfalls or brooks although the country has water in abundance. This desert-inspiring landscape was originated in order to visualize the *Zen* spirit, but nowadays it includes any garden or a part of the garden which is composed of stones and sand. The sand or gravel is formed into a variety of patterns by raking it in lines. Raked gravel patterns can suggest many natural scenes such as distant hills, streams, waves, or the sea. It is amazing that each pattern will give entirely different impression depending on the width and depth of the ridges.**

Gravels for Dry Streams

Usually, whitish sand or gravel are used for this purpose, such as *Shirakawa-suna*, *Mikawa-Shirakawa* suna, and *Ise* gravel.

Raking Patterns

Sazanami pattern (Ripples)

Ryusui pattern (Stream)

Ichimatsu pattern (Checkerboard)

Sazanami pattern (Ripples)

Seikaiha pattern (Sea waves)

Sui pattern (Water drop)

Sazanami pattern (Ripples)

Tatsunami pattern (High waves)

Aranami pattern (Rough waves)

Lay sand or gravel in the same manner as "Laying Gravel" on page 64.
Use a special rake to form the pattern on sand or gravel. If this type of rake is not available, you can make your own using a stick and a board of wood.

You will need:
Leveling tool (trowel or board)
Rake

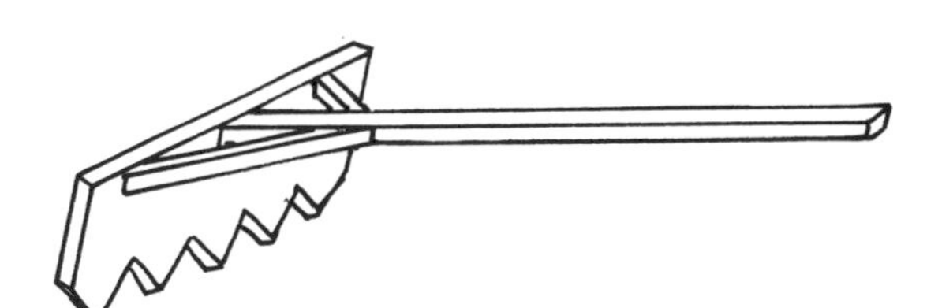

Instructions

1 Using a trowel or a flat board, level the sand in the whole area you are going to form the pattern.

2 Putting the rake deeply into the sand, draw it by stepping backwards to form the ridges.

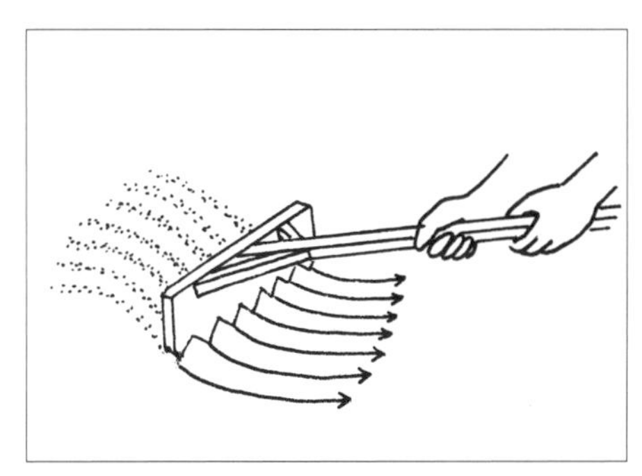

3 For a wave design, move the rake to left and right in a smooth motion.

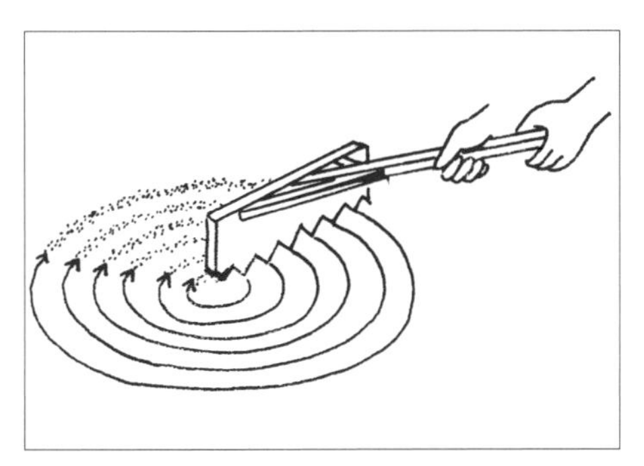

4 For a circular ripple design, fix one end of the rake at the center and rotate around.

5 When the patterns meet each other, erase the former pattern with the new lines.

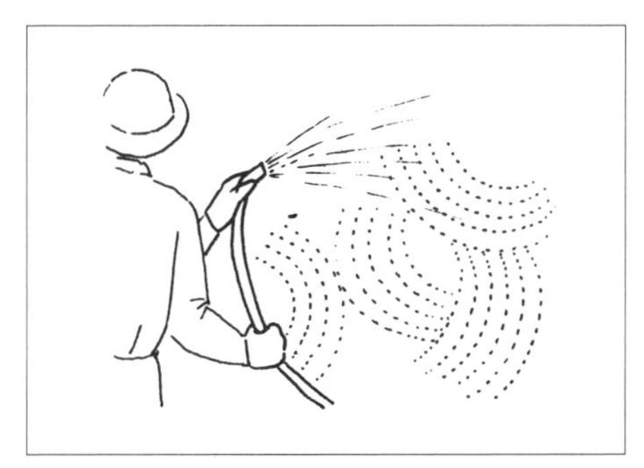

6 When the pattern is completed, sprinkle water to wash off the dirt. Do not gush the water as it may spoil the ridges.

PLANTING TREES AND SHRUBS

When you select the trees or shrubs to be planted in your garden, consider if the season, the soil, and the fertilizer are appropriate. The following is a method of planting a shop-bought nursery tree.

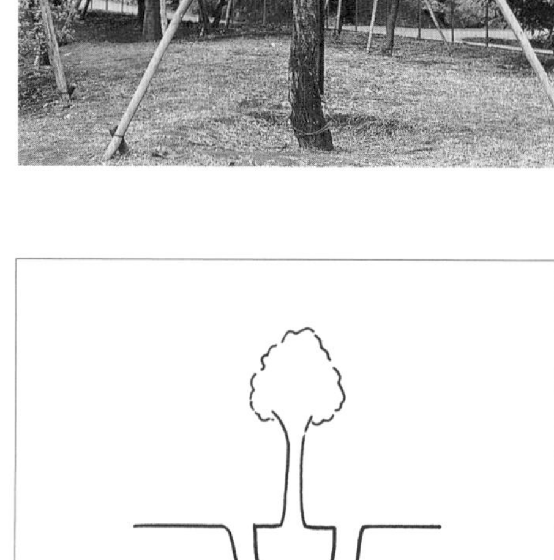

You will need:

Nursery tree
Shovel
Wooden pole
Prop
Rope(hemp palm)
Fertilizer

Instructions

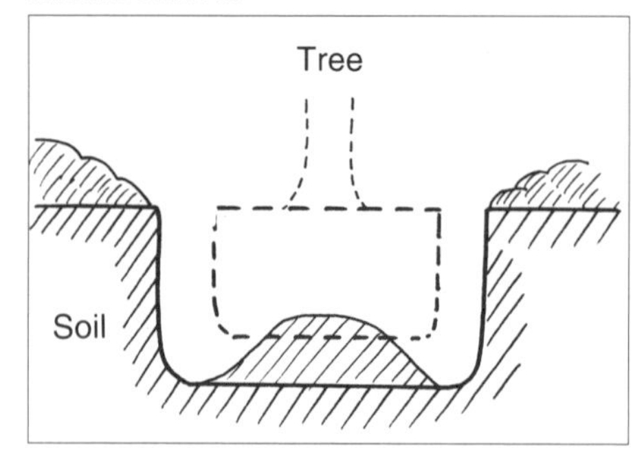

1 Dig a hole deeper and wider than the root of the tree to be planted.

2 Check the quality of the soil. If the soil is not of a good quality, the hole should be filled with a suitable type later. Spread fertilizer on the bottom.

3 Put some soil over fertilizer. Make the center higher so that the direction of the tree can be adjusted later.

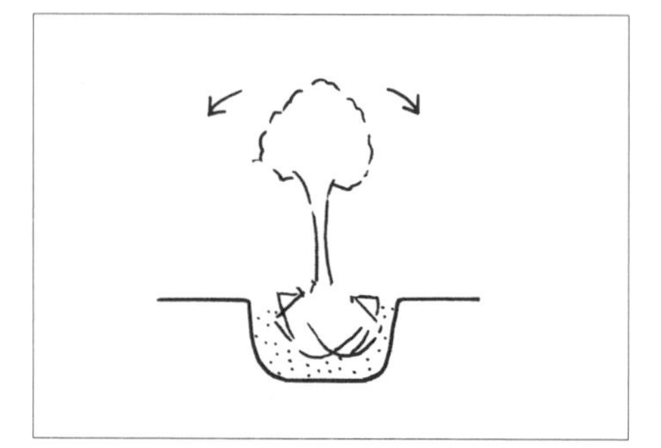

4 Place the nursery tree, add some more soil, and check the depth and direction of the tree.

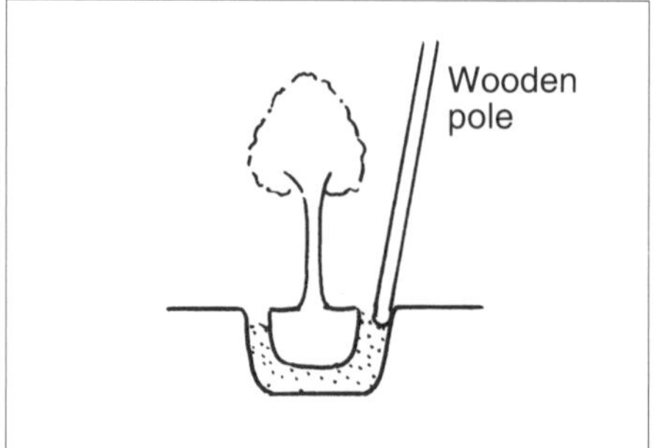

5 Press down the soil using a pole. In order to get the best result, do not put all the soil at one time, but tamp after each addition of the soil.

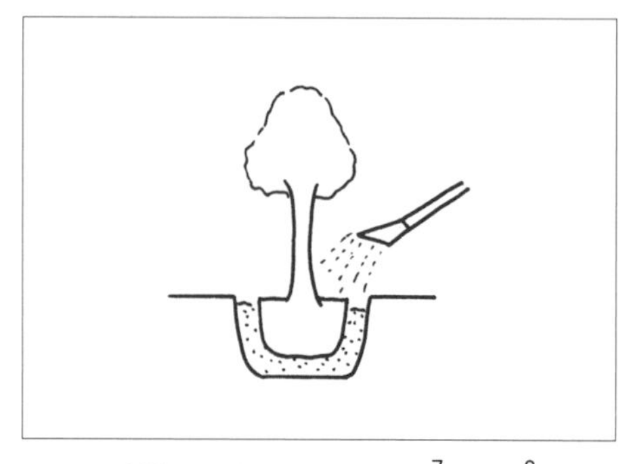

6 When the hole is $\frac{7}{10}$ to $\frac{8}{10}$ full, sprinkle with plenty of water.

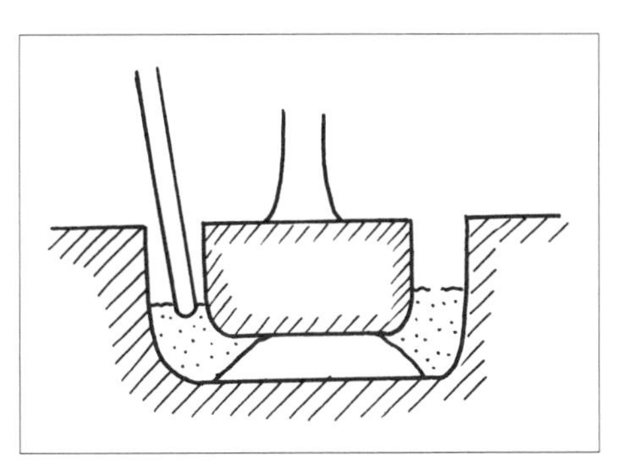

7 The soil will sink as it absorbs the water. Add more soil and tamp down.

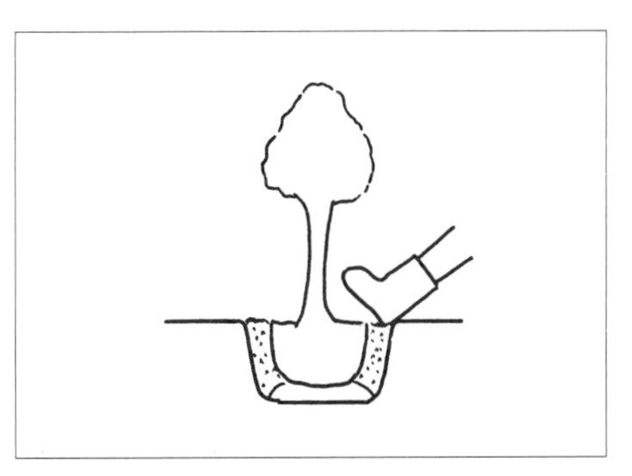

8 When the hole is filled, lightly stomp the ground. Add soil as necessary.

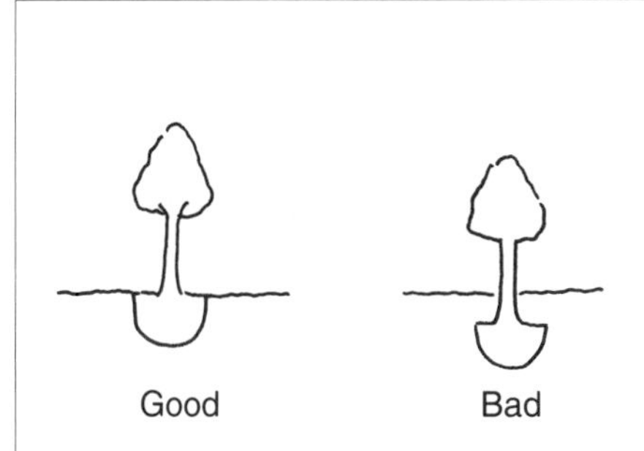

9 Do not plant the tree too deep because the new root will come out near the ground surface and the growth of the tree will become less vigorous.

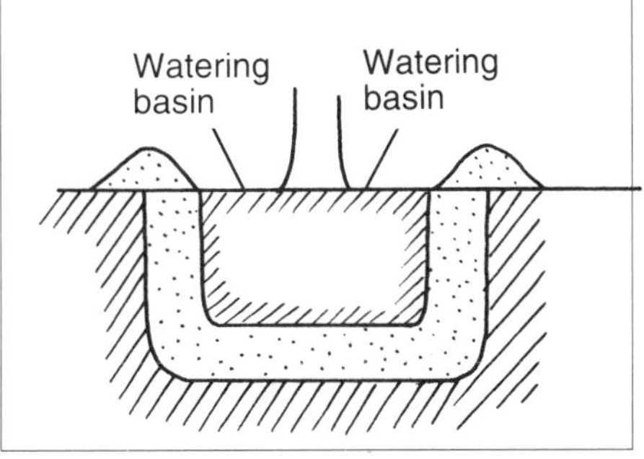

10 After the tree is watered and the correct level has been established, make a ridge of soil around the hole to form a watering basin.

Watering basin

By molding ridge of soil around the plant, the rainwater will not flow away and your watering chore will be lessened. Once the tree is rooted, it is not necessary to water regularly, but a watering basin will help to keep the soil wet even in the summer heat.

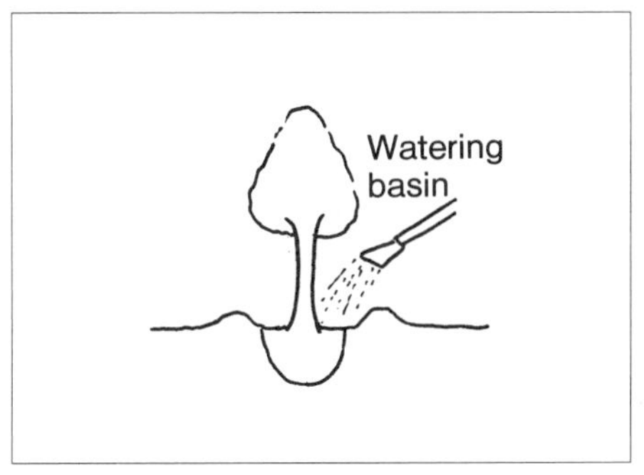

11 Pour plenty of water into the watering basin. Gently sprinkle water not to break down the ridge.

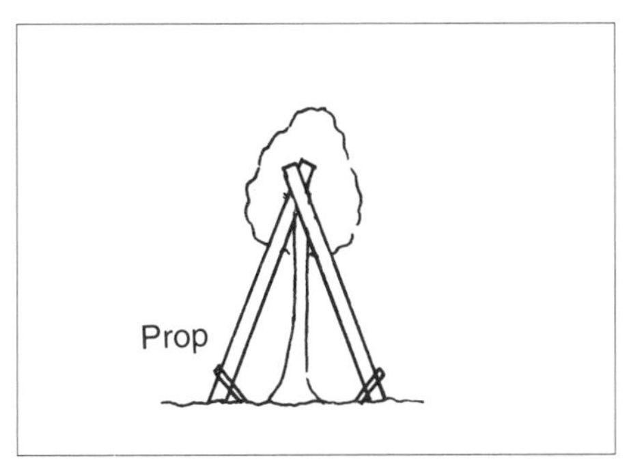

12 Set props until the tree has been securely rooted. Use bamboo stalks for short trees, logs for tall trees.

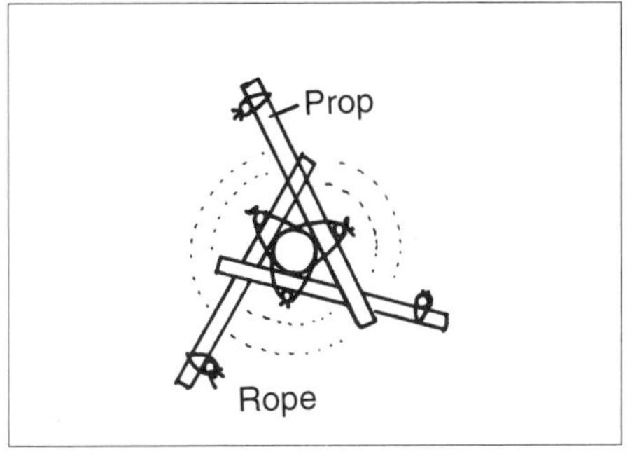

13 To prevent the tree from falling down, cross three props and bind each with the tree using a rope.

14 Attach short sticks to the props near the ground end binding with a rope, then hammer them into ground.

PLANTING GRASSES

In *tsuboniwa,* grass is often planted to cover the ground around the washing basin or among the arranged stones. Choose a ground cover which does not need much sunlight and maintenance. You can grow one portion of the grass until it covers the ground, but if you want a quick result, plant several portions at intervals and wait for the growth. The following is a planting method for *tamaryu,* or dwarf snake's beard, a typical Japanese ground cover.

You will need:
Tamaryu (Dwarf snake's beard)
Trowel

Potted dwarf snake's beard and its root

1 Measure the width and length of the ground where the grass is to be planted, and determine the necessary number of pots. Since dwarf snake's beard spreads in time, be sure to separate each plant.

2 Dig holes deep enough for the plant roots.

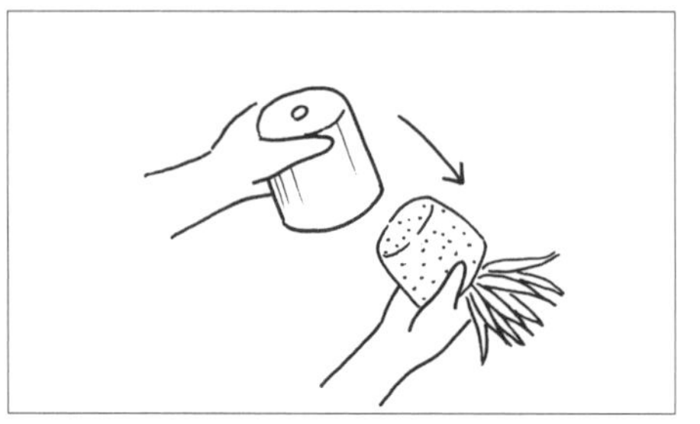

3 Take out the root, by holding the container upside down.

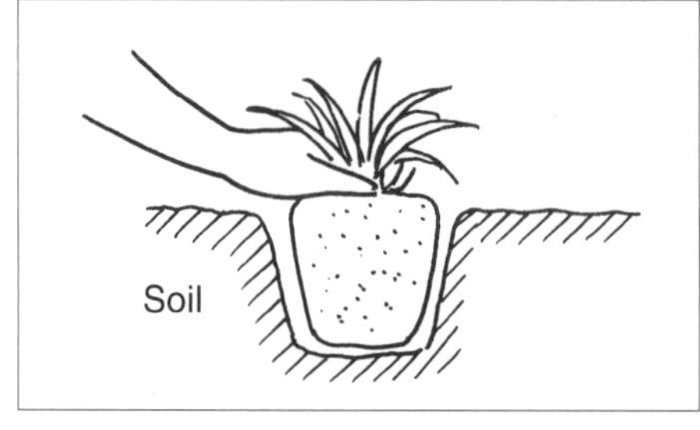

4 Set dwarf snake's beard into the planting hole, and press the top of soil with your hand.

5 Continue planting in rows towards you, so as not to tread on the plants.

6 After planting all the roots, gently water all over.

Maintenance

It is not necessary to water dwarf snake's beard, but instead, you will have to weed until the ground is completely covered with the plant. Once the ground is densely covered, the weed rarely comes out.

PLANTING MOSSES

Moss is another beautiful ground cover for *tsuboniwa*. Plant it during spring and enjoy the texture all year round. In order to encourage growth, choose a place with a certain amount of humidity and ventilation, preferably a shadowy, sandy ground. Here is a method of planting the popular hairmoss.

You will need:
Hairmoss
Trowel
Drop shank trowel
Basin

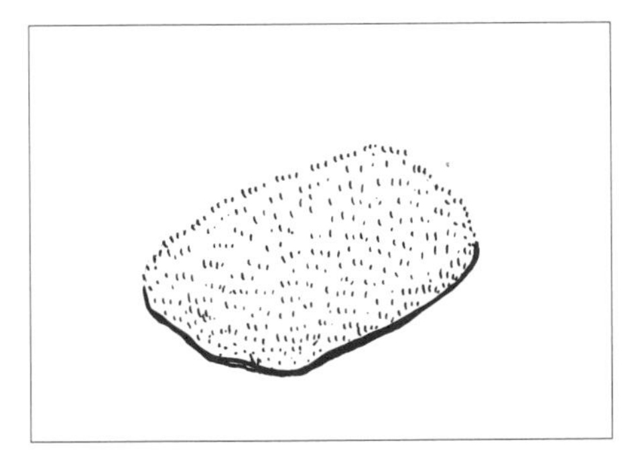

1 Measure the ground to determine how many portions of hairmoss are needed. Hairmoss is usually sold by 30cm^2 (1 ft^2) portion.

2 Dig a shallow hole for the hairmoss and fluff the soil. Remove weeds.

3 Fill a basin with water, and soak one portion of hairmoss so that it absorbs moisture.

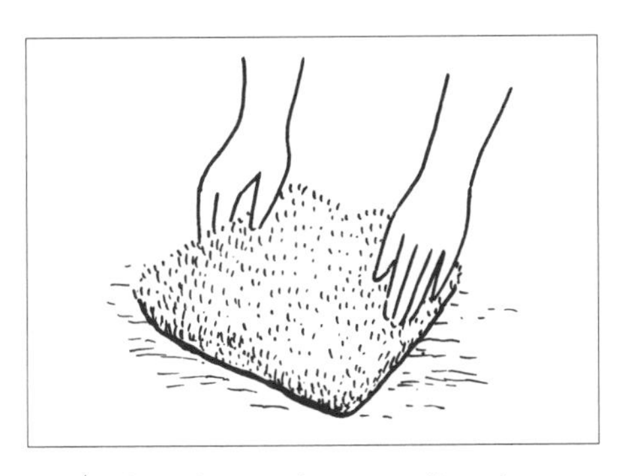

4 Lay the portion on soil and press gently but firmly to stick to the soil.

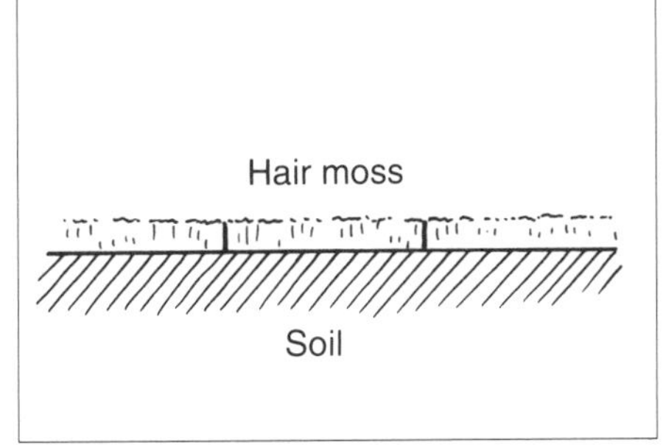

5 Lay another portion of hairmoss, butting with the first one. Continue in the same manner, leaving no space between each portion since mosses do not extend rapidly.

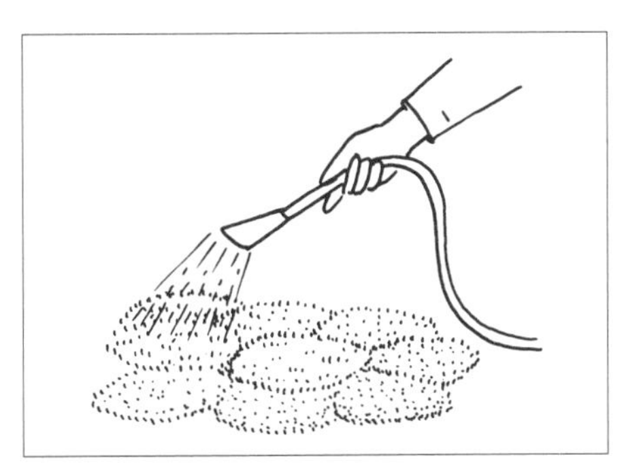

6 After planting all portions, water generously. The only maintenance will be occasional weeding until the ground is densely covered, in one to two years.

CONSTRUCTING *KENNINJI-GAKI*

The *Kenninji-gaki* bamboo fence is usually made wide rather than tall, so a longer stretch of fence or wall is possible in this style. One of the characteristics of this fence is the five or six tiers of horizontal crossbars. The five-tiered type is found mostly in western Japan whereas the six-tiered one is popular in the eastern regions. Although the figure on this page shows a six-tiered fence, the instructions are for the easier, narrower five-tiered style.

Blueprint

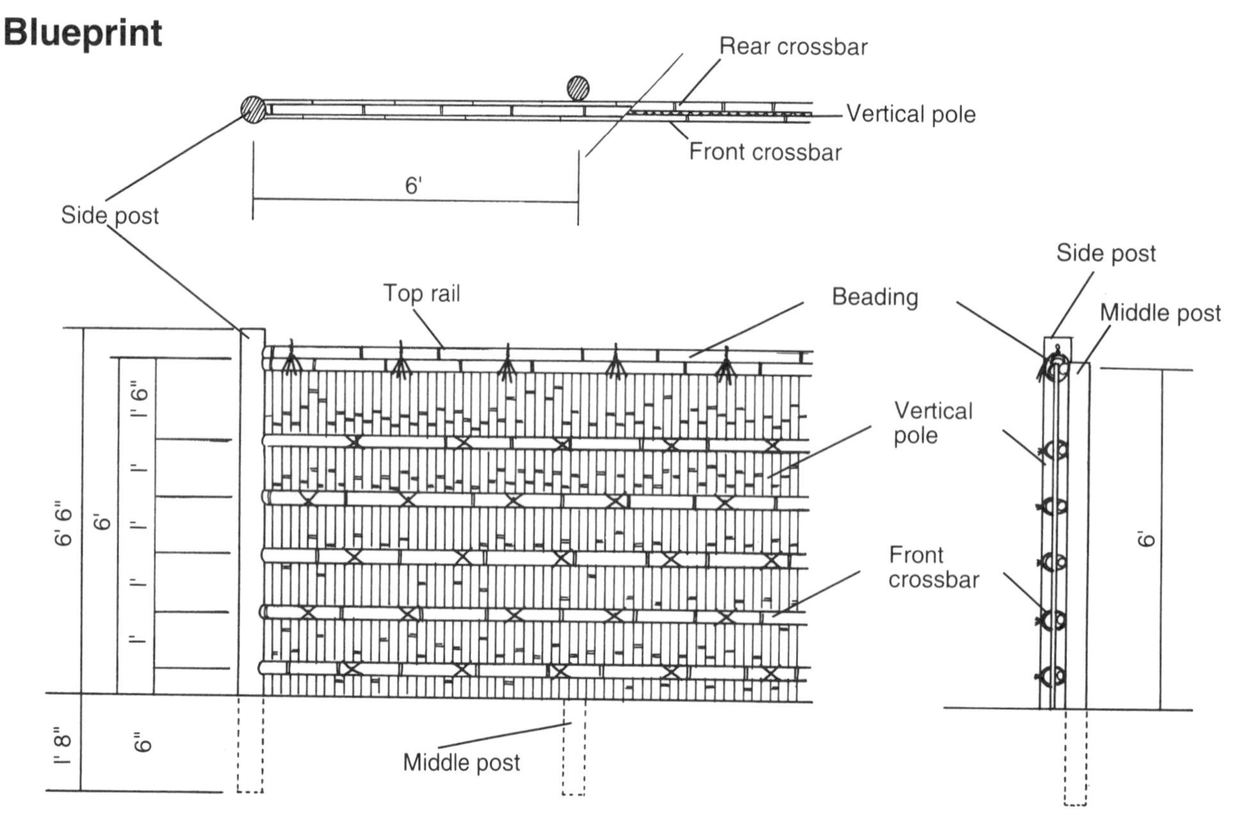

You will need:

Brush, Bucket, Post-hole digger, Tape measure, Wooden pole, Plumb bob, Level, Leveling string, Hammer, Saw for bamboo, Drill, Saw, Flat chisel, Paint brush, Lineman's pliers, Red marker, Hooked needle, Scissors, Axe

Side posts: 2 x 90-100cm(3'-3'3") diam, 1.8m(6') long scorched logs
Rear crossbars: 6 x 1.8m(6') long, narrow bamboo
Vertical poles: 40(approx) x 1.8m(6') long, split bamboo
Front crossbars: 6 x 1.8m(6') long, thick bamboo halves
Top rail: 1 x 1.8m(6') long, thick bamboo halves
Black hemp rope, Nail, Wire, Antiseptic wood stain

Procedure:

1. Prepare logs and bamboo.
2. Implant supporting posts.
3. Attach crossbars on reverse side.
4. Set base board.
5. Tie with hemp rope.

1 Pour water over scorched logs and wash off the carbonized surface using a brush.

2 Mark the ground with positions of side posts, 1.8m(6') apart.

3 Using a post-hole digger, make a hole in position. Bring the digger deep down to catch the soil.

4 Remove the soil.

5 Dig until the hole is approximately 50cm(20") deep.

6 Set the poles to check that they settle at the same height. Fill any space with soil and tamp down with a pole.

7 Using a plumb bob, check that the posts stand perpendicular to the ground. Adjust so that the thread falls through the center of the post.

8 Tamp down the soil around the posts.

9 Using a level, recheck that the post is vertical. Hold the level with its top apart from the post since the posts are tapered toward the tips.

10 Place a board on both posts and nail down temporarily; do not drive completely.

11 Now the posts are temporarily fixed with the board, which will make the later work easier.

12 Stretch leveling string between the posts, at any height.

13 Using a level, adjust the string to make it horizontal.

14 Make a ruler: On a long and narrow board, mark the positions for crossbars above the ground (or in the middle). Transfer the marks onto posts.

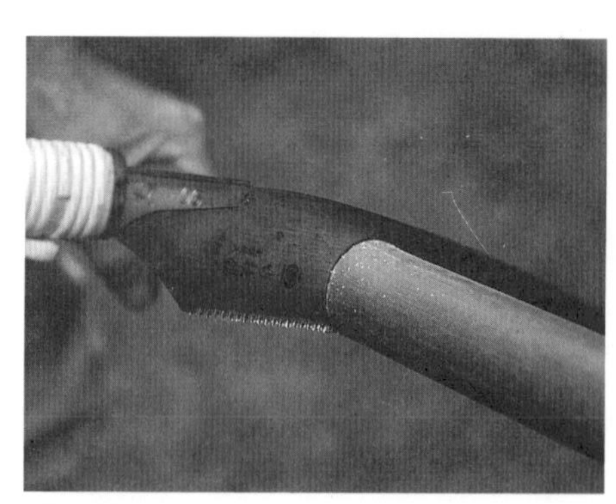

15 Prepare a bamboo stalk for the back, to be set as the second crossbar from the top.

16 Cut away the root end diagonally so as to fit the left-side post.

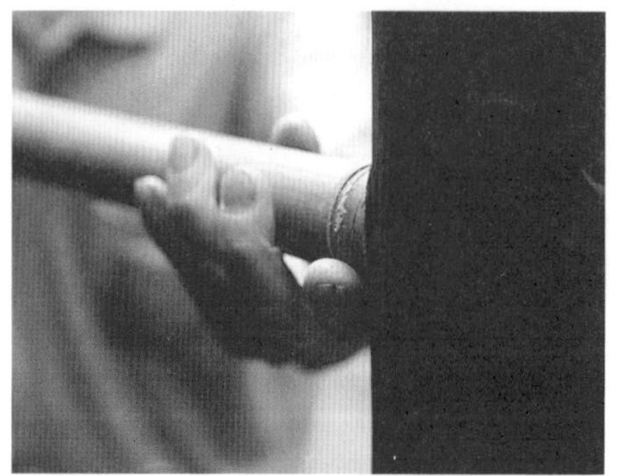

17 Set the pole between the marks on the posts and check the length.

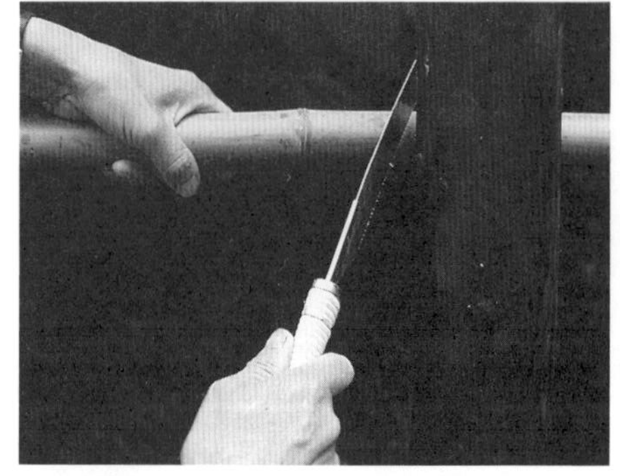

18 Cut off the right-hand end diagonally.

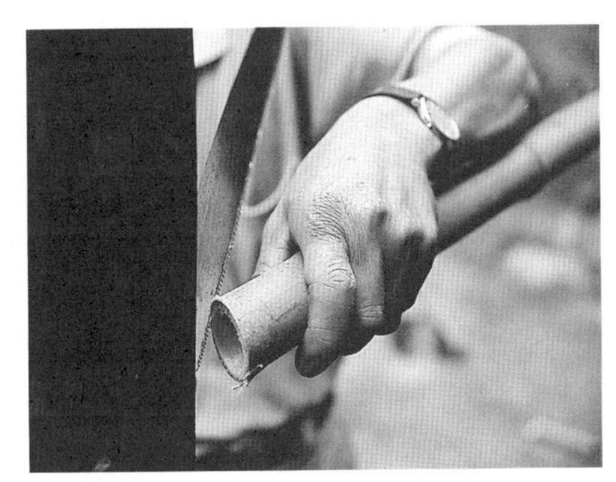

19 The right-hand end has been cut.

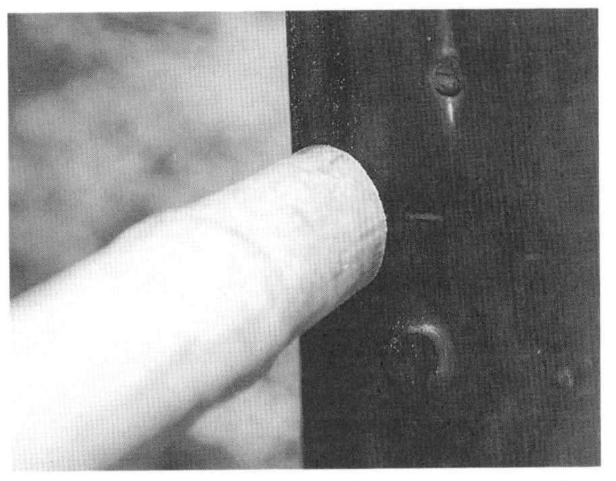

20 It is best if the front side of the crossbar meets the center line of the side post.

21 Drill a hole at a slant, through to the post.

22 Nail down. Hammer carefully since the bamboo stalks may split unless hammering near the joints.

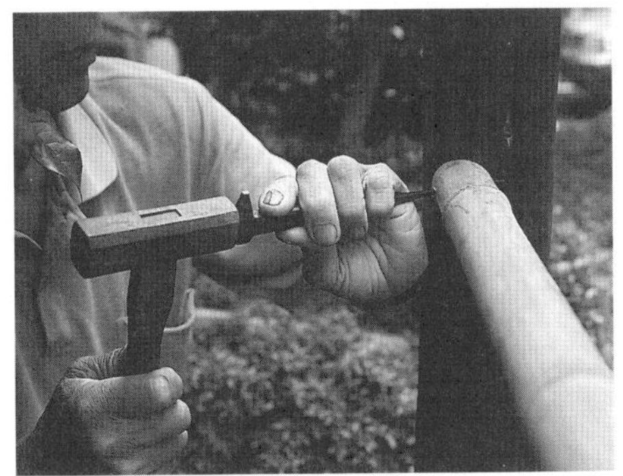

23 Finish by hammering onto a nail set. A nail set can be substituted with another nail.

24 The crossbar is nailed to the side post (seen from behind).

25 There is a space between the crossbar and the side post.

26 Prepare and set the third crossbar in the same manner, but alternate the direction of the bamboo.

27 Set the fourth pole in the same manner, alternating the direction again.

28 Set the fifth pole in the same manner. By alternating the directions of bamboo stalks, the whole panel will look well-balanced.

29 Now set the base board. This board not only supports the vertical poles, but keeps the bamboo poles from decaying. Mark the setting positions onto the side posts.

30 Using a flat chisel, cut a dado.

31 Chisel out wood so that the board edge fits flush.

32 Trim ends of the board as shown, not to show the gap between the board and the post.

33 Check if the fit is tight.

34 Using a wide paint brush, apply antiseptic wood stain over the dado.

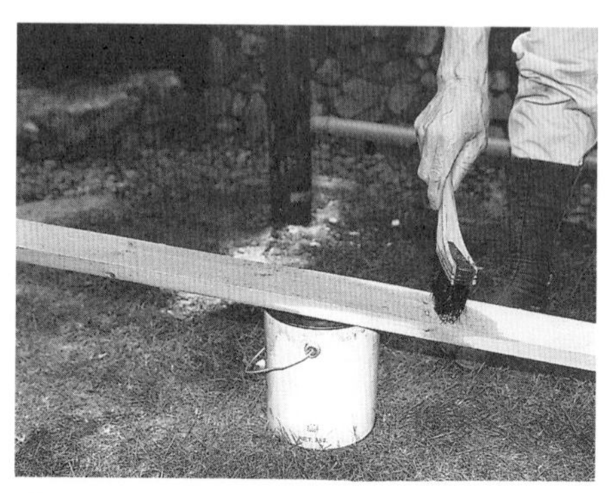

35 Also apply antiseptic wood stain all over the base board.

36 Insert the ends of the board into the dadoes, hammering on a piece of wood to protect the surface of the board.

37 Drill a hole at a slant, through to the post.

38 Nail the board to the post.

39 The four rear crossbars and two boards are fixed to the posts.

40 Finally attach the top crossbar, alternating the direction with the second crossbar.

41 Fix a hooked nail at the post, next to the third crossbar to use as a hook.

42 Tie a temporary string around the hooked nail. Hemp rope is ideal although any string will do.

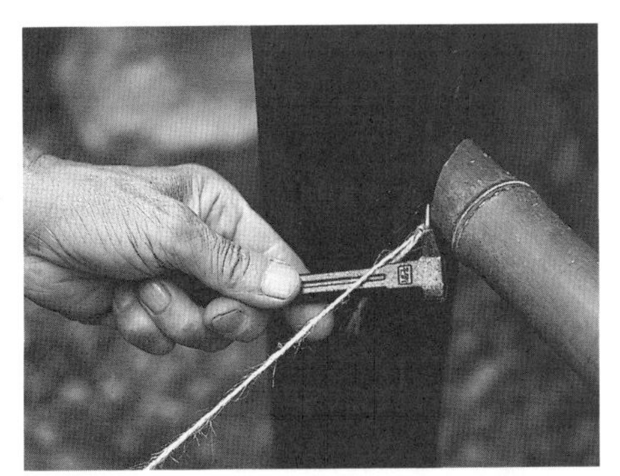

43 Drive down the hooked nail deeply.

44 Using a plumb bob, mark each crossbar at an interval of about six vertical poles.

45 Cut the bamboo for vertical poles according to the indicated length.

46 Stand the first vertical pole and hold with hemp rope.

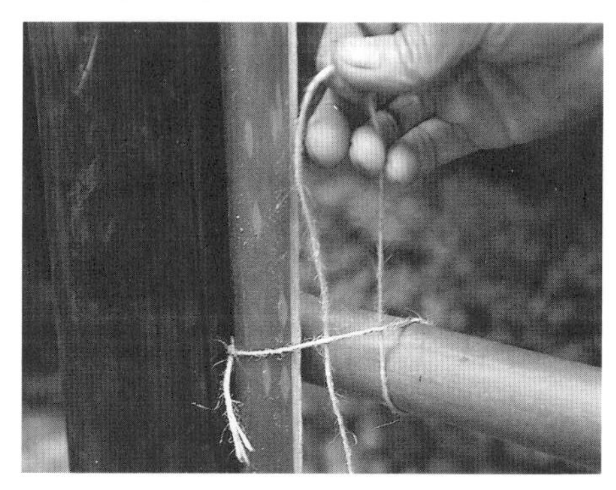

47 Pass the rope over the crossbar and bring under it, as shown.

48 Pull the rope upwards.

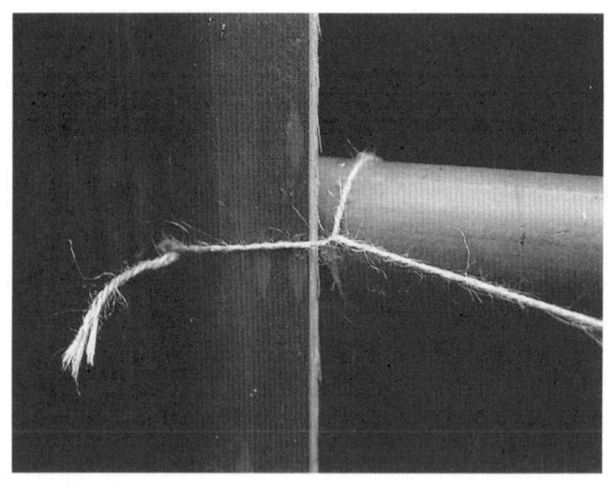

49 Tighten by pulling the end towards right.

50 Now stand the second pole and bind with the same rope. Prepare enough number of poles and place within your reach for efficiency.

51 The second pole has been held with the rope. Do not "tie" with rope.

52 Set the poles so that the joints do not meet each other. This way, the surface of the fence will look attractive.

53 The third rear crossbar seen from the back.

54 When six vertical poles are held, check if the side of the sixth pole meets the marks on the crossbars.

55 Reverse side of the vertical poles that are being held with the rope.

56 Continue catching the poles until the pole reaches the other post.

57 When the last pole is held, tie the rope onto the rear crossbar.

58 The vertical poles are all set. Remove the top board at this stage.

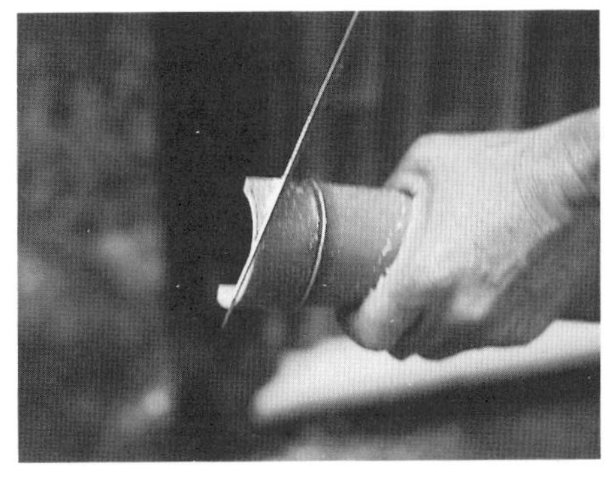

59 Prepare the front crossbar. Cut the root end of bamboo in half, at a slant.

60 Hold it at the level of the third (middle) crossbar and adjust the end to fit the curve of the side post.

61 Holding the bar, cut the other end at a slant.

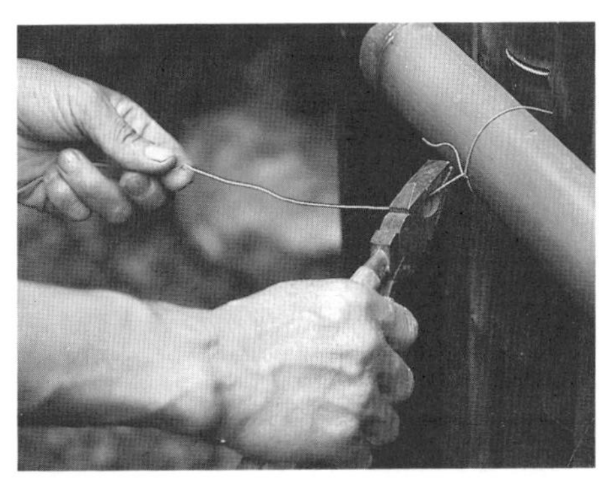

62 Using wire, bind the front crossbar to its matching rear crossbar.

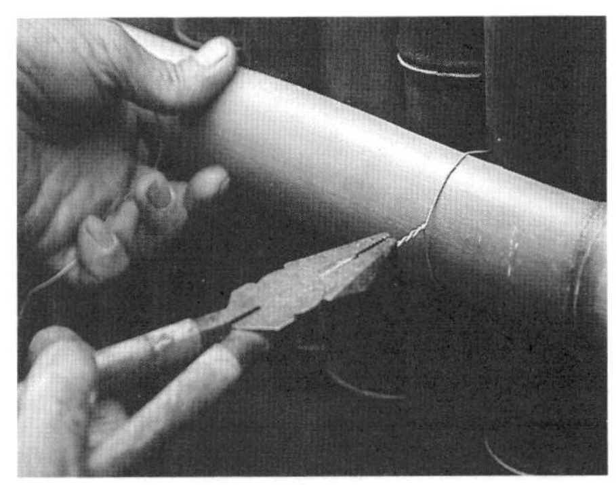

63 Twist the ends of wire together. Do not twist too tight.

64 The third crossbar is temporarily fixed.

65 In the same manner, bind the fifth crossbar.

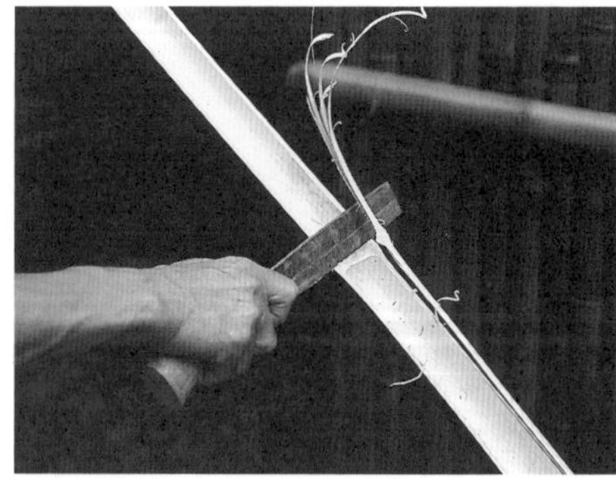

66 When adjusting the width of the vertical pole, shave off toward the root. (When splitting the bamboo, work towards the tip).

67 Bind the fourth crossbar temporarily in the same manner.

68 Bind the second crossbar temporarily in the same manner.

69 Finally bind the top crossbar temporarily in the same manner.

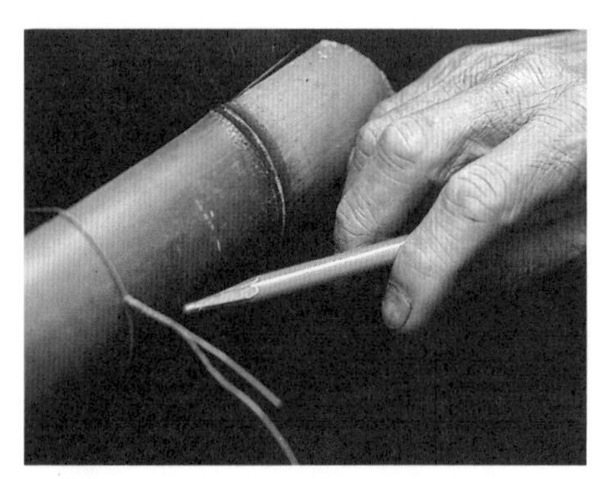

70 Mark the tying position onto the second crossbar, at the end of the second vertical pole.

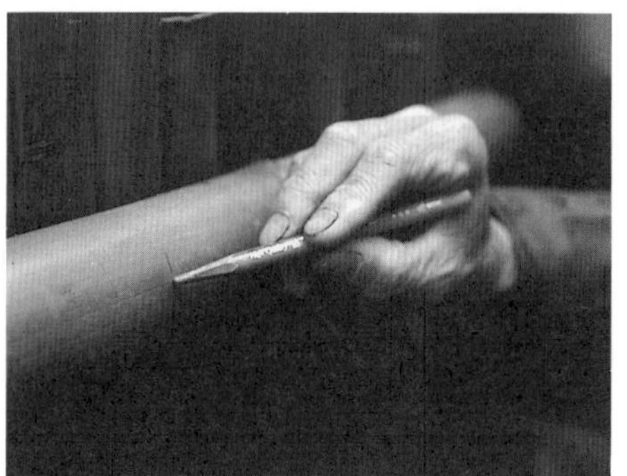

71 Mark the same position onto every other crossbar, downwards.

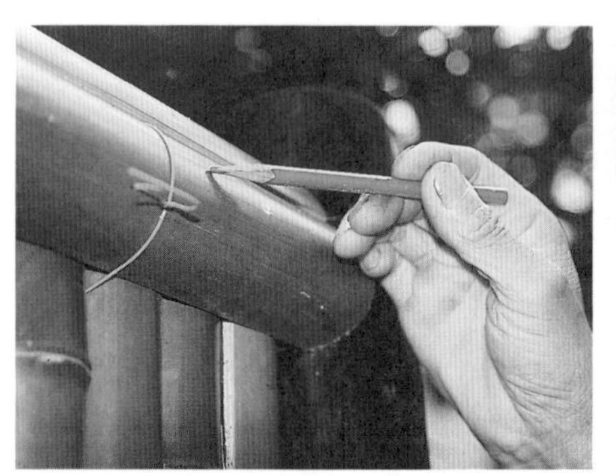

72 Mark the same position onto every other crossbar, upwards.

73 Soak hemp rope in water to soften the fibers, for easy handling.

74 Take the rope out.

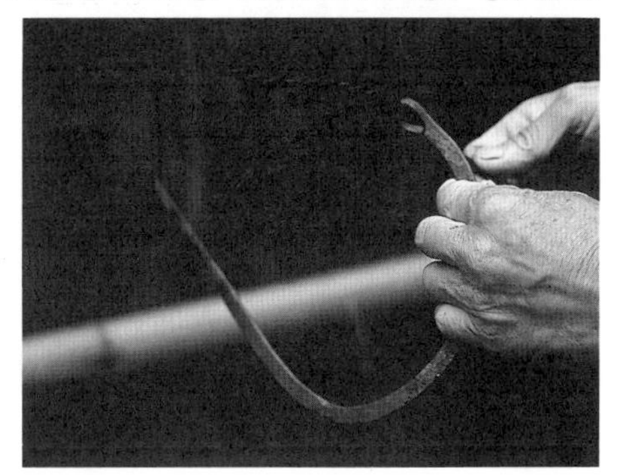

75 Thread two strands of hemp rope into the eye of a hooked needle.

76 Thrust the hooked needle between the poles at the spot marked on the crossbar.

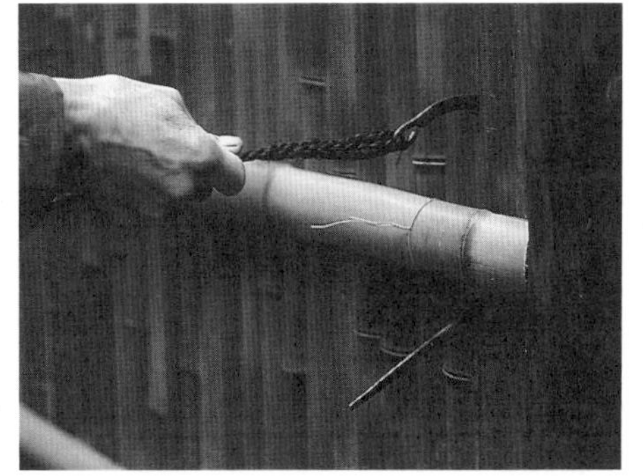

77 Rotate the needle to bring the tip back between the poles, below the crossbar.

78 If the space between the poles is too narrow, insert a bamboo stick to widen the space.

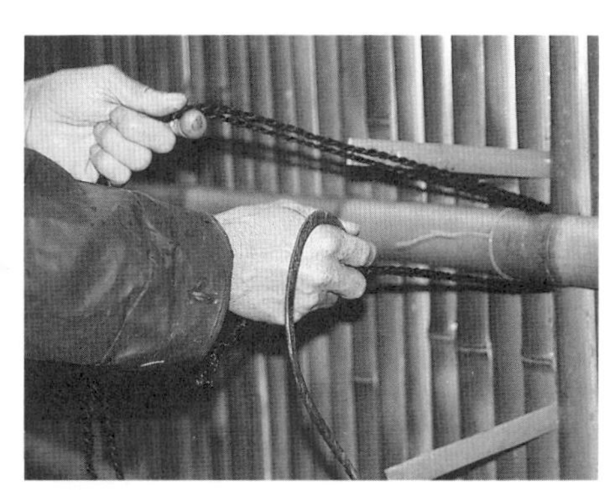

79 Pull out the whole needle.

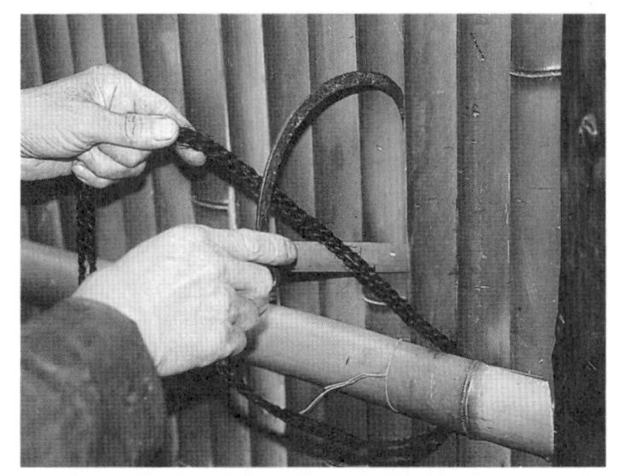

80 Then cross the needle over the rope and insert again immediately to the left of the previous spot.

81 Rotate and bring back below the crossbar, towards you.

82 Remove the needle and pull the rope tight.

83 Tie ends into *tokkuri*-tie. See page 35 for tying directions.

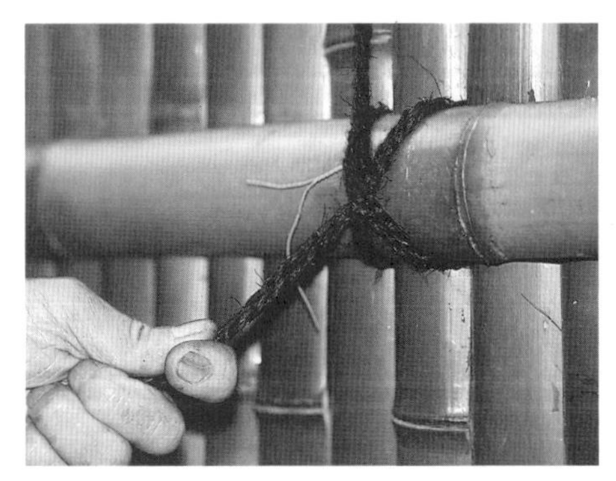

84 Pull the ends tight.

85 Tie into an *ibo-musubi* knot. See page 34 for the knot.

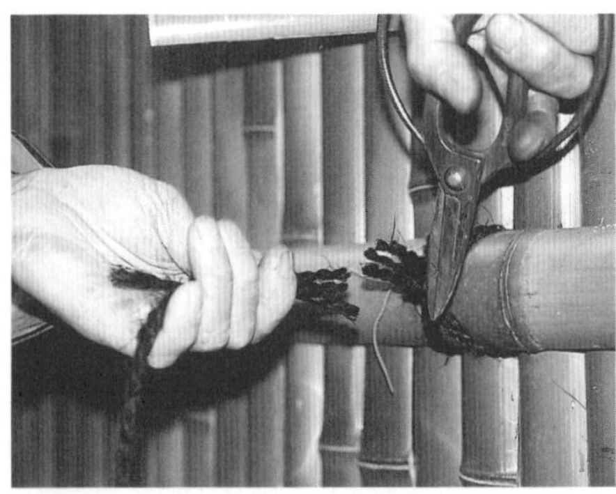

86 Cut off excess rope.

87 Remove the wire.

88 Finished knot.

89 In the same manner, tie all crossbars so that the knot alternates the position on each row.

90 Prepare the beading (top rail). First, cut the bamboo at right angle.

91 Shave off the left end diagonally so as to fit the curve of the side post.

92 Prepare the top rail by removing the joints.

93 Place the top rail.

94 Tie the top rail together with the crossbar, making a decorative knots, starting at the left end.
See page 36 for directions.

95 Tie four decorative knots according to the marks.

96 As for rope ends, make a single knot on each and trim the ends away.

97 Finished decorative knots.

98 Wipe off dirt for the finished *Kenninji-gaki*.

CONSTRUCTING *TOKUSA-GAKI*

Tokusa-gaki **fence shows the simple beauty of vertical bamboo stalks by using no horizontal bars in the front. Therefore, it is important to secure the vertical poles to the rear crossbars.**

Blueprint

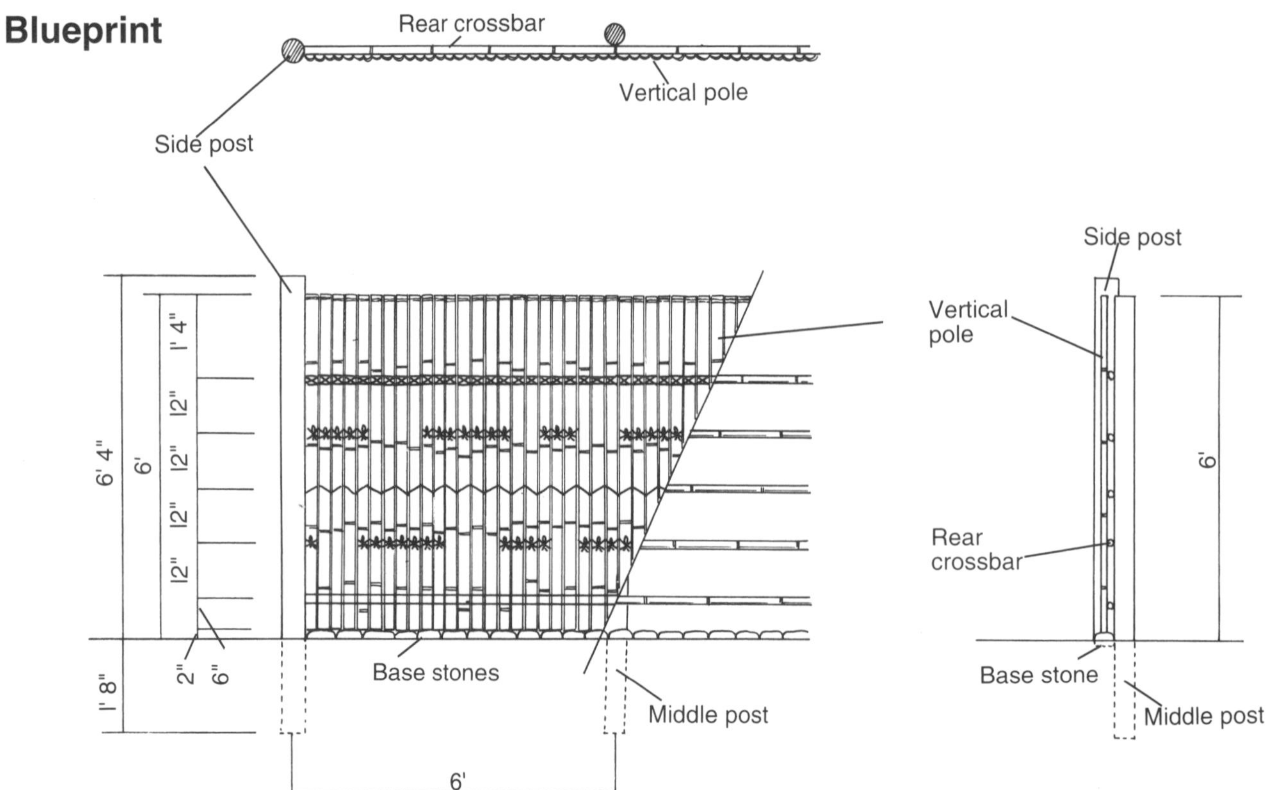

You will need:

Post-hole digger or shovel, Tamping pole, Brass brush, Brush, Marker, Drill, Hammer, Round chisel, Saw, Level, Leveling thread, Saw for bamboo, Axe, Knife, Tape measure, Bucket

Side posts: 2 x 90-100mm($3\frac{1}{2}$"-4") diam, 2.4m(8') long scorched logs

Middle post: 1 x 70-80mm($2\frac{3}{4}$"-3") diam, 2.3m($7\frac{1}{2}$') long scorched log

Crossbars: 5 x 3.6m(12') long *garadake* bamboo

Vertical poles: 25 x 70-80mm($2\frac{3}{4}$"-3") diam, l.75m(5'10") bamboo

Base stones: 10-15 flat stones

Black hemp rope, Nail

Procedure:

1 Prepare logs and bamboo.
2 Implant supporting posts.
3 Attach crossbars on reverse side.
4 Set base stones.
5 Tie with hemp rope.

1 Pour water over scorched logs and wash off the carbonized surface using a brush.

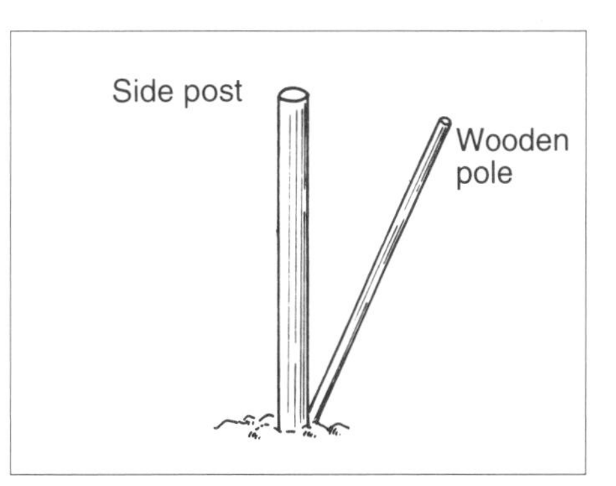

2 Dig about 50cm(20") deep hole and implant the washed log as a side post. Fill any space with soil and tamp down.

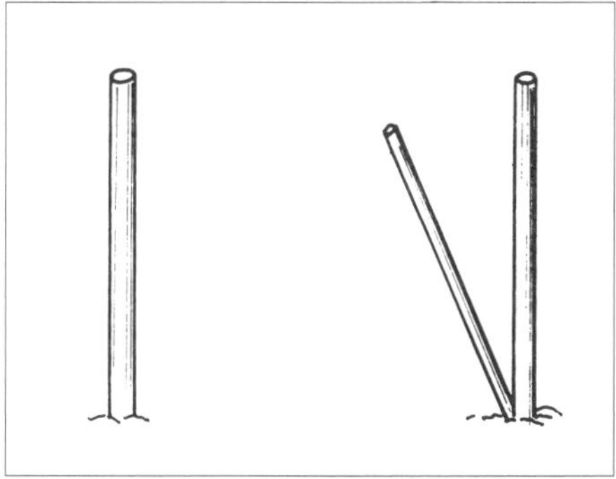

3 Set the other side post in position, in the same manner.

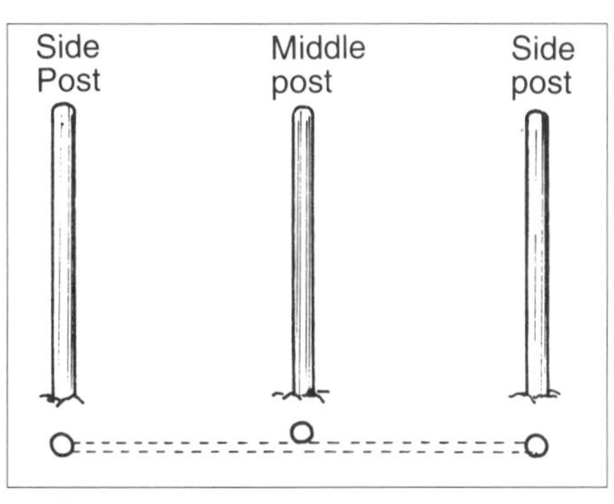

4 Set a middle post. Recess the position so that this post does not show when completed.

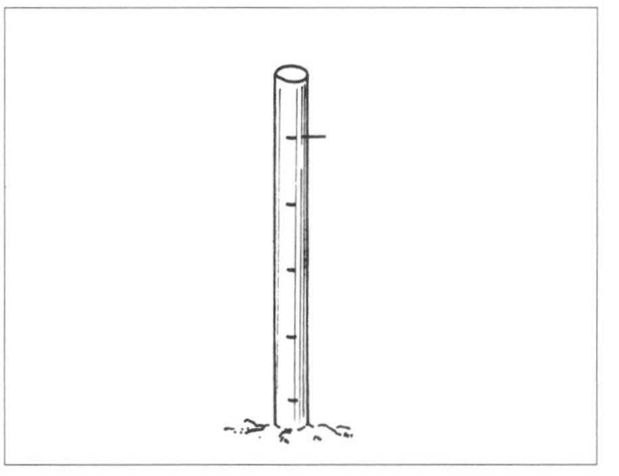

5 Mark each post with the positions to attach to the horizontal crossbars.

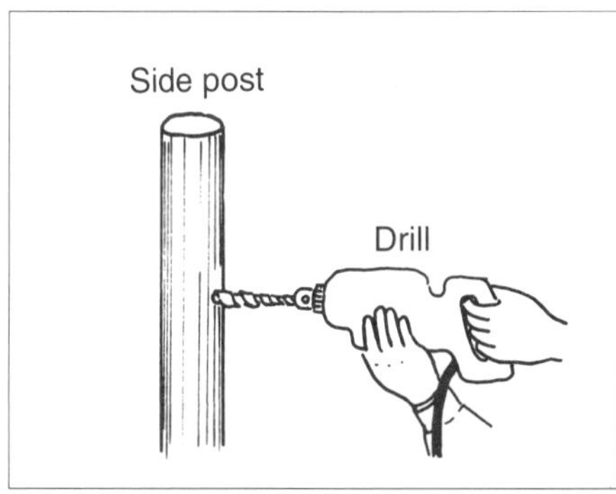

6 Drill a mortise 3-5cm($1\frac{1}{4}$"-2") deep into each post.

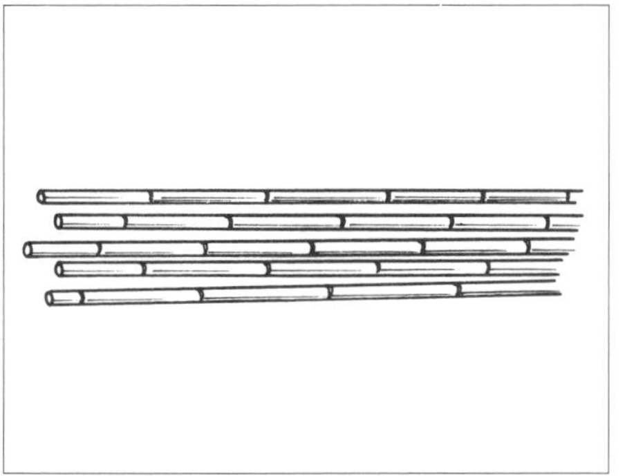

7 Select bamboo stalks for rear crossbars. Take five stalks with less curves.

8 If the surface of bamboo is soiled, wash with water using a brass brush.

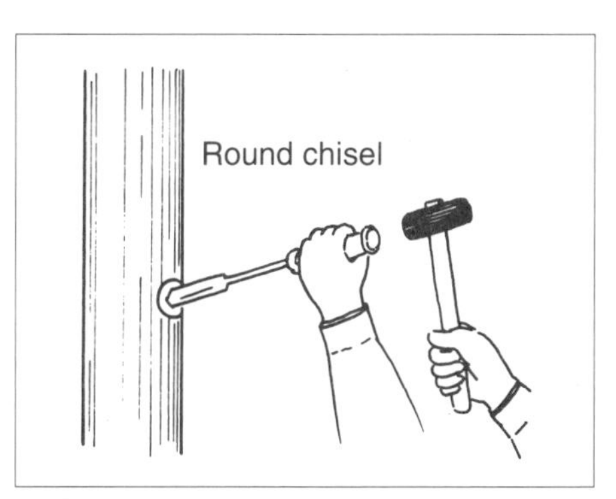

9 Adjust the hole to the size of a crossbar: Drill a hole, then enlarge it using a round chisel.

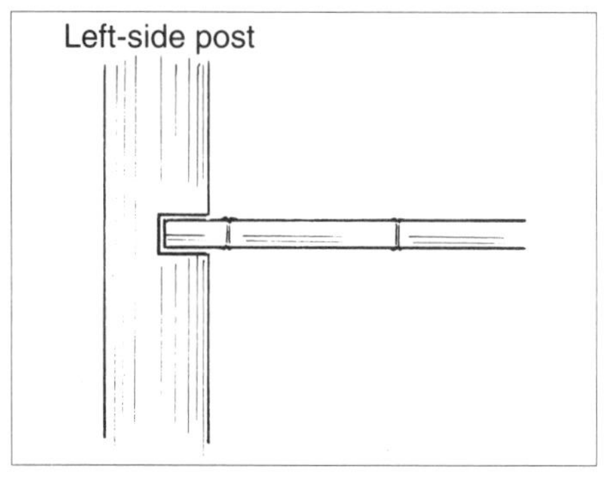

10 Insert the root end of crossbar into the hole of left-side post. Make sure that the end fits flush.

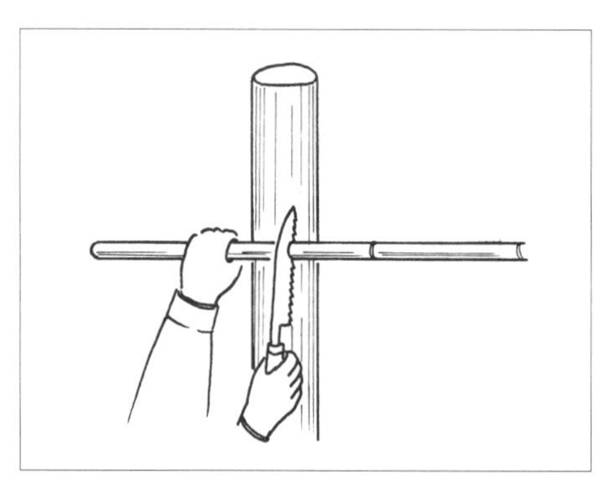

11 Hold it and place the other end at the right-side post. Cut this end a little shorter than the depth of the hole.

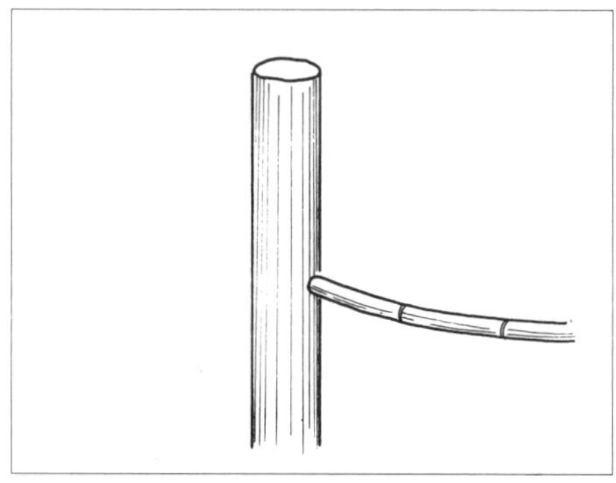

12 Set the end in the hole, bending the crossbar.

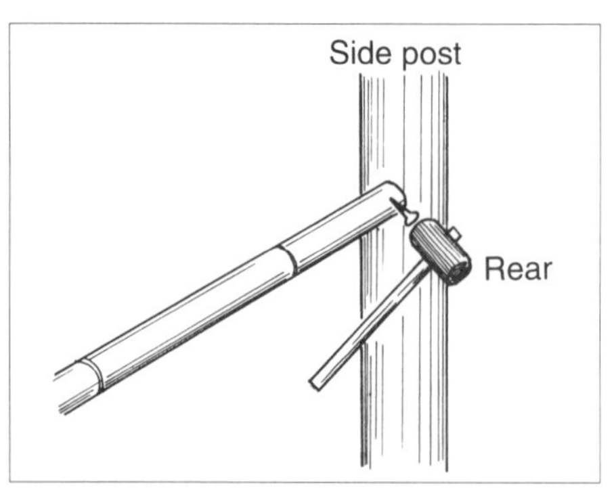

13 Fix onto reverse side; drill a hole and nail at a slant, through to the post.

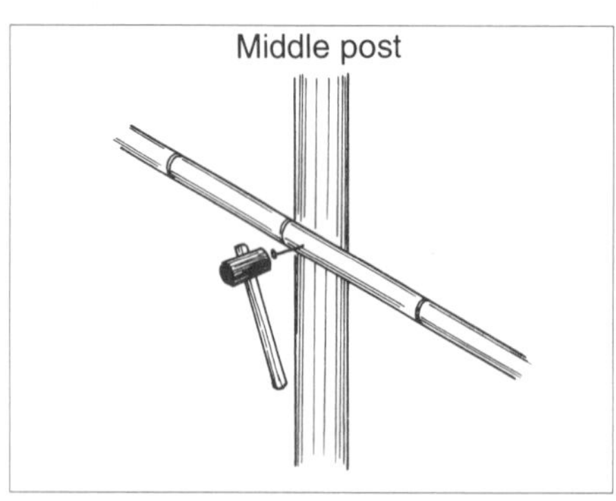

14 Fix the crossbar to the middle post. Check the horizontal line and nail the crossbar to the post.

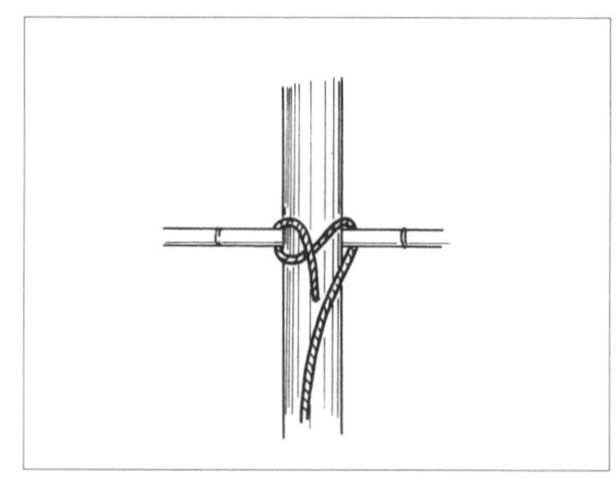

15 Pass hemp rope across the post and make a crisscross. This is called *Kuigake*-tie.

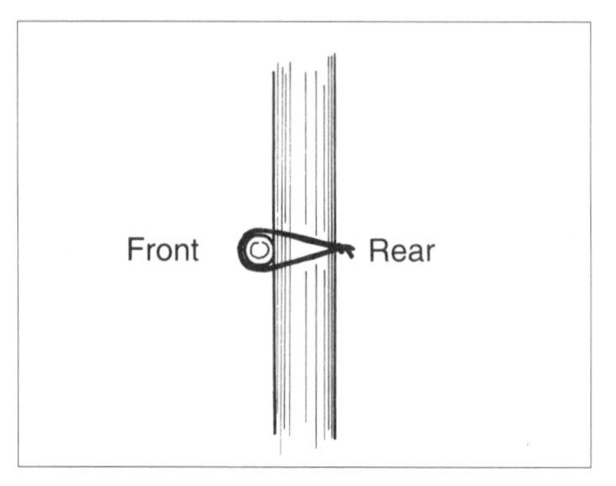

16 *Kuigake*-tie seen from the side.

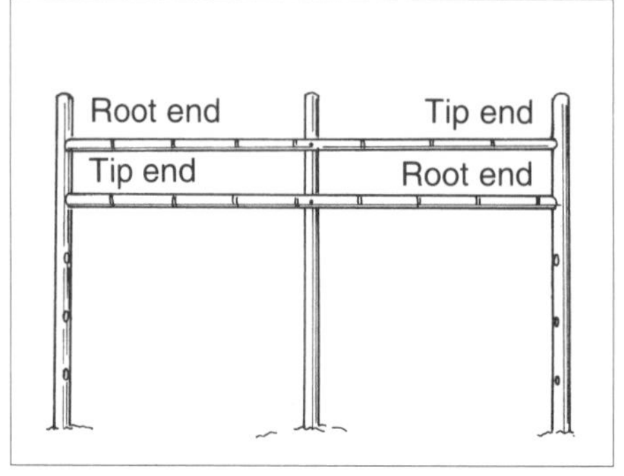

17 Attach other crossbars in the same manner, alternating the direction.

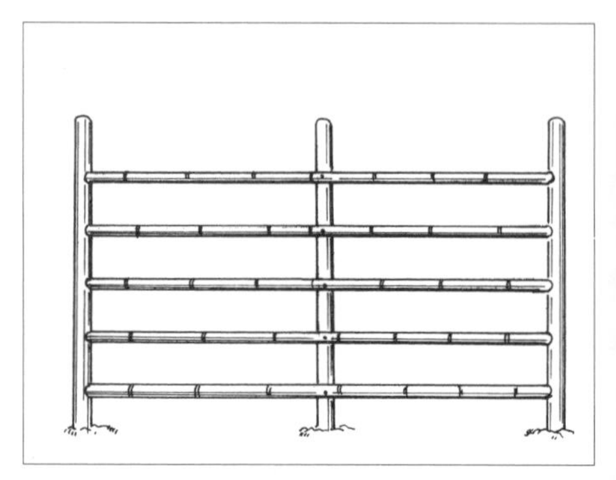

18 All five crossbars are attached.

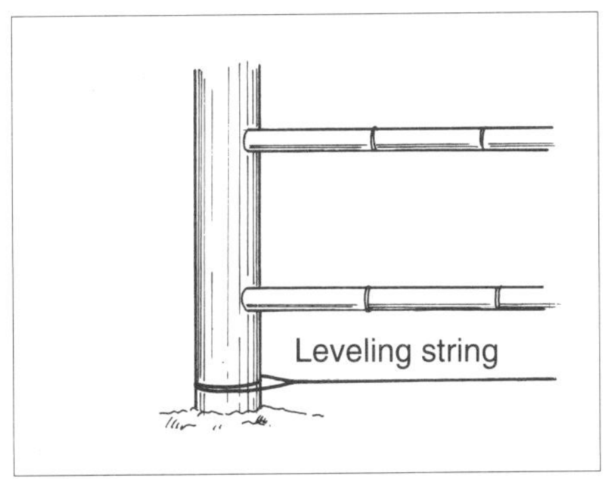

19 To set base stones horizontally, stretch leveling string between the side posts.

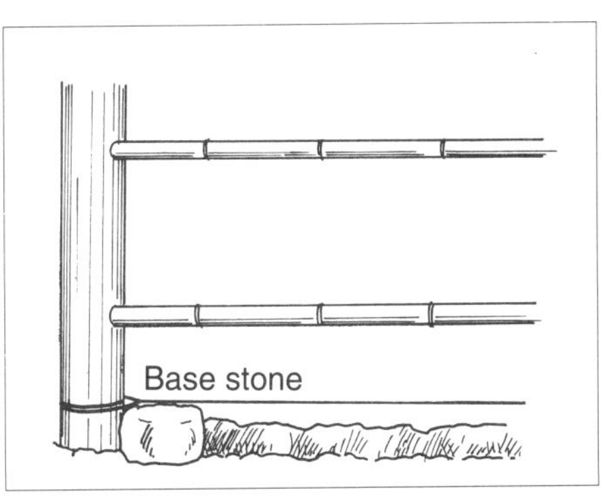

20 Dig a ditch to adjust the height of base stones.

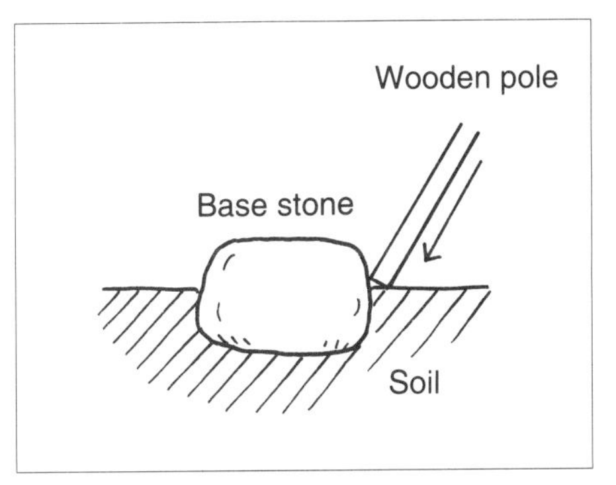

21 Tamp down the soil to stabilize the stone.

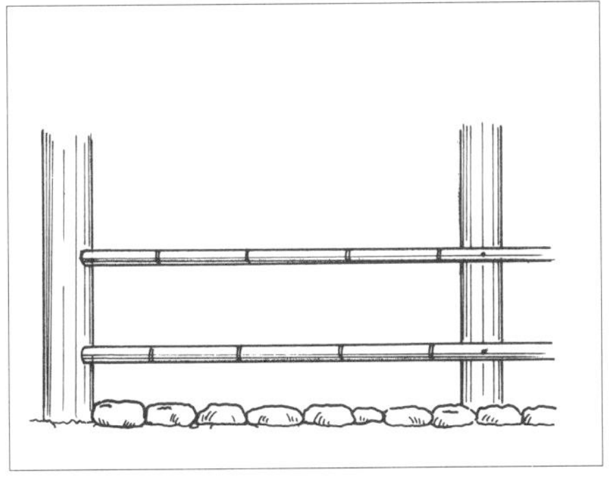

22 Set all the stones in the same manner.

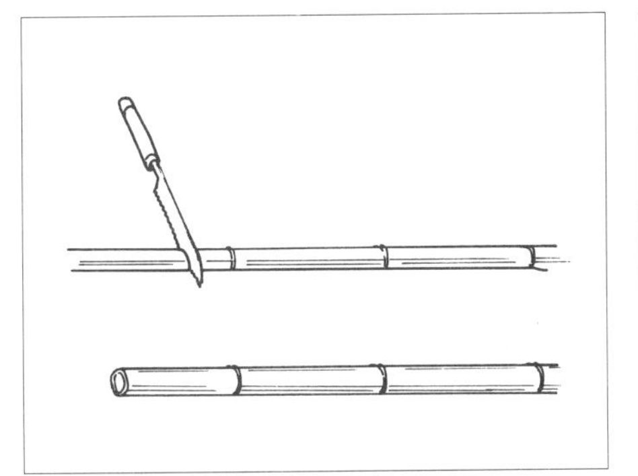

23 Prepare the vertical poles. Cut the bamboo stalks somewhat longer than the size so that you can adjust the directions and the joints.

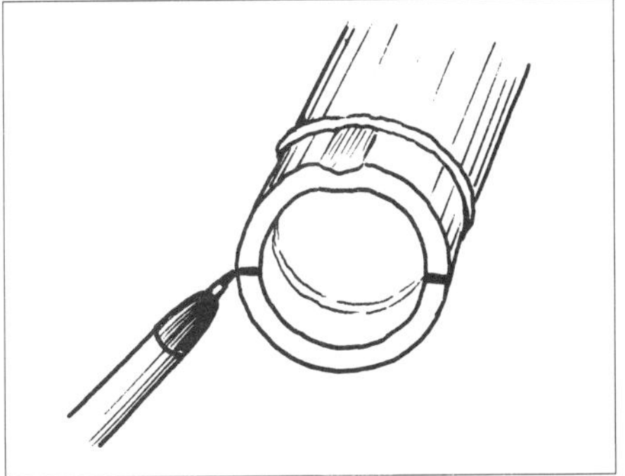

24 Mark the end of bamboo so as to split bamboo precisely in two.

25 Cut with a hatchet, aiming at the marks.

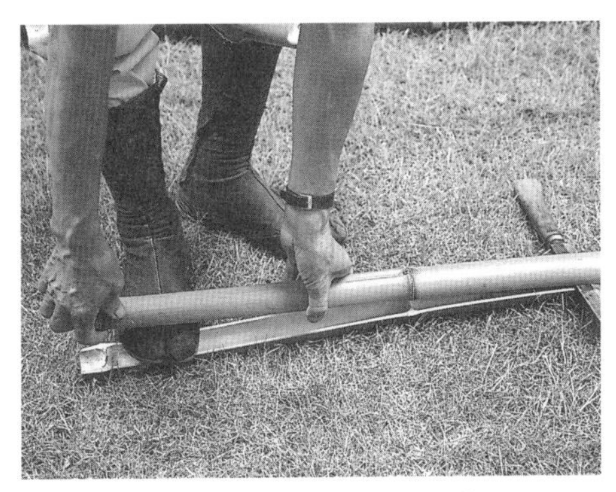

26 When the bamboo splits open, remove the hatchet and pull each half with your foot and hand. Turn over occasionally so as to split precisely.

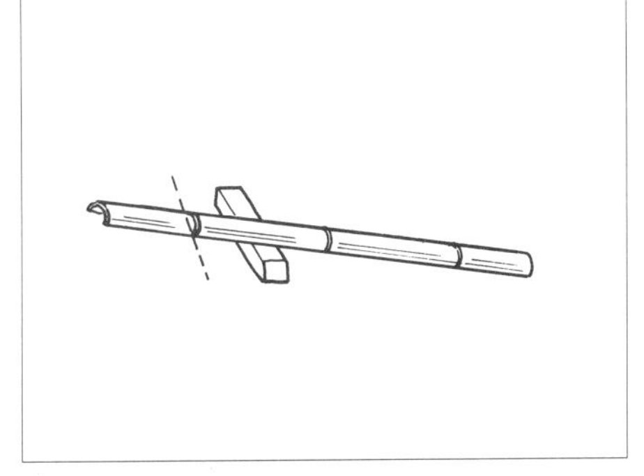

27 Cut the root end just above the joint. The poles next to the side posts should be stood root ends up, so that they can be fixed vertically.

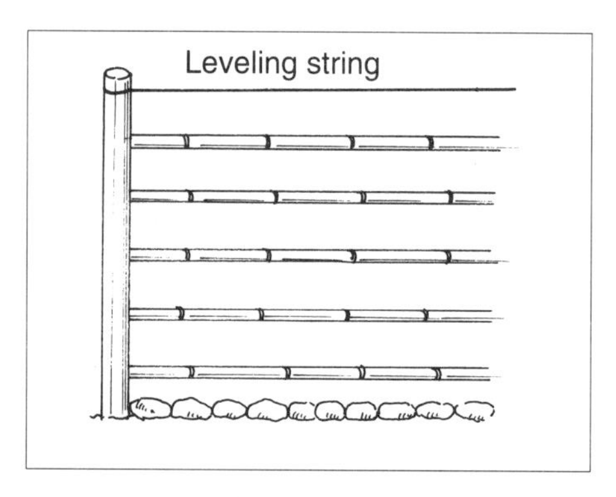

28 Stretch leveling string to mark the height of vertical poles. Use a level to check if the string is horizontal.

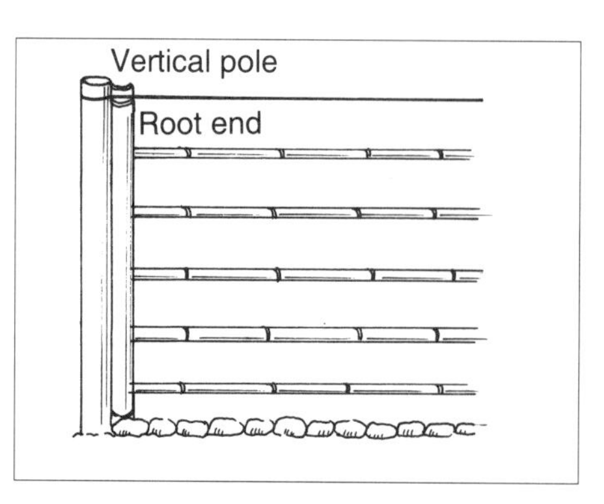

29 Stand a vertical pole, root end up, and adjust the height to match the leveling string.

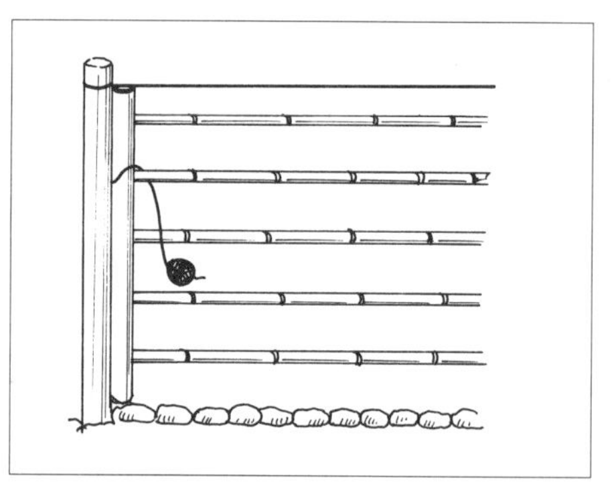

30 Bind the pole to the crossbars temporarily: Drive a nail into left post and tie hemp rope onto it. Pass rope over the second bar as shown.

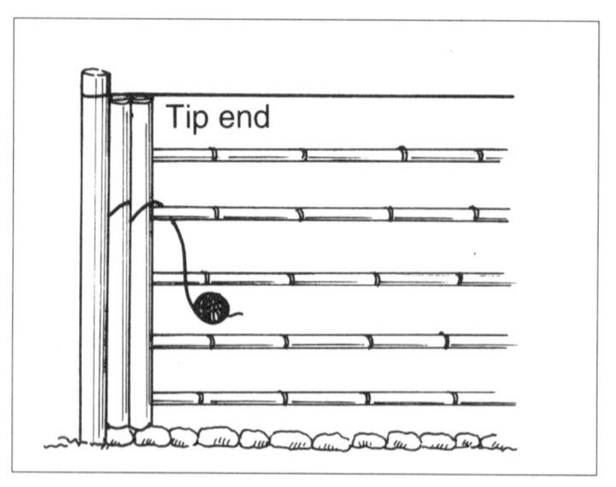

31 Stand the second vertical pole, tip end up. Be sure to cut this end just above the joint to keep away from rainwater. Pass rope across this bar.

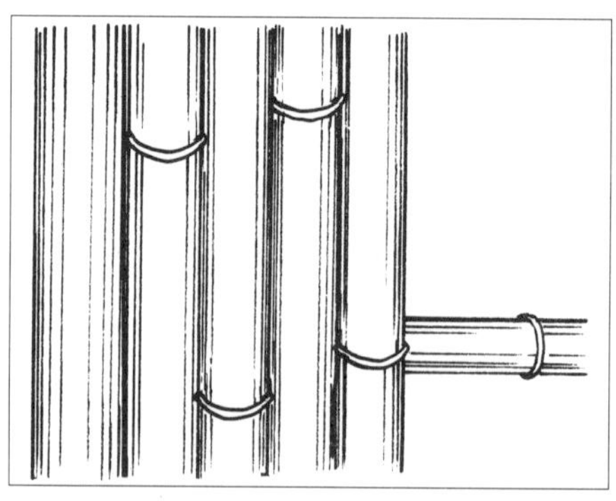

32 Continue standing vertical poles, alternating the directions so they stand vertically.

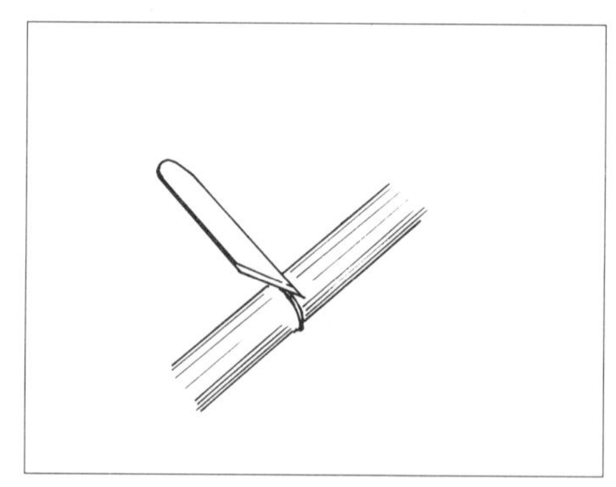

33 Shave off protruding joints so as to pack the poles side to side.

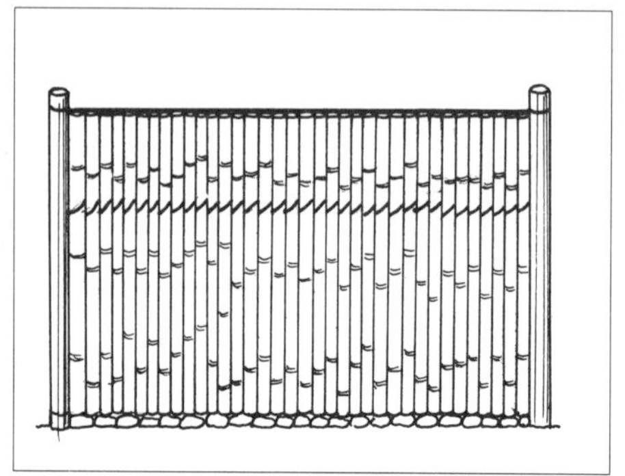

34 Continue until the poles fill the space, passing rope across each pole as shown. Bind the end of rope to the right post.

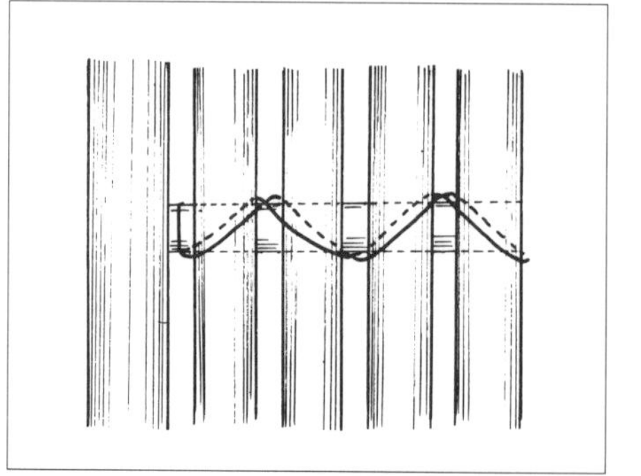

35 Secure the poles to the third bar using black hemp rope. Use two strands of rope and "weave", crossing them between poles to form a zigzag.

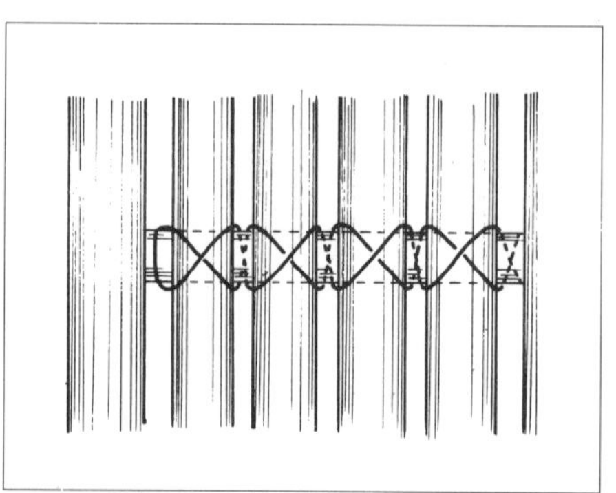

36 Secure the poles to the top bar. Use two strands of rope and cross them on back and front.

37 Using two strands, cross at back (see figure of Step 38) so two straight lines frame the previous front crosses.

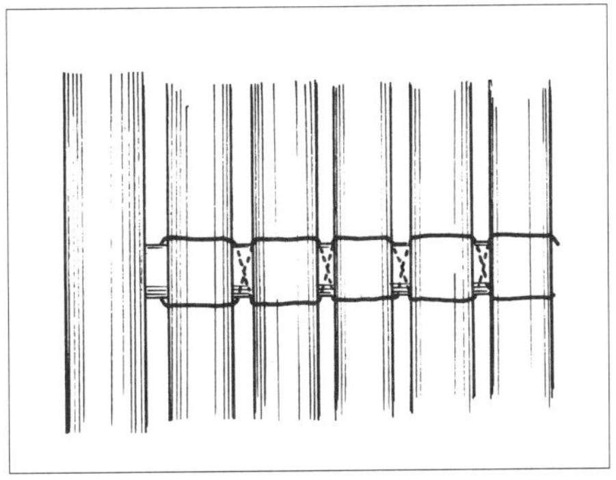

38 Fix the poles to the fifth(bottom) crossbar. Use two strands and cross at back.

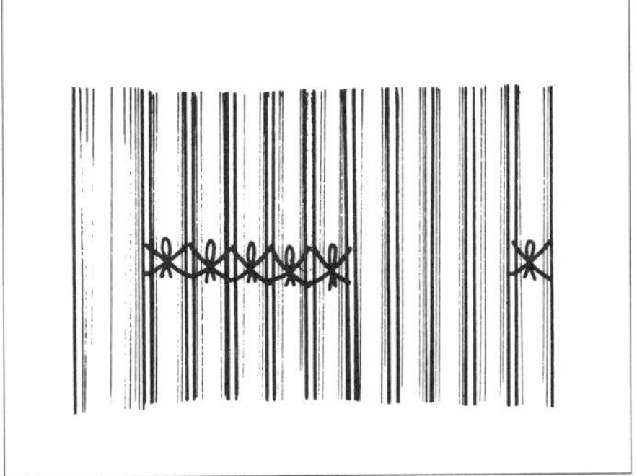

39 Finally make random ties, fixing to the second and the fourth crossbars. Tie rope across four or five poles, after every few poles.

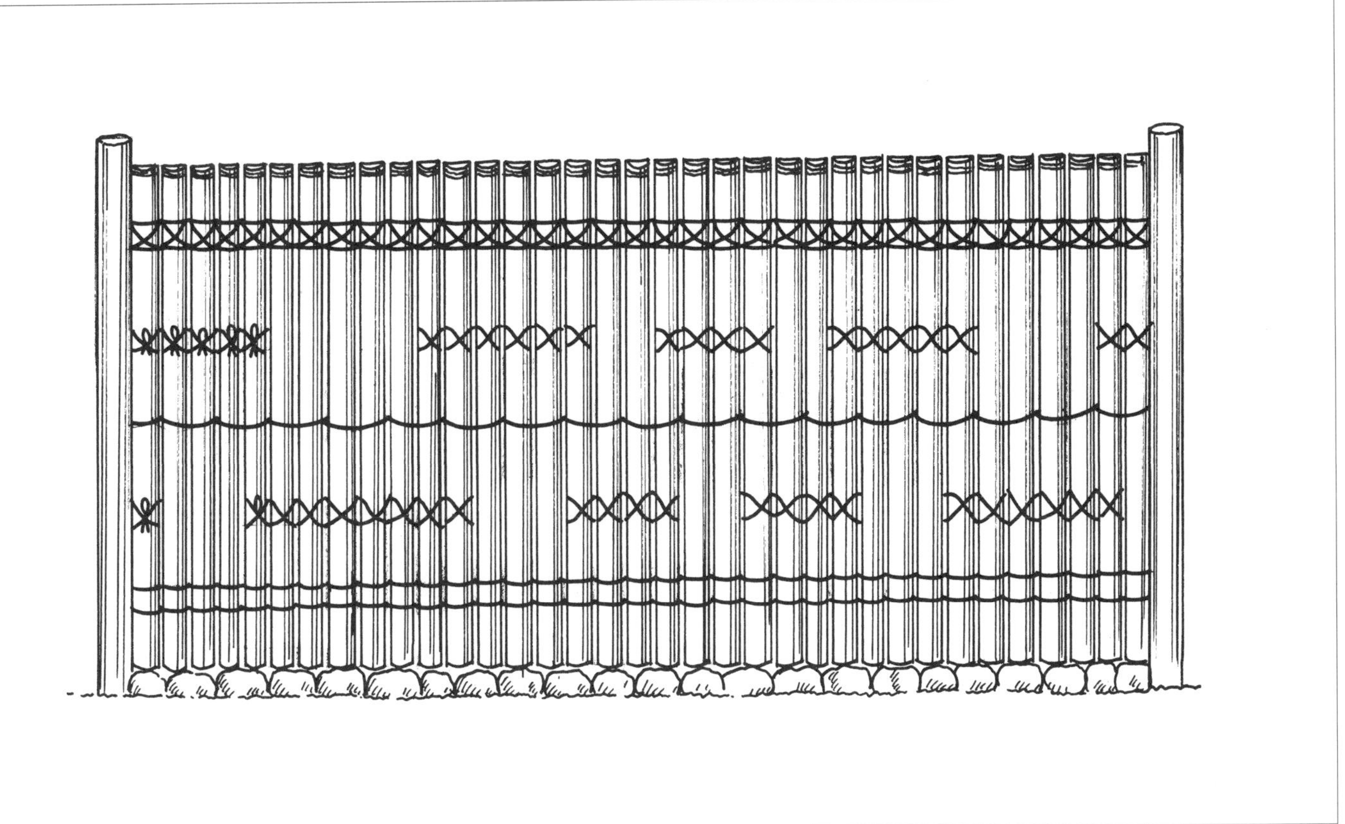

40 Wipe off dirt for the finished *Tokusa-gaki.*

CONSTRUCTING *MISU-GAKI*

Narrow, horizontally piled bamboo poles are supported by thick vertical poles in this noble, delicate screen fence. The bamboo frets are inserted into the grooves made in the posts.

Blueprint

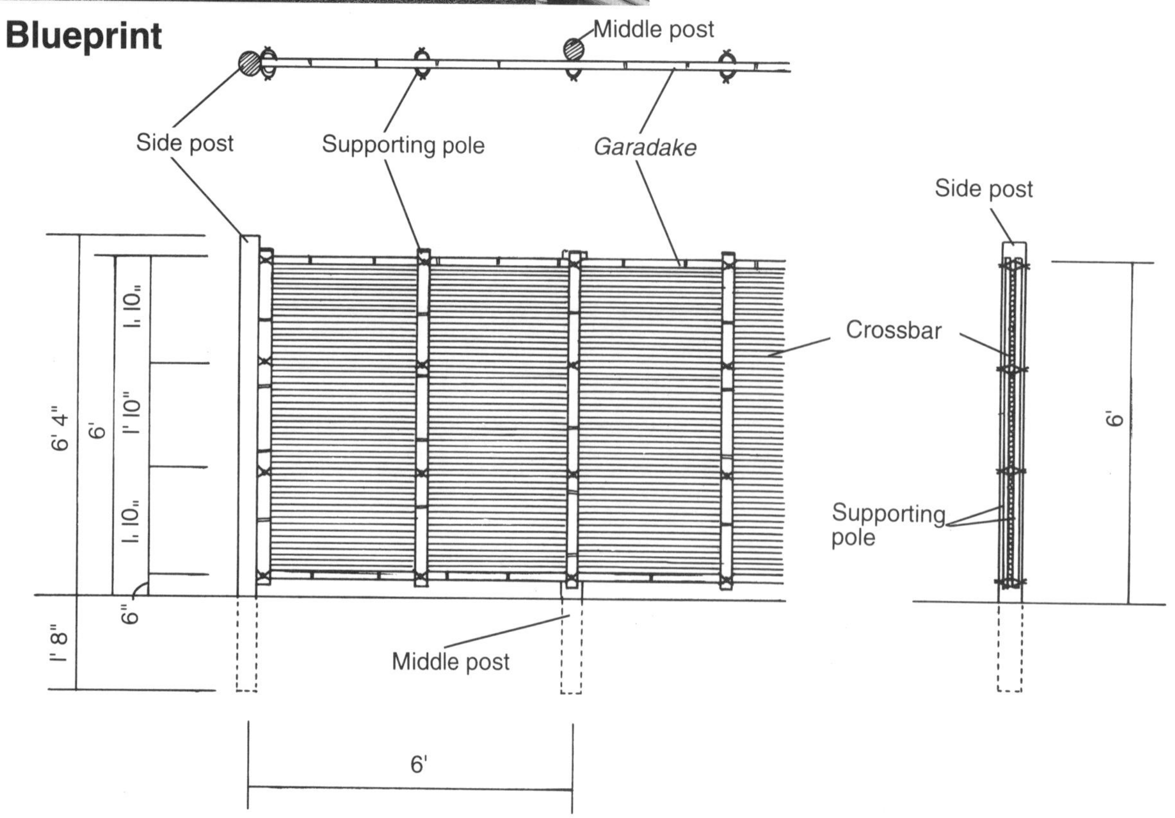

You will need:

Brass brush, Brush, Marker, Electric saw, Flat chisel, Round chisel, Post-hole digger or shovel, Wooden pole, Leveling string, Hammer, saw, Hatchet, Saw for bamboo, Drill or gimlet, Level, Knife, Needle, Rippping claw, Tape measure, Bucket

Side posts: 2 x 90-100mm($3\frac{1}{2}$"-4") diam, 2.4m(8') long scorched logs
Middle post: 1 x 70-80mm($2\frac{3}{4}$"-$3\frac{1}{8}$") diam, 2.3m($7\frac{1}{2}$') long scorched log
Rear Supporting poles: 2 x 3.6m(12') long *garadake* bamboo
Horizontal poles: 140 x 1.8m(6') long oiled bamboo
Front supporting poles: 5 x 1.8m(6') long bamboo halves

Black hemp rope, Nail, Wire

Procedure

1. Prepare logs and bamboo.
2. Implant side and middle posts.
3. Set crossbars.
4. Set supporting poles.
5. Tie with hemp rope.

1 Pour water over scorched logs and wash off the carbonized surface using a brush.

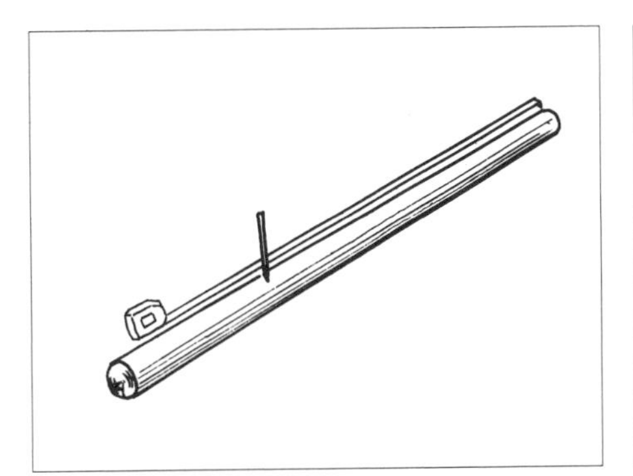

2 According to the blueprint, mark groove lines along the inner side of the washed logs.

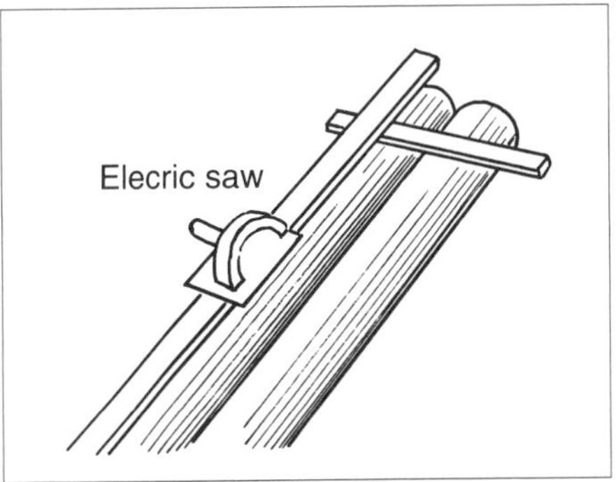

3 Cut a groove along each log. An electric saw does this job very well.

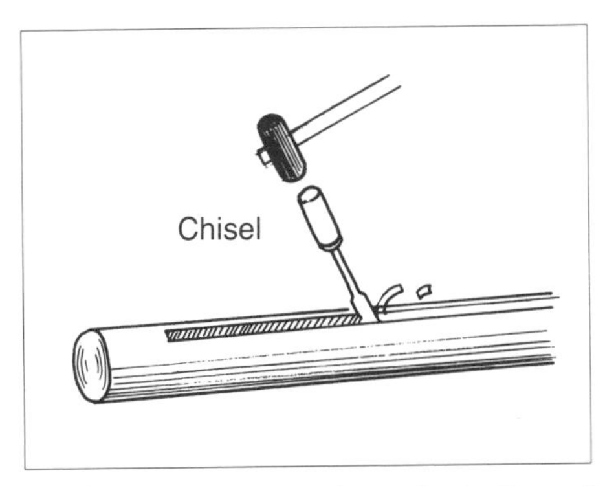

4 Using a chisel, shave the bottom of the groove flat.

5 Dig holes for the side posts. Drive a digger or shovel into the ground at right angle, and remove soil until a 50cm(20") deep hole is made for each.

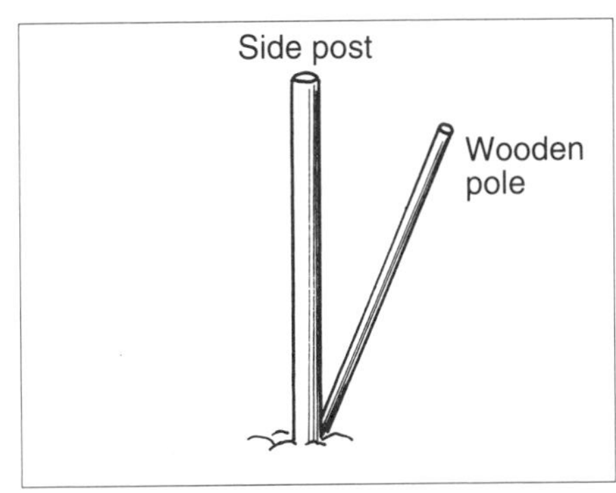

6 Set the side posts and tamp down the soil around it. Implant both posts.

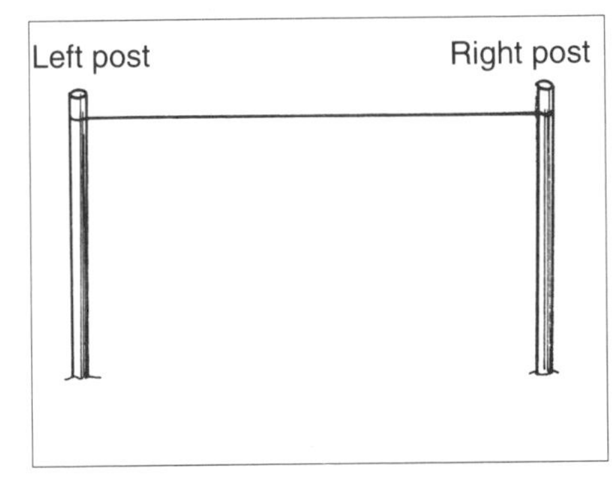

7 Stretch a leveling thread between the side posts, above the grooves. Use a level to set it horizontally.

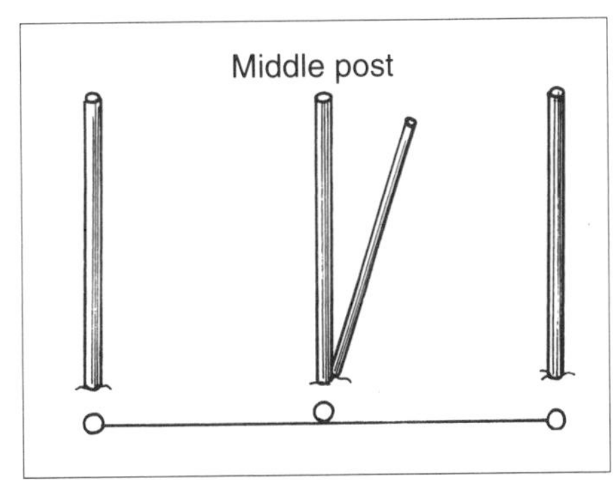

8 Implant the middle post in center, recessing slightly so as not to show when the fence is completed.

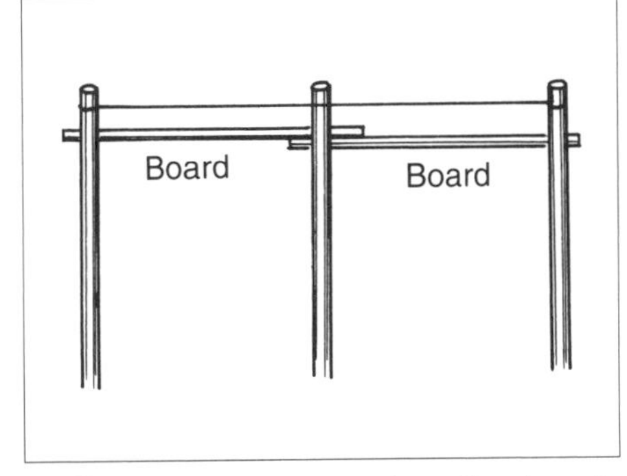

9 Stabilize the posts by nailing boards at back, temporarily. This will make the later work easier.

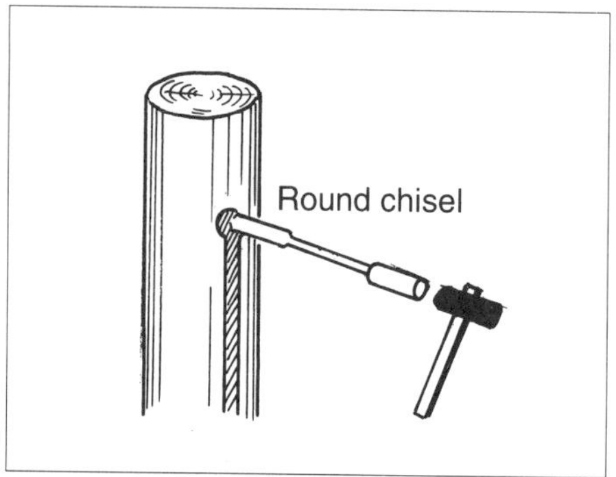

10 Using a round chisel, cut a hole to insert *garadake* bamboo stalks. Make a 3-5cm($1\frac{1}{4}$"~2") deep hole in each side post.

11 If the *garadake* bamboo stalks are soiled, wash with water using a brass brush.

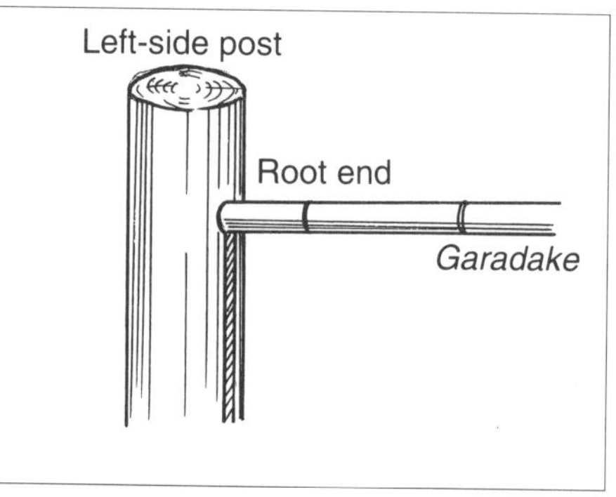

12 Insert the root end of bamboo stalk into the hole and check the fit.

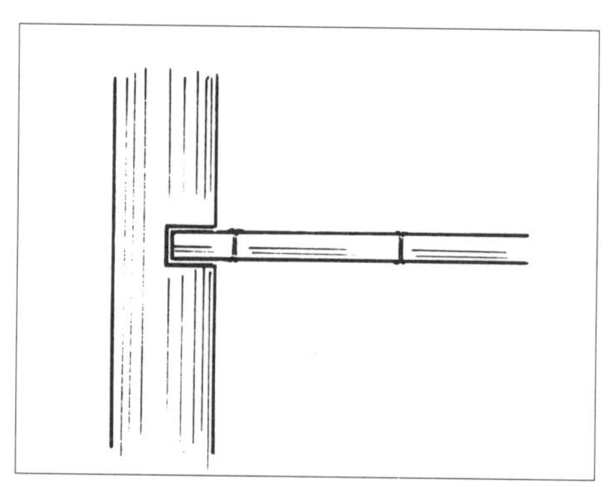

13 If the bamboo slips out easily, make the hole deeper.

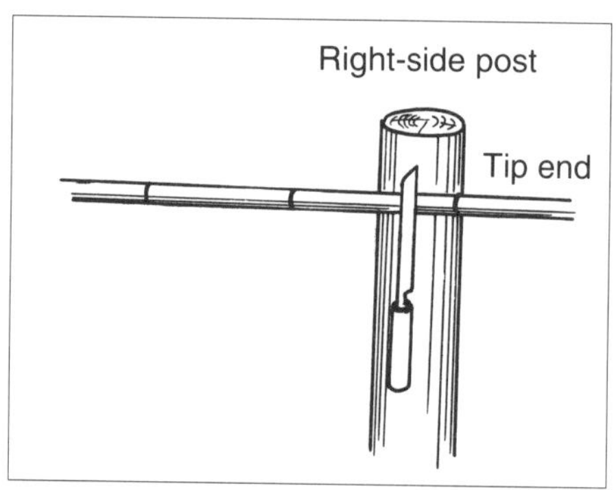

14 Holding the inserted bamboo, cut the other end slightly longer, including the inserting depth.

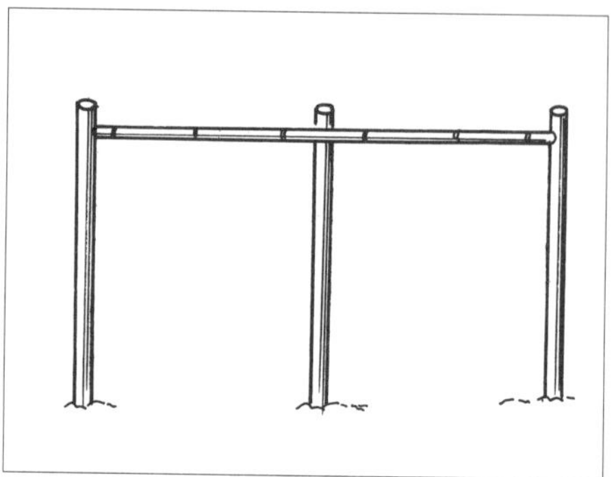

15 Bending the bamboo, insert the other end into the hole.

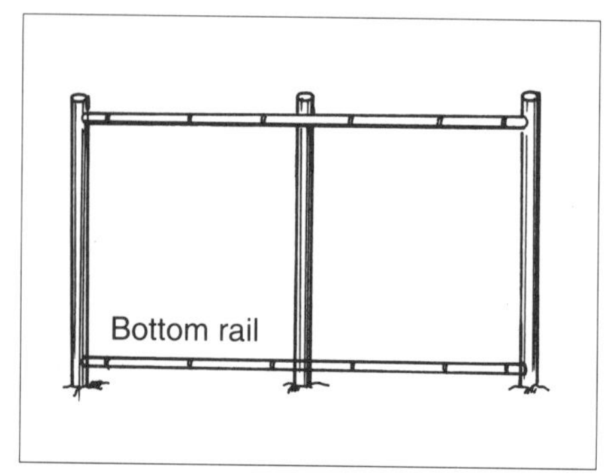

16 Set the bottom rail in the same manner.

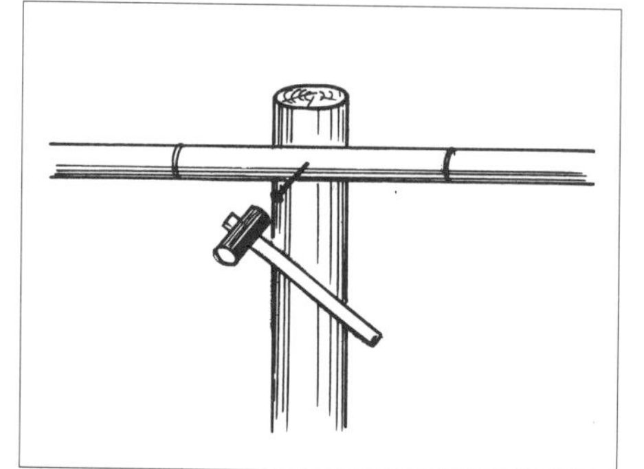

17 Fix the bamboo rails onto the posts. Nail them into the side posts, then into the middle post, checking the horizontal line with level. Remove the boards.

18 Now prepare the oiled bamboo for horizontal poles.

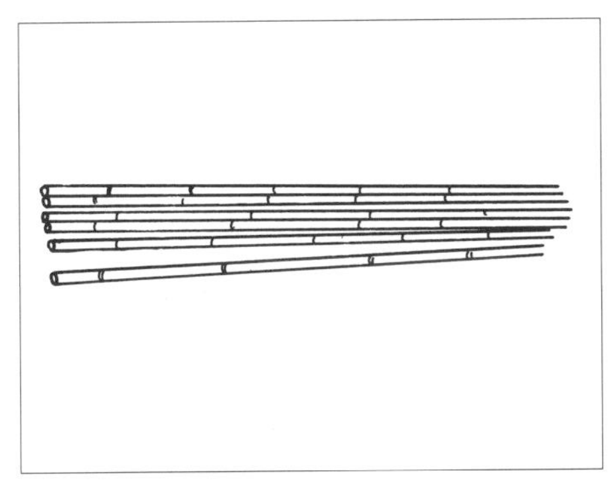

19 Select the stalks of similar thickness for horizontal poles. Adjust the length slightly longer than the distance between the side posts.

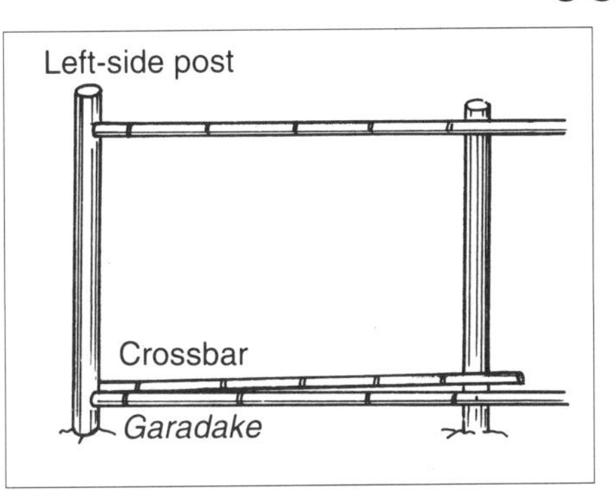

20 Set poles starting at the left post: Insert a fret into the groove.

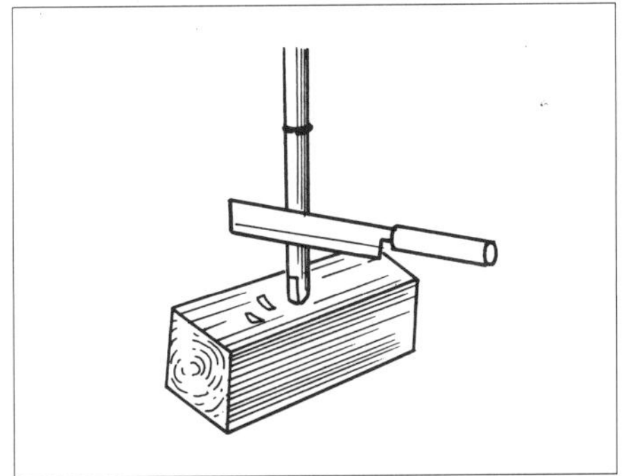

21 If the stalk is too thick to insert, shave both sides of each end.

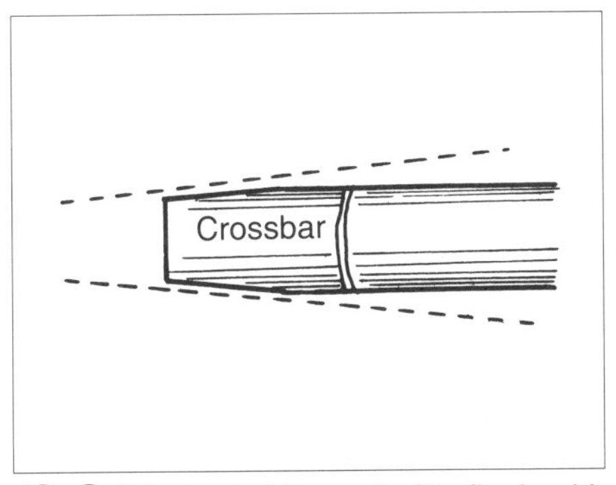

22 It is best if the pole fits flush with the groove.

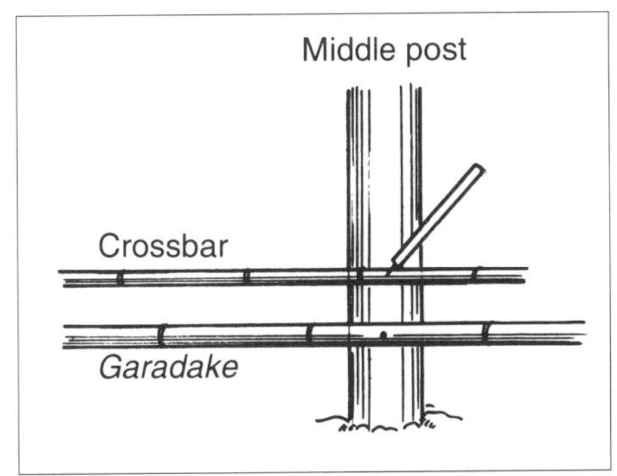

23 Mark the other end of pole at the center of the middle post to cut off.

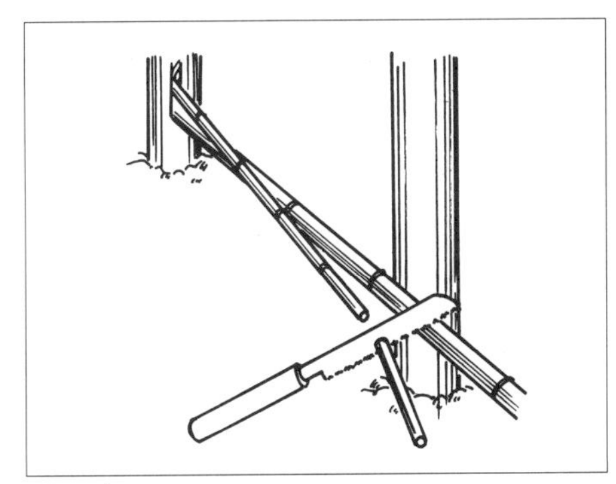

24 Holding the inserted pole, cut off excess.

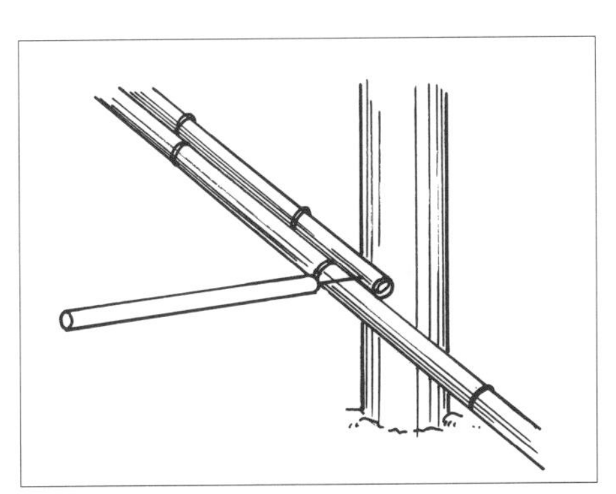

25 To fix the pole to the middle post, make a hole using a gimlet or drill.

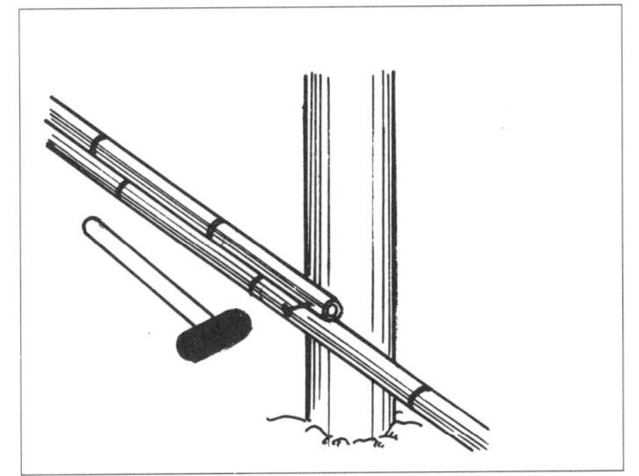

26 Nail the pole to the middle post. Drive gently so as not to split the bamboo.

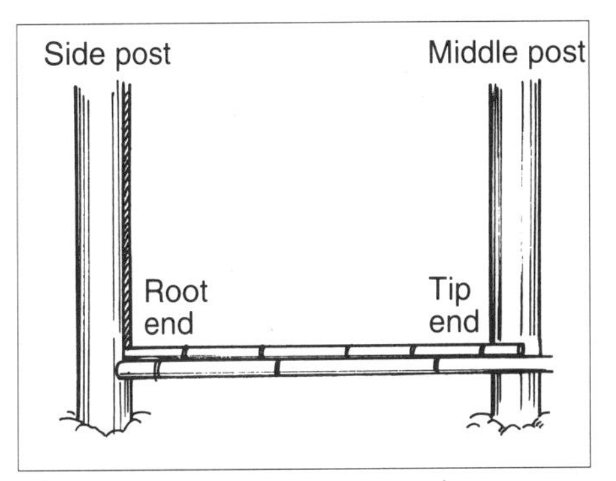

27 The bottom pole is set between the side and the middle posts. It is best if the pole is nailed to the center of the middle post.

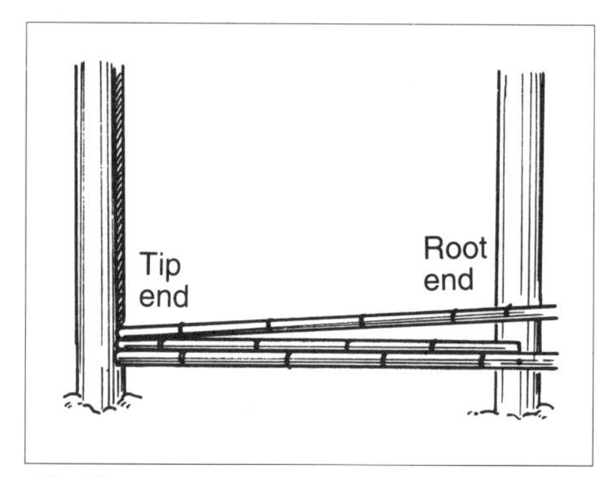

28 Set the second pole. Lay in the other direction to the previous one.

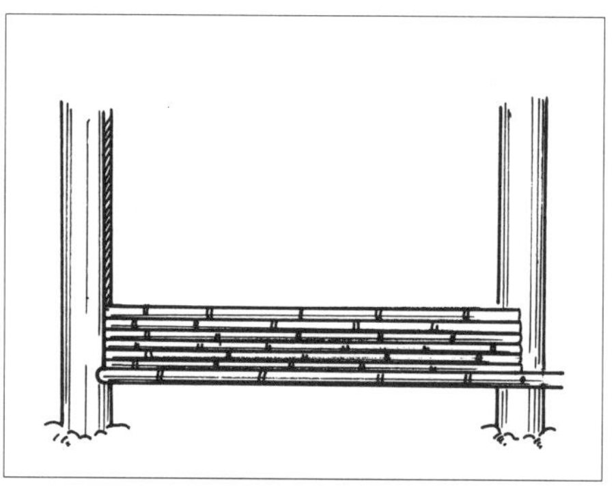

29 Continue setting poles alternating the direction on each row. This way the finished surface will look orderly.

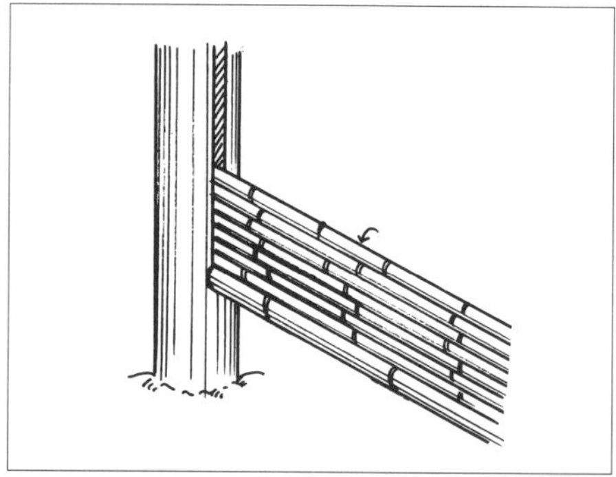

30 Be sure to pack the poles tightly. If there is any odd space in between, rotate to fit to the previous pole.

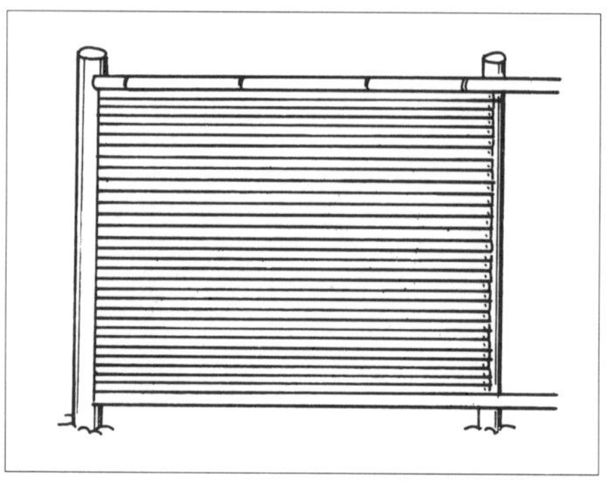

31 Continue until you reach the top rail.

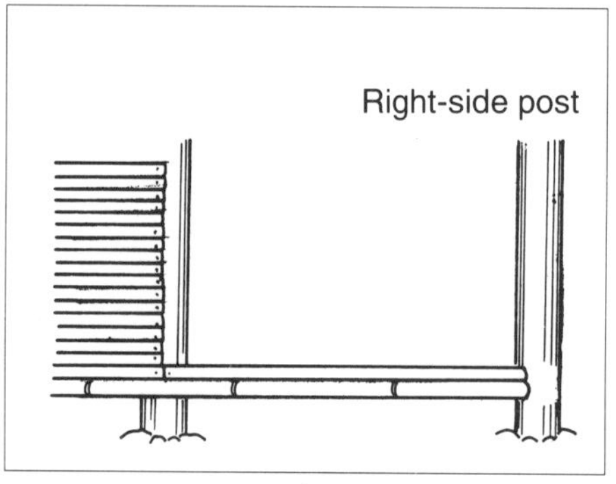

32 Work the right panel in the same manner; insert an end into the right post and cut the other end to meet the center of the middle post; nail down.

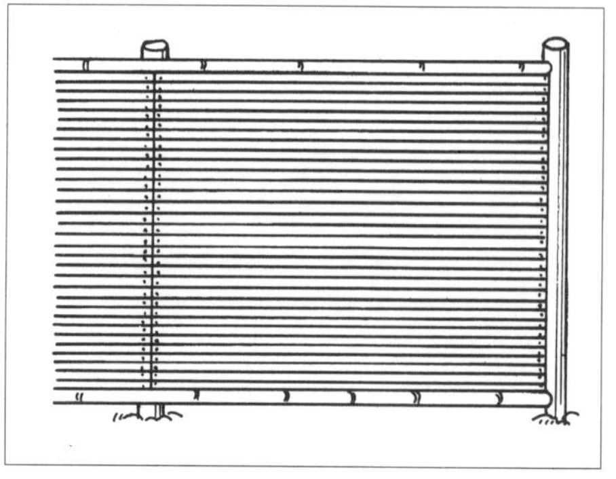

33 Both panels are filled with horizontal poles.

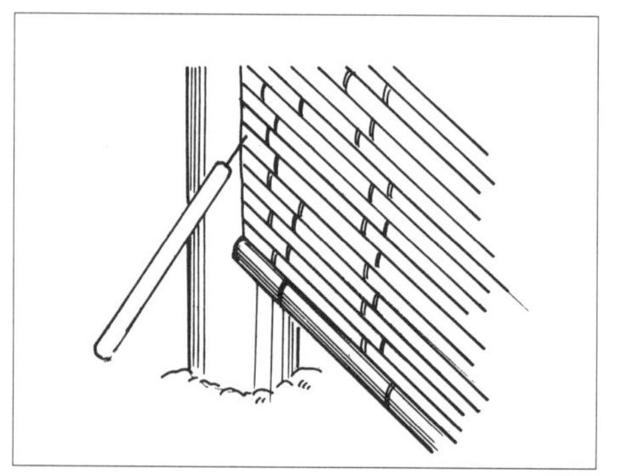

34 Fix the poles to side posts; drill a hole through each pole into the post.

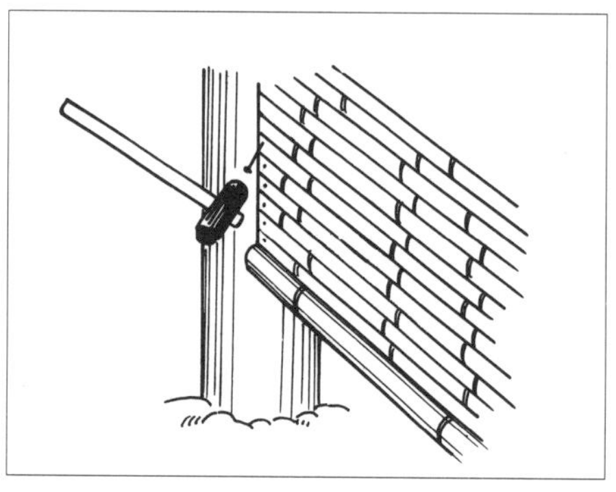

35 Hammer a nail into each pole.

36 Prepare supporting poles. Take thick bamboo stalks and wash if necessary, using a brass brush.

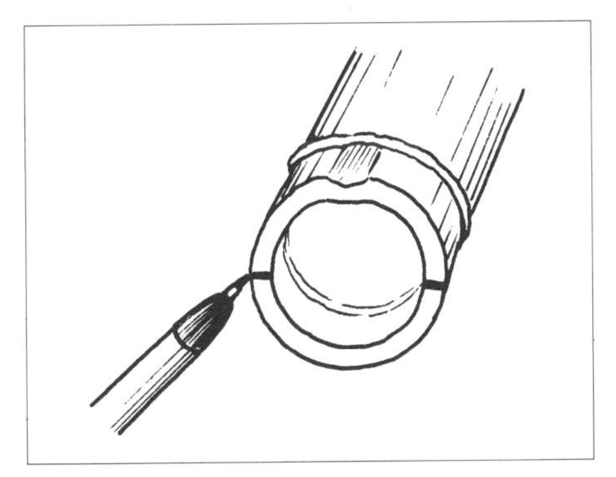

37 Place marks to split the bamboo in two.

38 Apply a hatchet onto the marks.

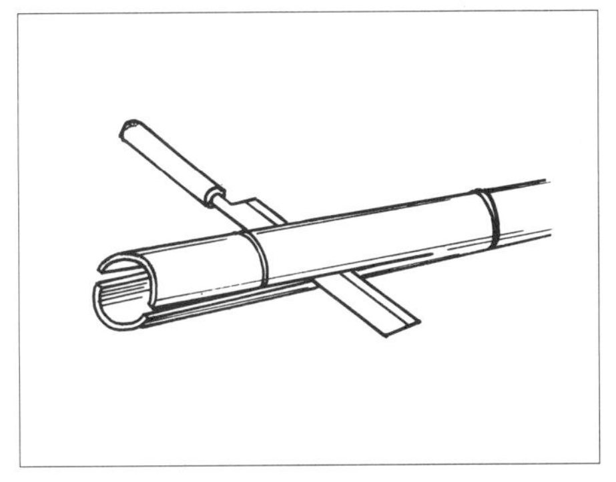

39 Carefully cut into the bamboo, checking the width of each half.

40 When split to some extent, pull apart using your foot and hand. Turn the bamboo occasionally to split precisely in two.

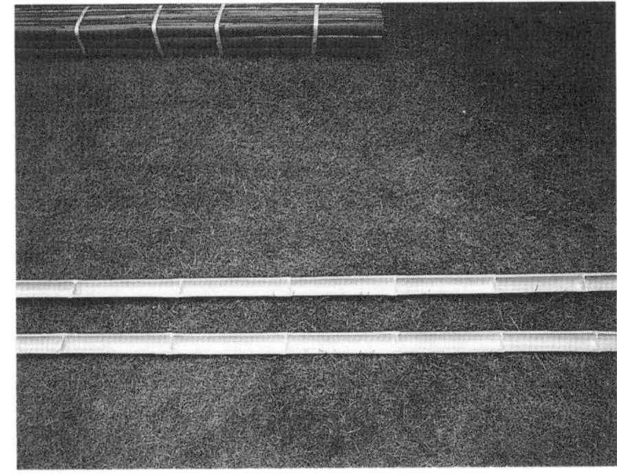

41 Precisely halved bamboo stalks, ready for use.

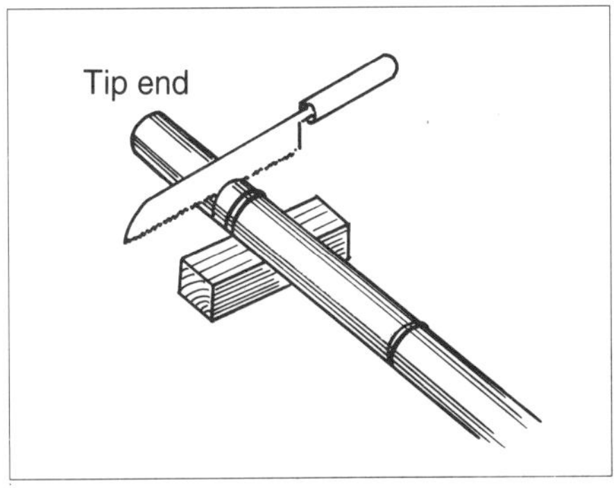

42 Trim the end of supporting pole, cutting just above a joint.

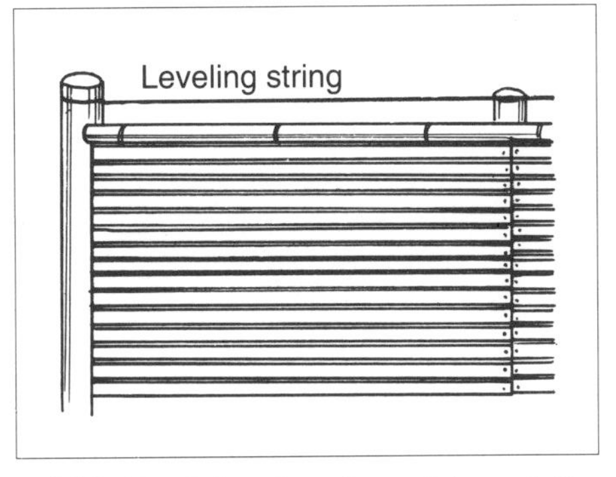

43 Stretch a leveling string at the indicated height for the top rail.

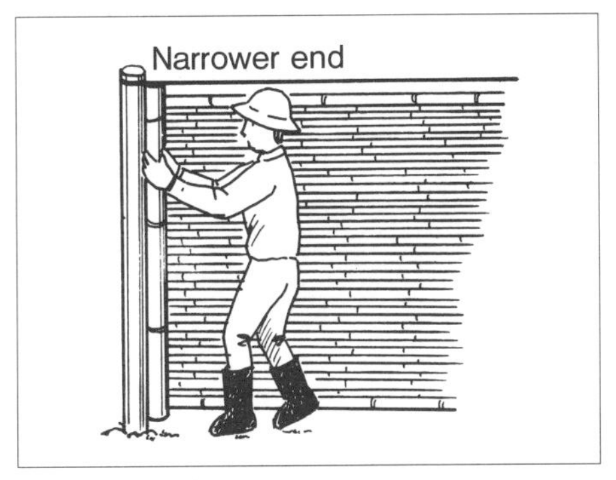

44 Set a supporting pole next to the left post, narrower end up.

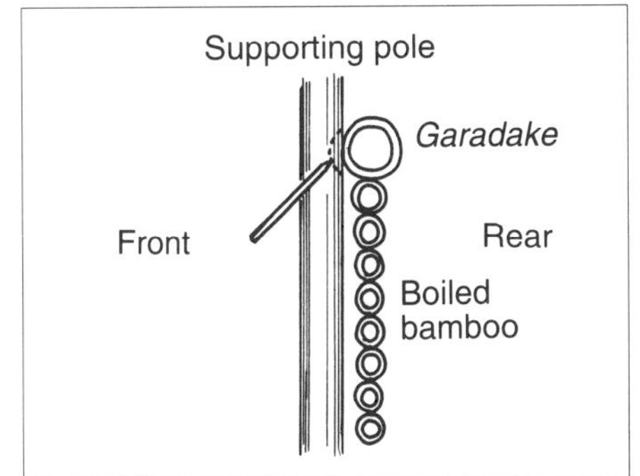

45 Mark where the supporting pole touches the top rail.

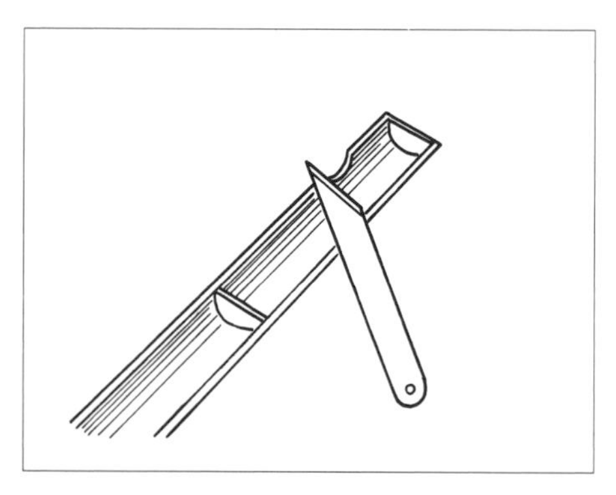

46 Using a knife, shave off the part that touches the top rail.

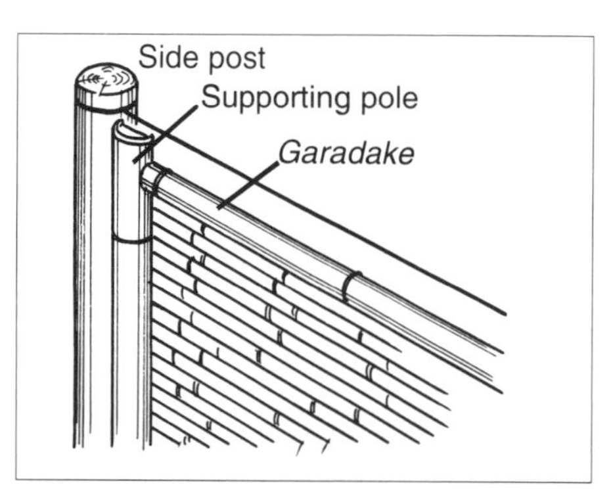

47 Check that the curve fits the top rail.

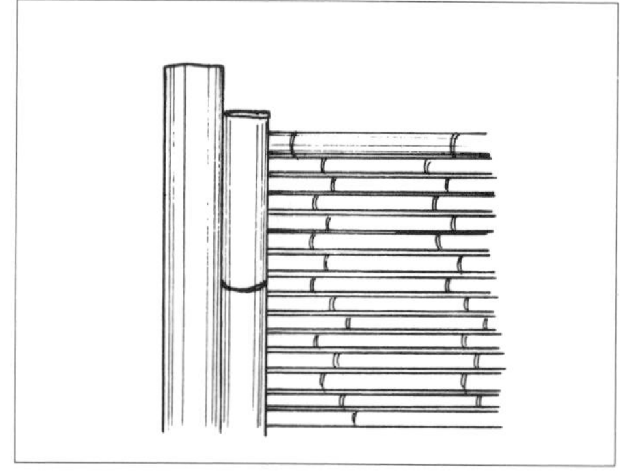

48 If necessary, shave the side of supporting pole to fit the side post.

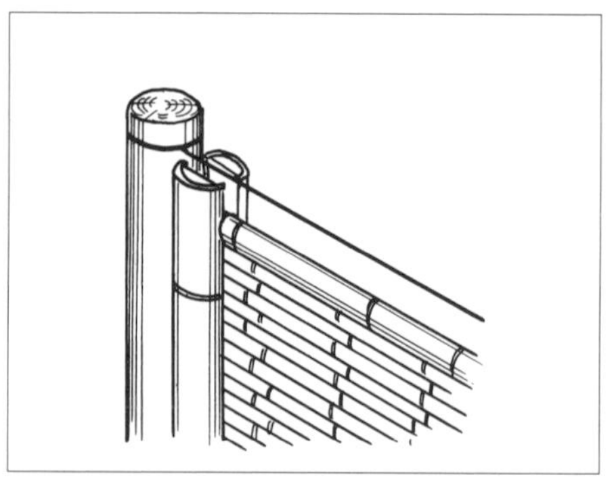

49 Adjust the rear supporting pole in the same manner. If the fit is correct, nail both poles temporarily.

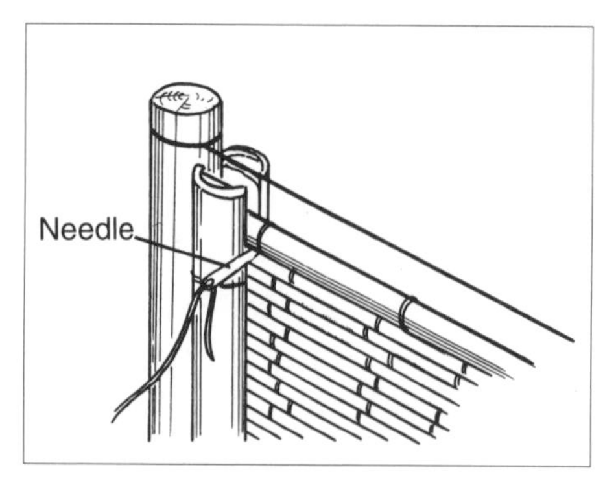

50 Bind the supporting poles and the top rail using black hemp rope. Insert a threaded needle under the top rail.

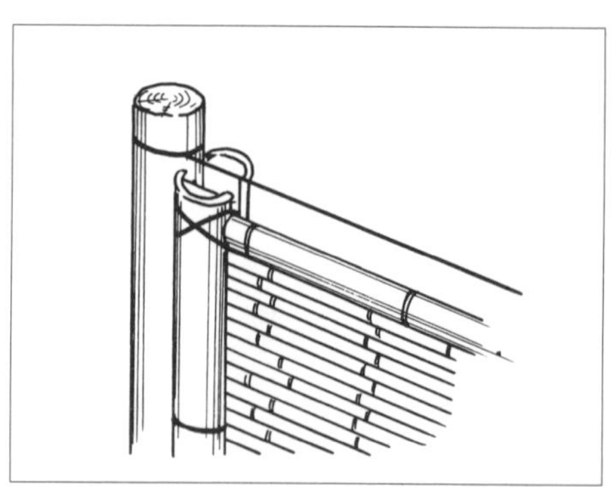

51 Tie the rope into an *ibo* knot. See page 34 for instructions.

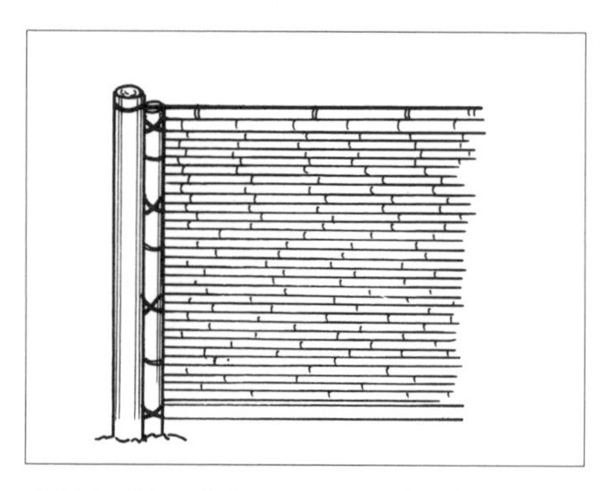

52 Tie at three spots in the same manner.

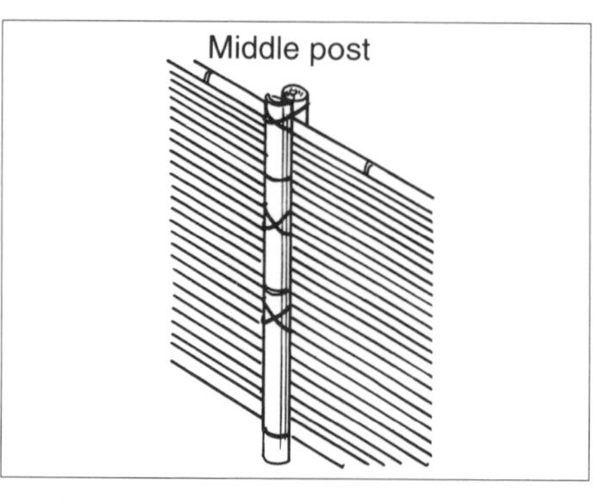

53 As for the middle post, set the supporting pole only to the front.

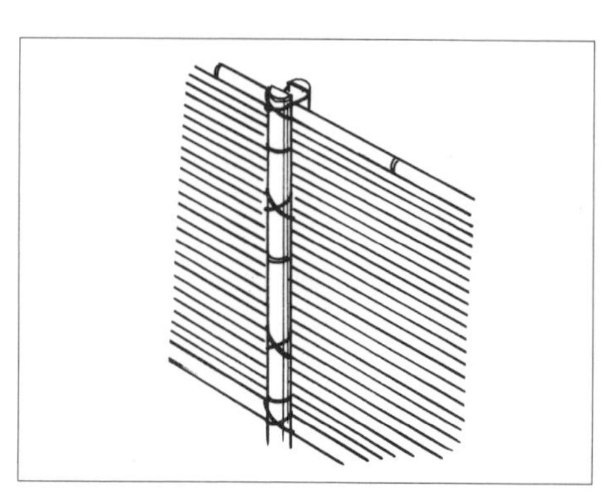

54 Set front and rear supporting poles between the side post and middle post.

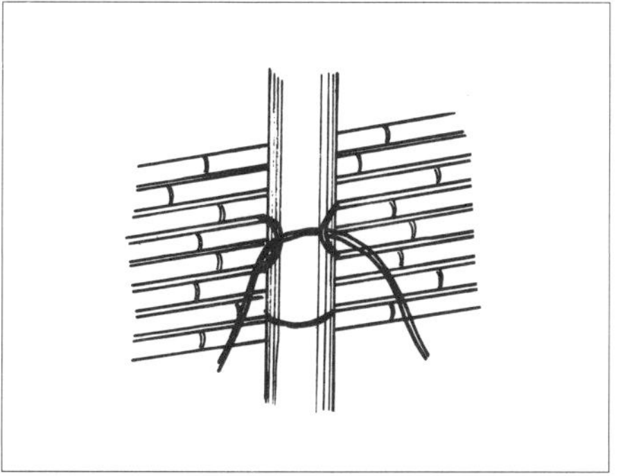

55 If tying knots on the reverse side, work with another piece of rope at back.

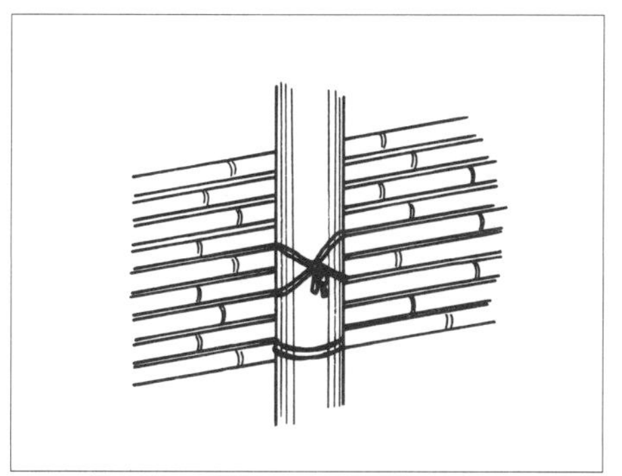

56 For the best result, ask a helper who can work on the other side of the fence.

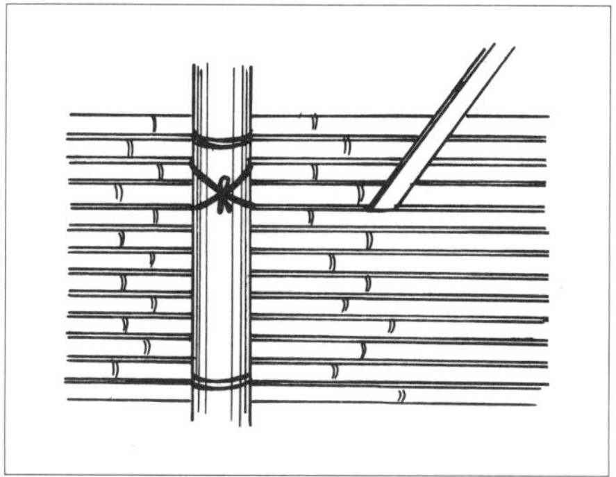

57 When all the supporting poles are bound with hemp rope, remove the wire and check the surface of the horizontal poles.

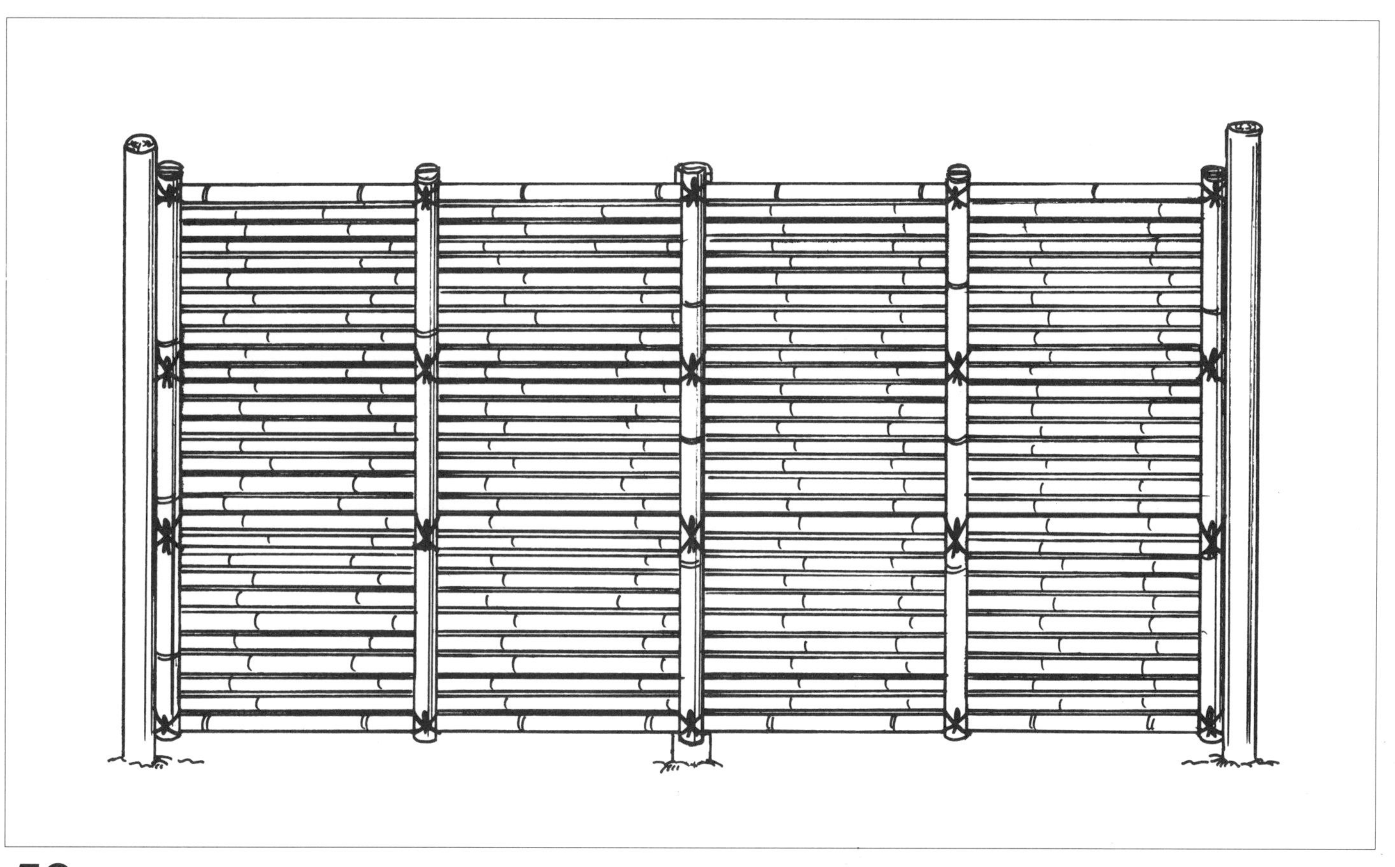

58 Wipe off dirt for the finished *Misu-gaki*.

CONSTRUCTING *KOETSU-GAKI*

The distinctive feature of this elegant see-through fence is the thick, round beading which curves down to the ground. In order to form a gentle curving line, vinyl chloride pipe is used for the core of beading. Since many narrow-split bamboo stalks are used, this is quite a challenging project for a beginner.

Blueprint

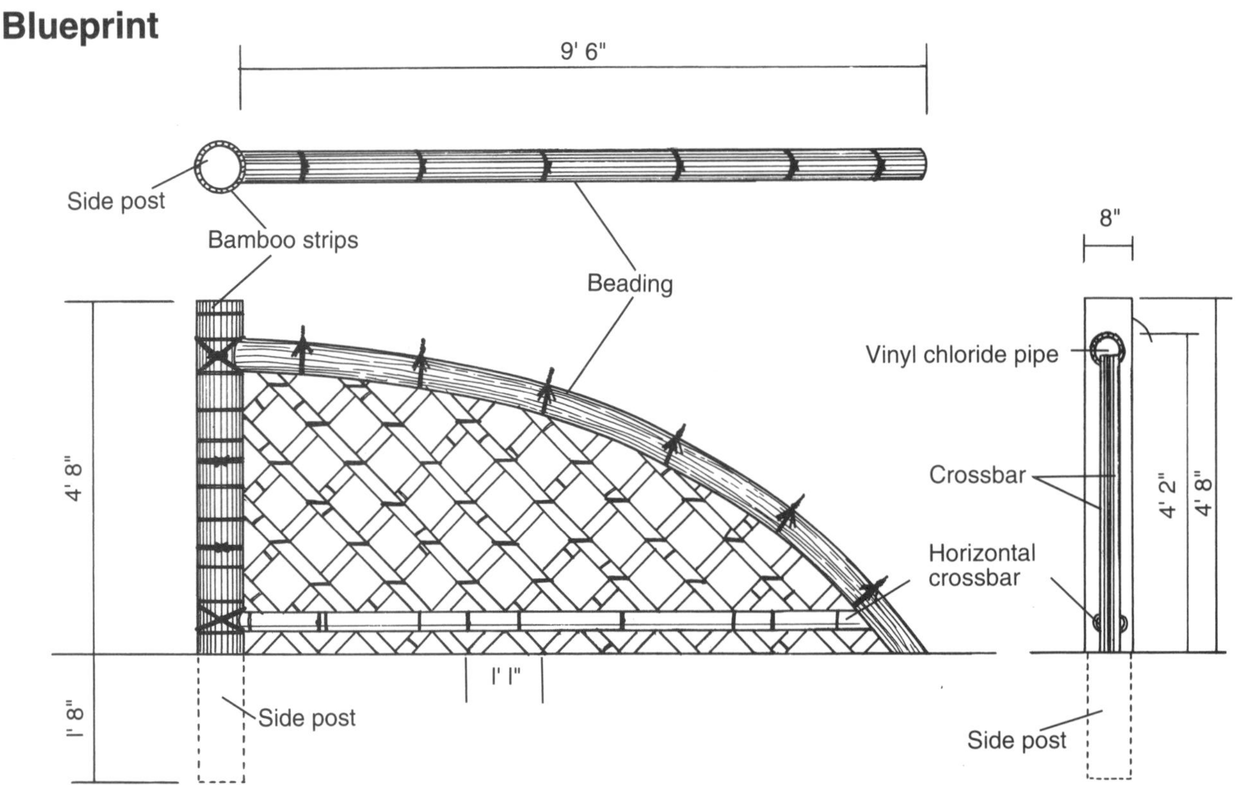

You will need:

Marker, Hammer, Round chisel, Post-hole digger or shovel, Tamping pole, Blowtorch, Bucket, Hatchet, Knife, Lineman's pliers, Gimlet, Drill, Saw, Saw for bamboo

Side post: 1 x 170-180mm($6\frac{3}{4}$"-7') diam, 1.9m (6'4") long scorched log
Beading: 1 x 100mm(4") diam, 3m(10') long vinyl chloride pipe
Approx.20 x 100-150mm(4"-6") wide, 3m(10') long bamboo strips
Crossbars: Approx. 30 x 40mm($1\frac{1}{2}$") wide, 1m(3' 4") long bamboo strips
Post: Approx 35 x 100-150mm(4"-6") wide, 1.4m(4'8") long bamboo strips
Horizontal crossbar: 1 x 70-80mm($2\frac{3}{4}$"-3") diam, 2.8m(9'4") long bamboo strips

Black hemp rope, Nail, Wire

Procedure:

1. Implant supporting post.
2. Bend vinyl chloride pipe.
3. Set crossbars.
4. Wrap post and beading with bamboo strips.
5. Attach horizontal crossbar.
6. Tie with hemp rope.

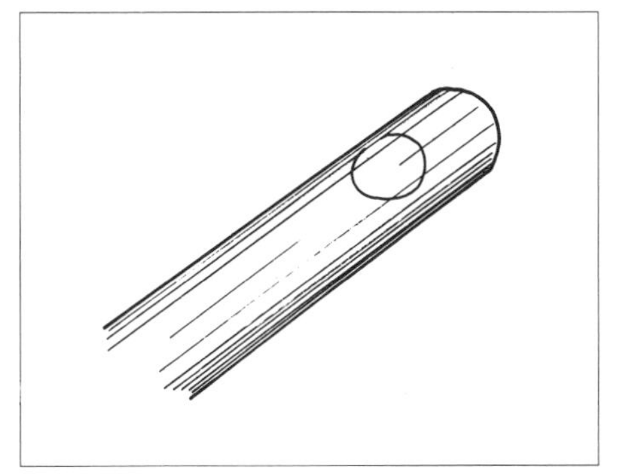

1 Cut scorched long log into the indicated size. Mark a hole to insert the beading.

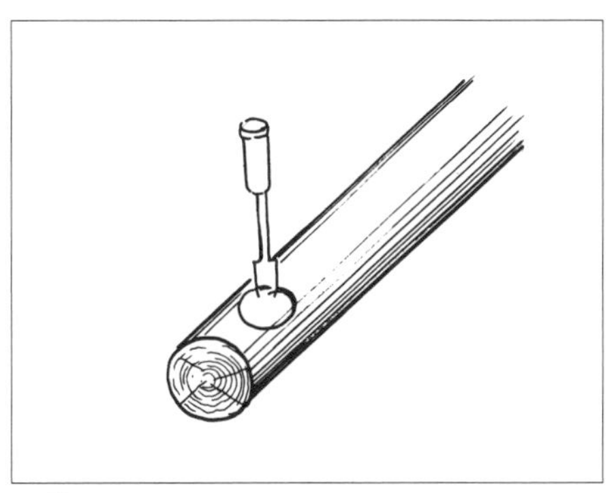

2 Chisel out wood and make a 8cm ($3\frac{1}{8}$") deep hole.

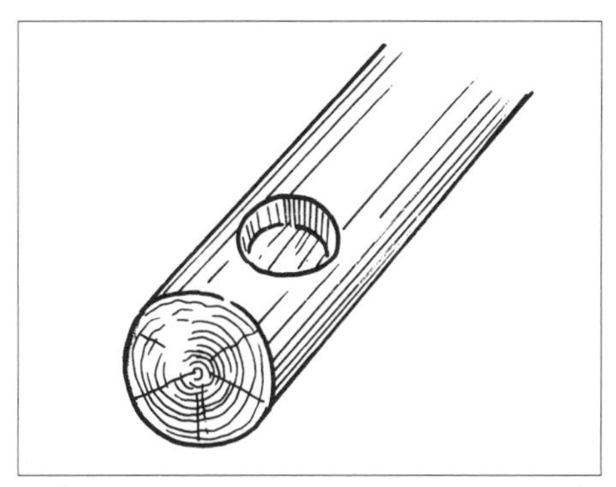

3 Make sure the hole is large enough for the vinyl chloride pipe.

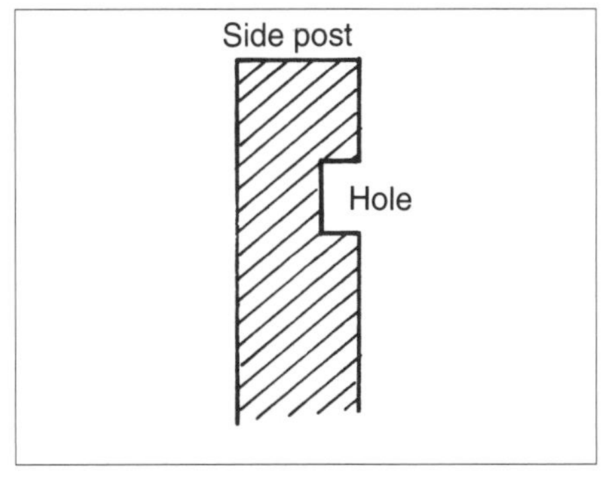

4 Insert an end of vinyl chloride pipe into this hole.

5 Using a post-hole digger or shovel, dig a hole for the post.

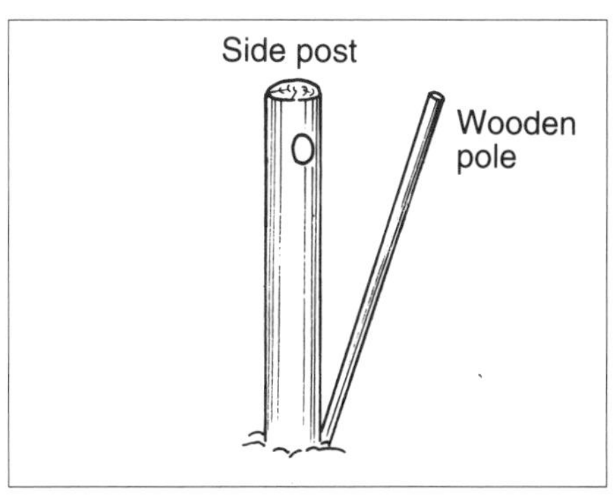

6 Implant the post securely, thrusting pebbles or gravel around the post.

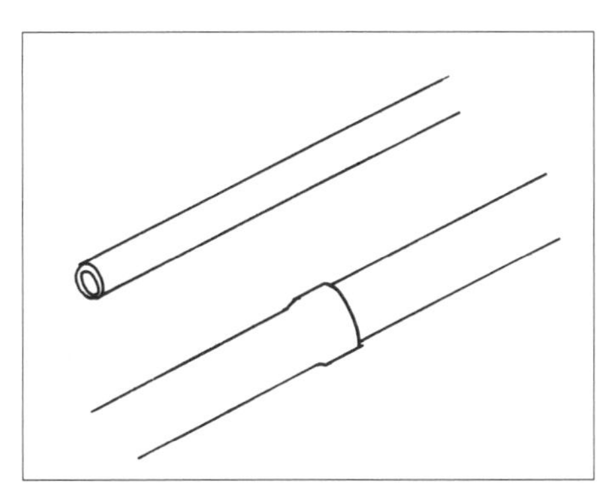

7 Prepare the vinyl chloride pipe. If necessary, join another pipe, heating with a blowtorch.

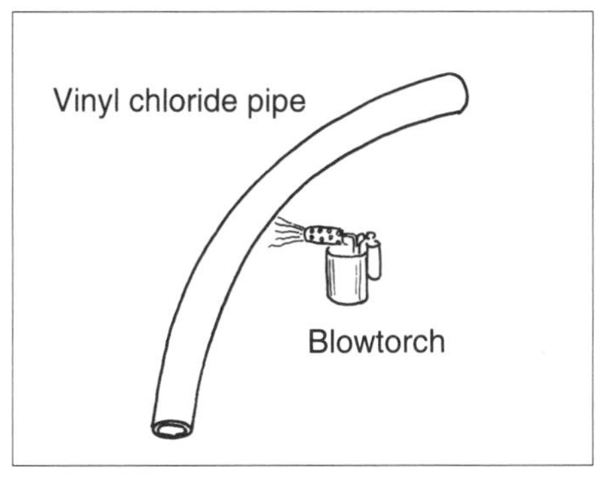

8 Bend the pipe according to the blueprint. Make a smooth curve heating with the blowtorch.

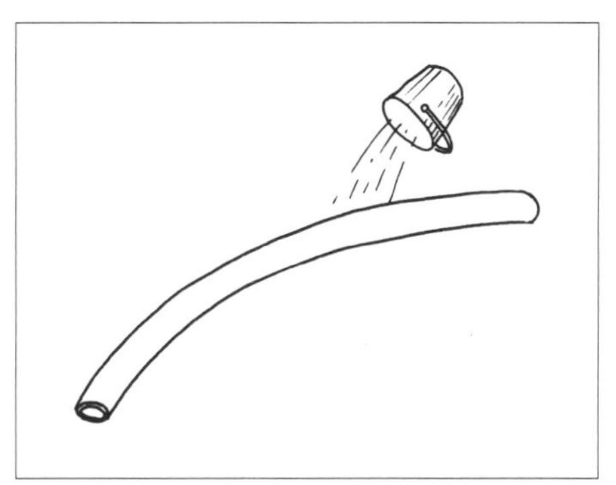

9 When bent into the desired shape, pour over water to cool down; the curve will be fixed.

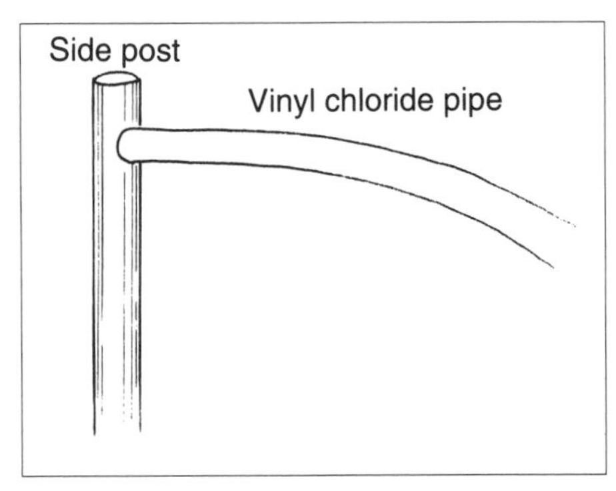

10 Insert an end of vinyl chloride pipe into the hole, and check the size.

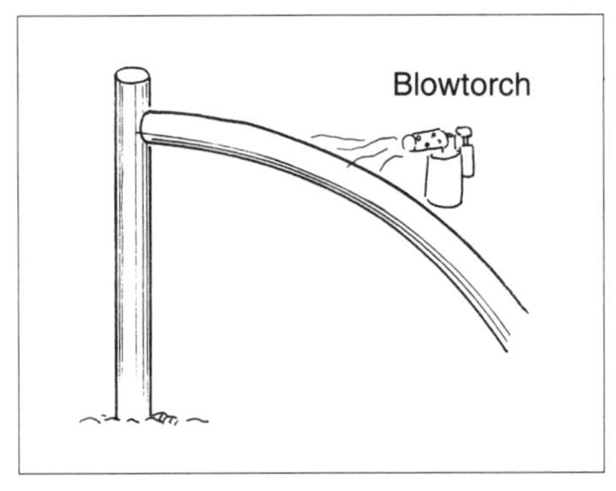

11 Adjust the curve using the blowtorch as needed.

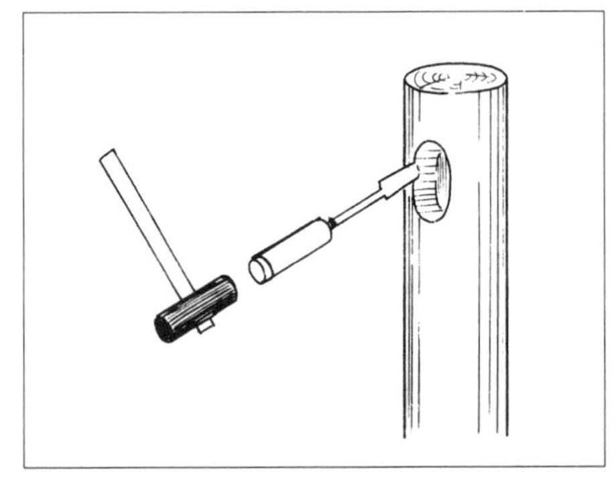

12 Cut a ditch around the hole to insert bamboo strips.

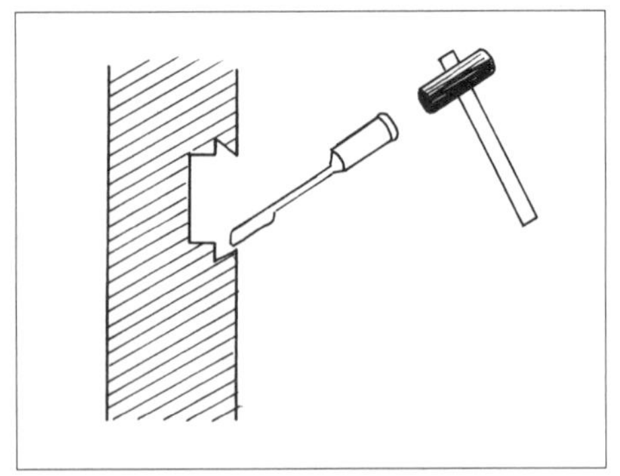

13 Make the ditch progressively wider towards the bottom. This way the bamboo strips will be caught securely.

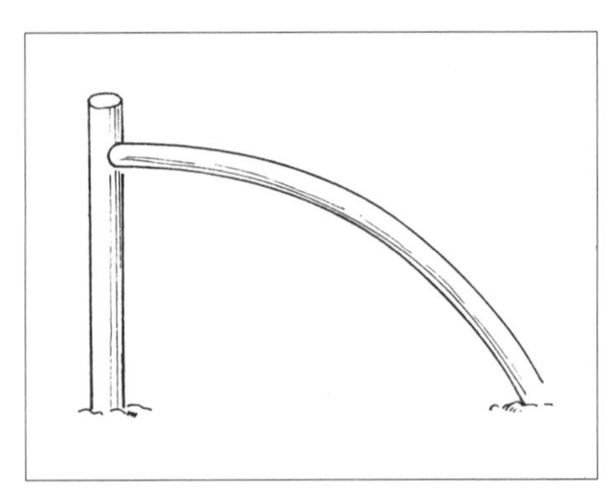

14 Insert one end into the post, and the other end into the ground.

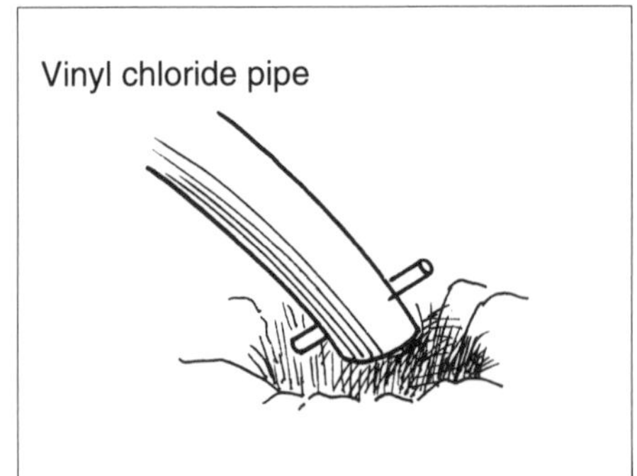

15 Stabilize the pipe by piercing a metal stick or thick nail through the end.

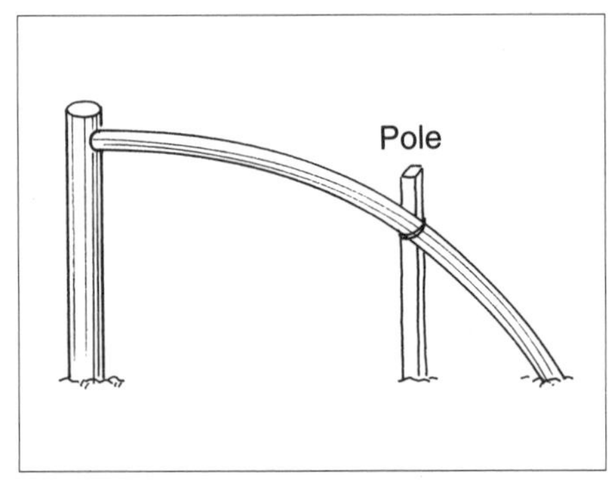

16 Implant a pole to support the pipe. This will make the later work easier.

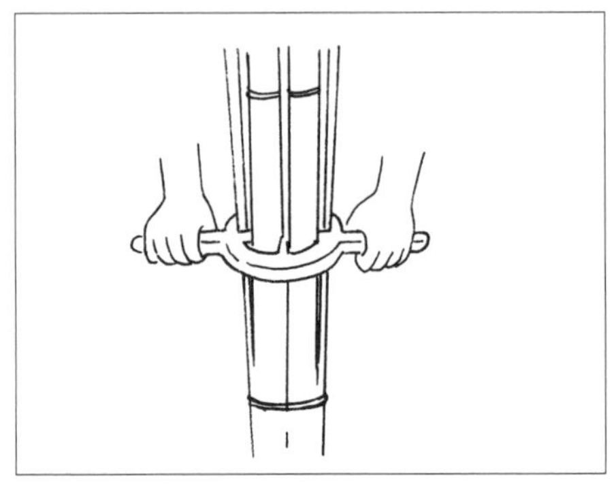

17 Prepare crossbars. Split thick *madake* bamboo or use purchased bamboo strips.

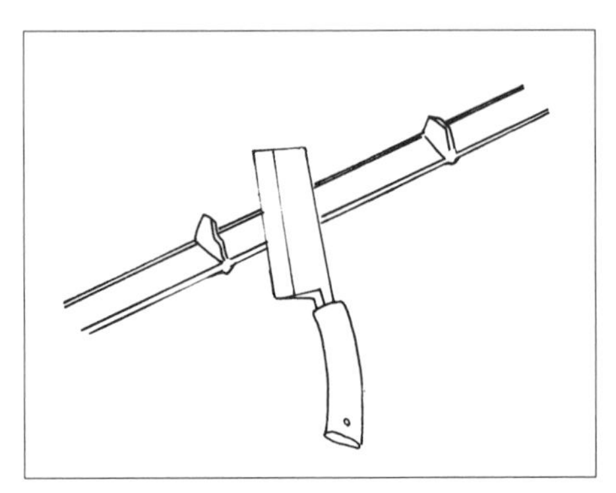

18 Remove joints from split bamboo stalks to make the surface flat.

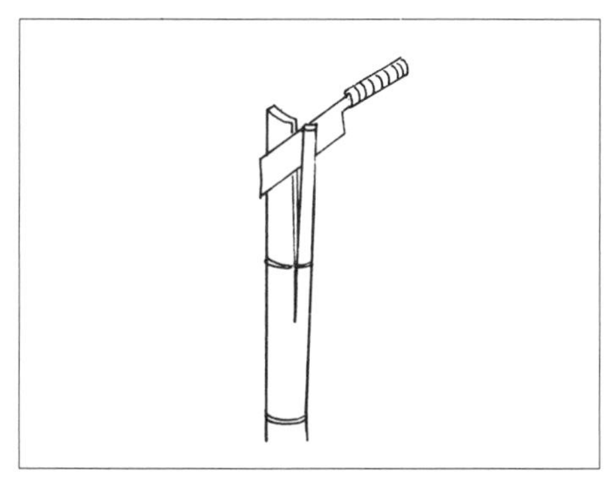

19 Cut the bamboo in the same width, approximately 4cm($1\frac{3}{5}$"), and slightly longer than indicated.

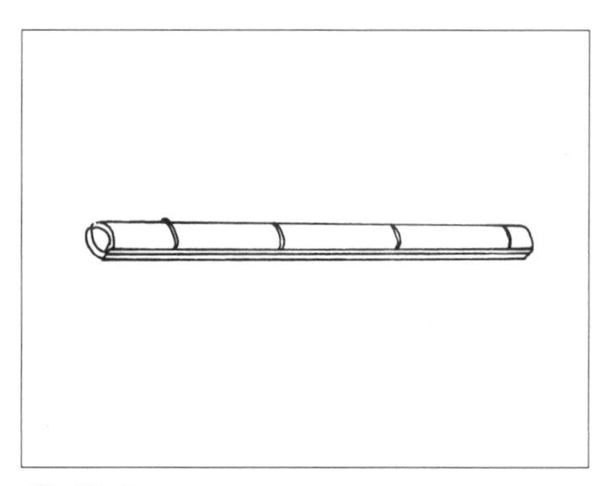

20 Sort the strips into pairs taken from the same stalk so as to use in pairs.

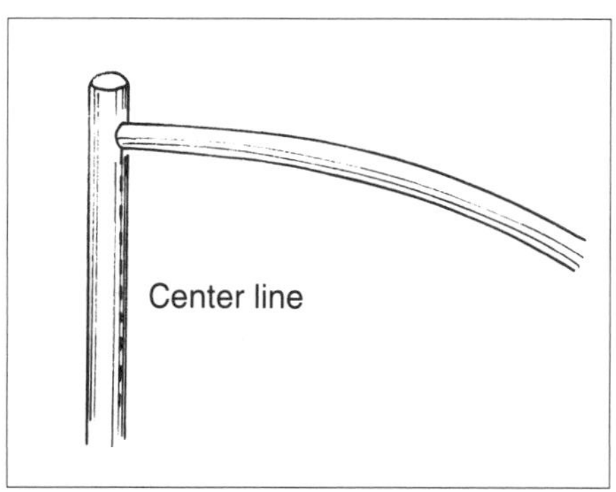

21 Mark the center line on the post.

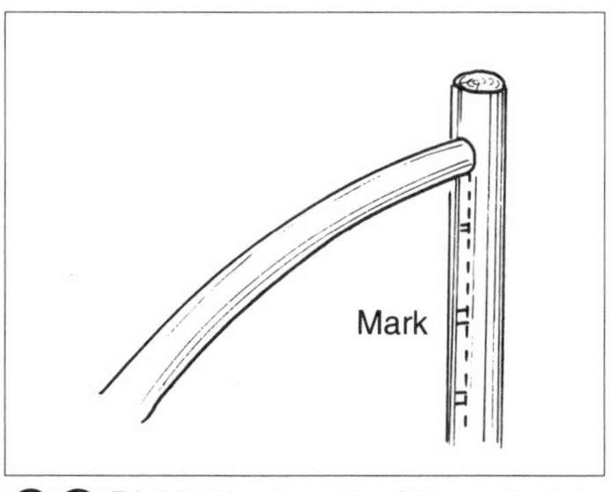

22 Divide the length of the pole into equal length and mark on it.

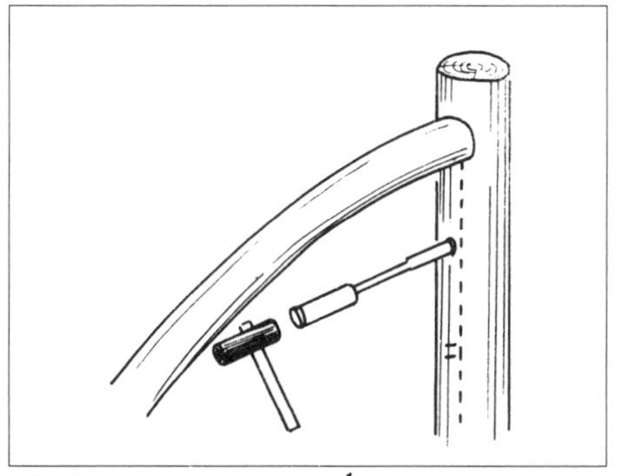

23 Make a 3cm ($1\frac{1}{4}$") deep hole at each mark, in a width just enough to insert the tips of two bamboo strips.

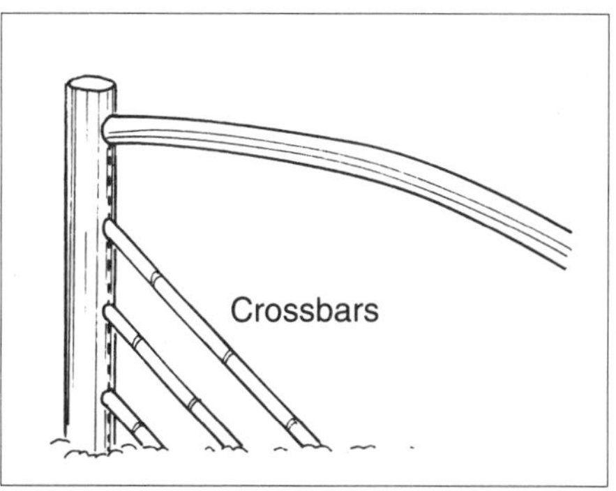

24 Set the crossbars for front. Select a certain angle from the ground. Inset one end into the post, the other into the ground.

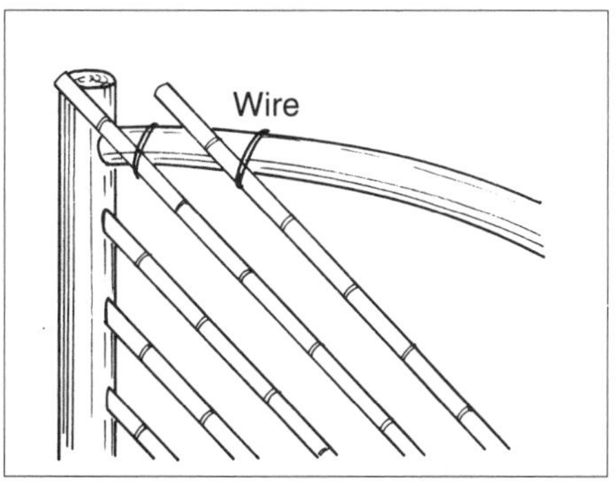

25 Secure each crossbar by implanting deeply into the ground. Bind the upper ends with wire to be inserted into the beading later.

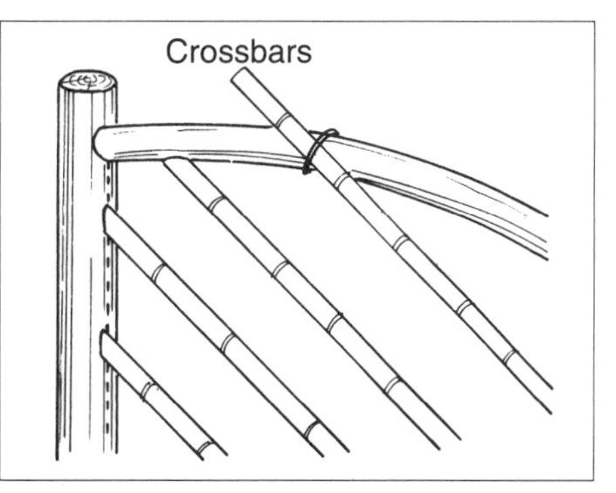

26 Cut the upper ends diagonally to fit the pipe. Leave enough length to insert into it.

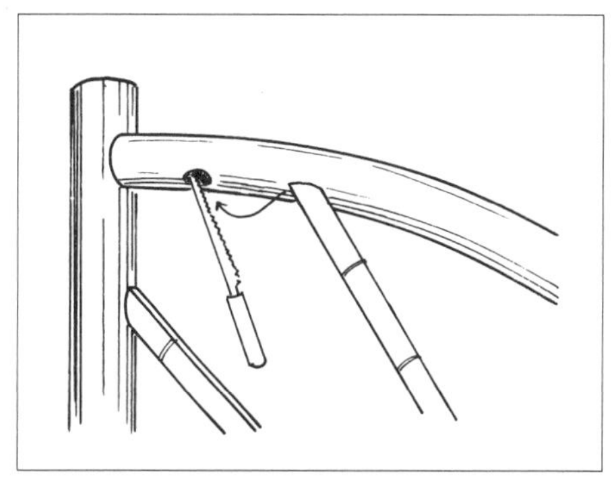

27 Make holes underneath the pipe. Do not make oversized holes.

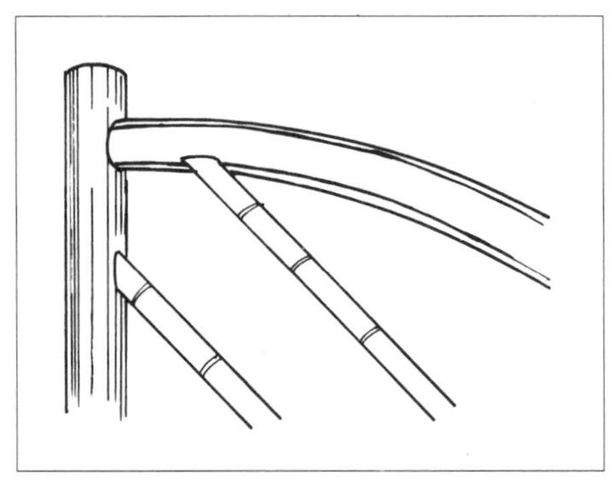

28 Insert the upper end of fret into the holes of the pipe.

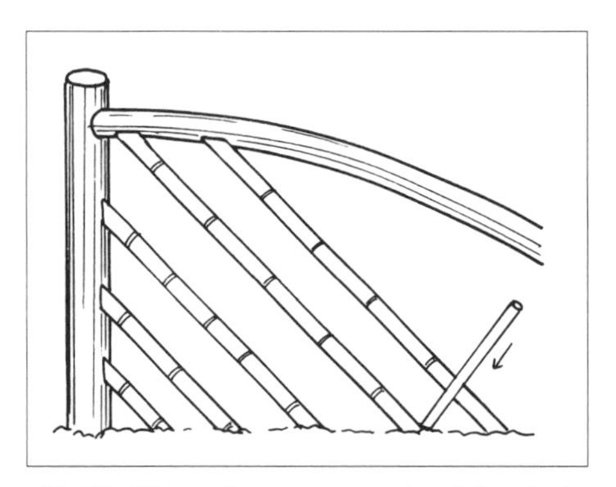

29 When the upper ends of the frets are fixed, press down the soil to stabilize the lower ends.

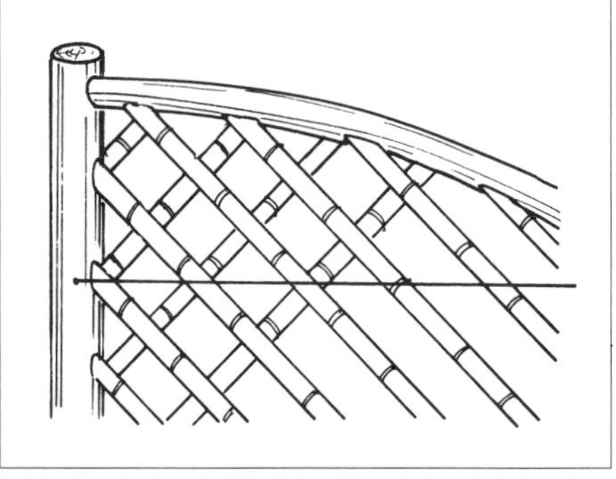

30 When the front frets are fixed, set frets to reverse side to form a lattice.

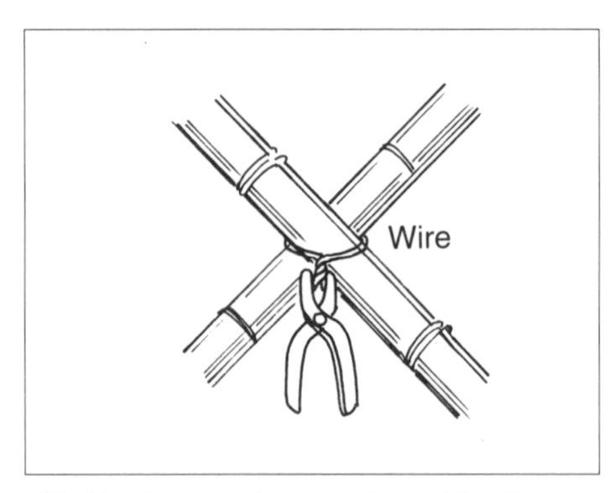

31 Secure the crossing with wire.

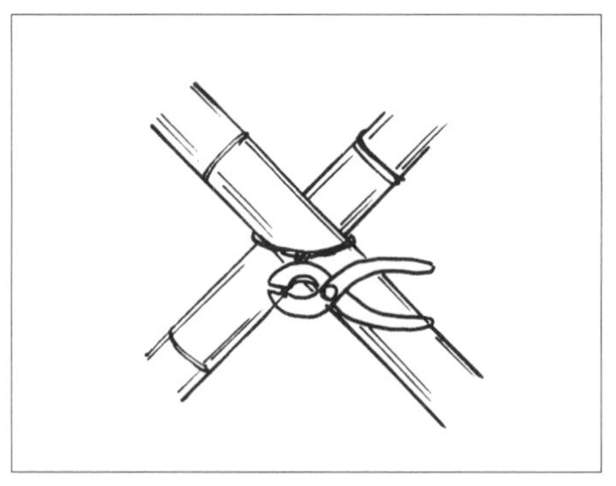

32 Using lineman's pliers, twist the ends of wire tightly.

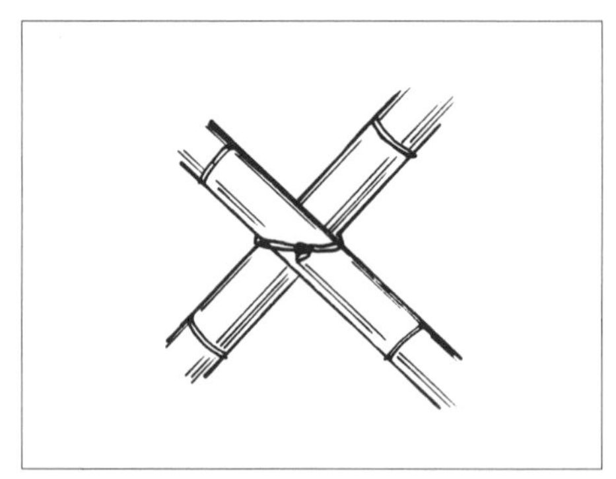

33 Trim away the excess wire and bend any remainder to a side.

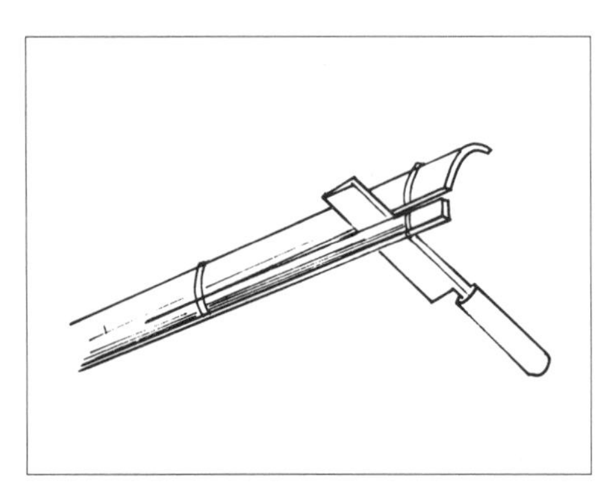

34 Prepare bamboo strips to cover the beading. Split *madake* bamboo into narrow strips of 1-1.5cm($\frac{3}{8}$"-$\frac{5}{8}$") width.

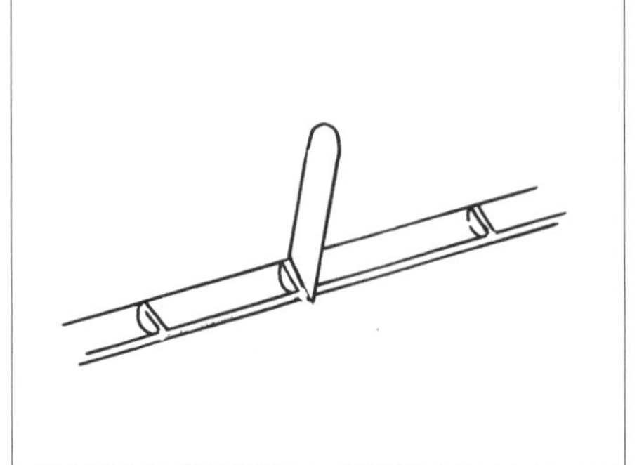

35 Since these strips should cling onto the beading, shave off any joints on the wrong side.

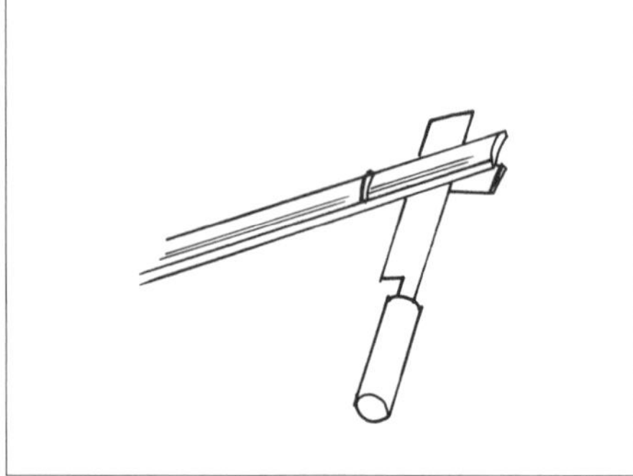

36 Adjust the thickness of strips, if necessary. Thick bamboo is difficult to bend, and irregular thicknesses will make a bumpy surface.

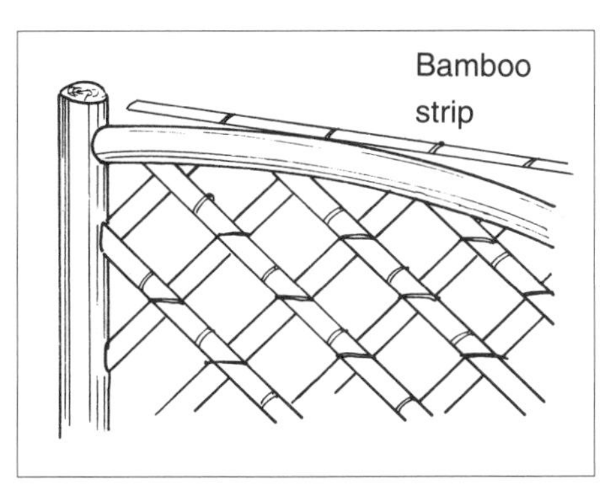

37 Set the strips on the beading. First, place a strip on the beading and check the size.

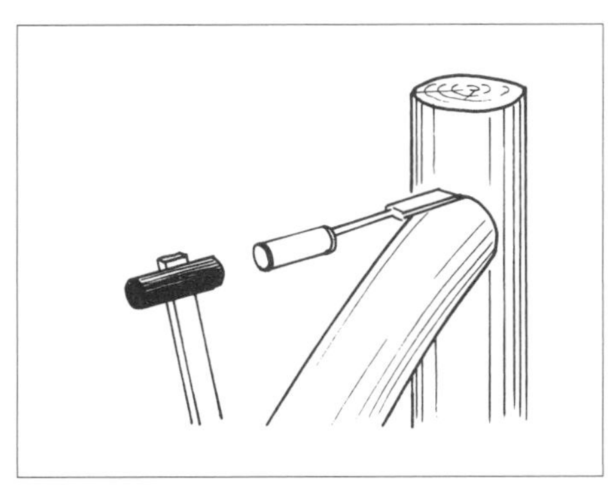

38 Cut a groove around the pipe so that the bamboo strips can be inserted.

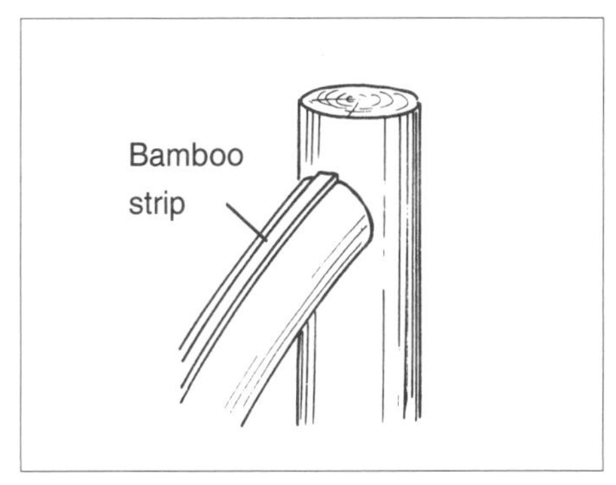

39 Insert an end of bamboo strip into the space between the post and the pipe.

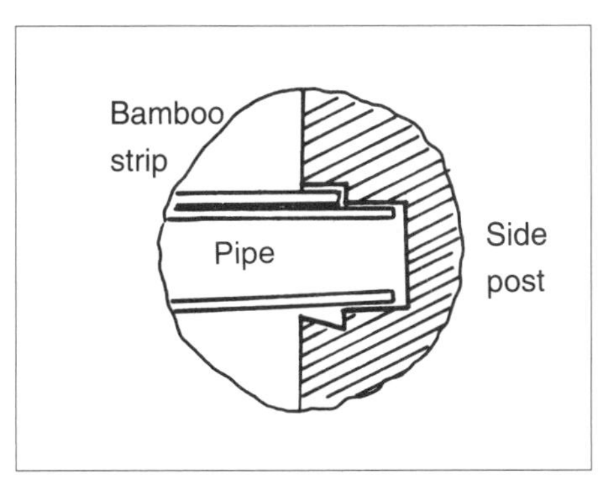

40 The bamboo strips are secured if caught in the ditch.

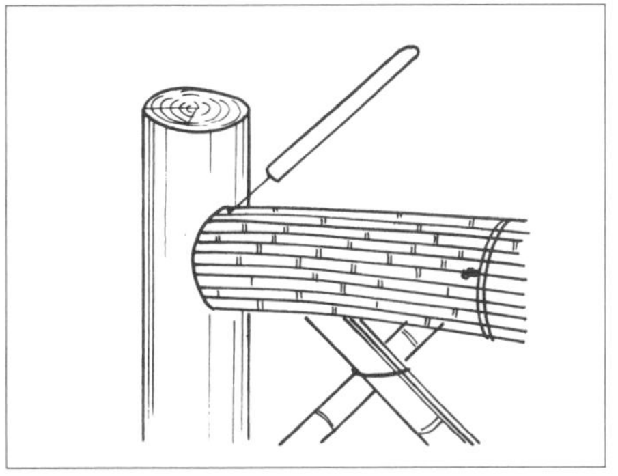

41 When the pipe is completely covered by the bamboo strips, wire the pipe. Drill a hole to fix the strips to the pipe.

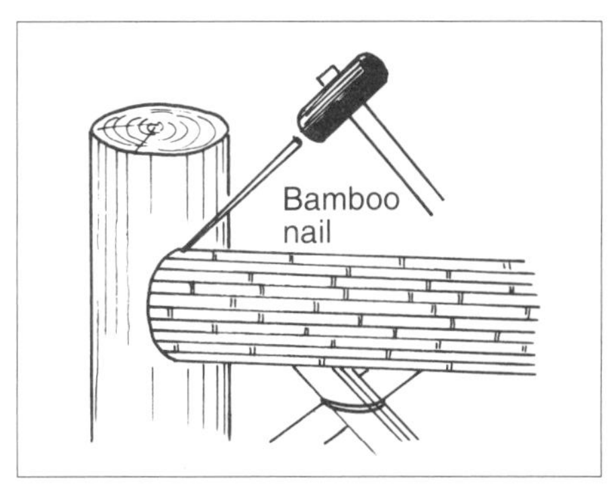

42 Using bamboo nails, secure the ends of bamboo strips to the pipe.

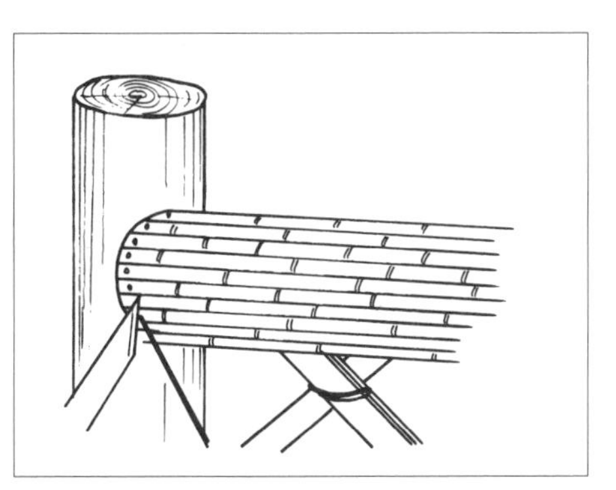

43 After each nailing, cut away excess and shave the tip to form a new nail.

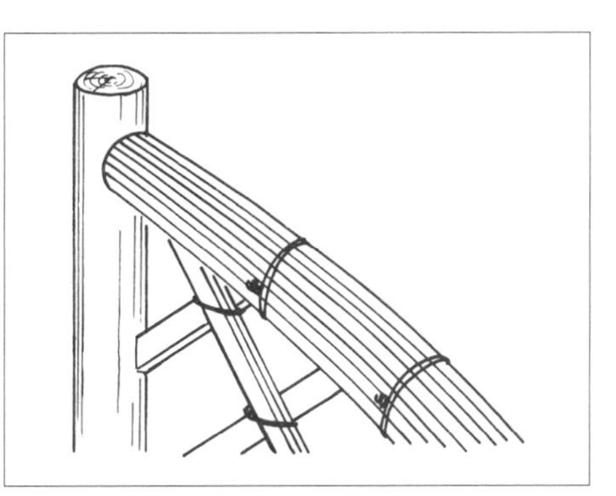

44 When all the ends are fixed, bind the strips with wire, at an interval.

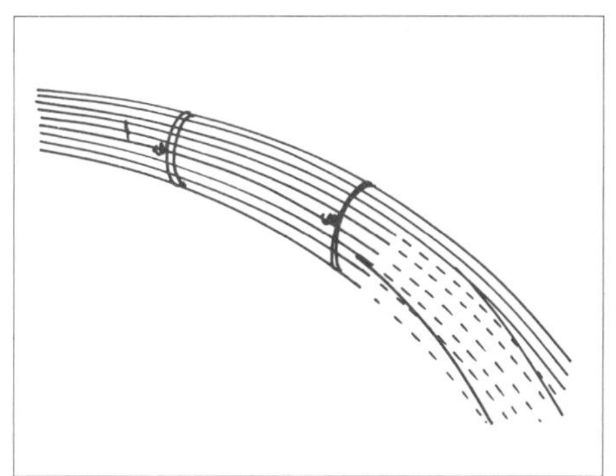

45 Bind the bamboo strips tightly, especially at a sharp bend. If the binding is loose, the strips will come apart.

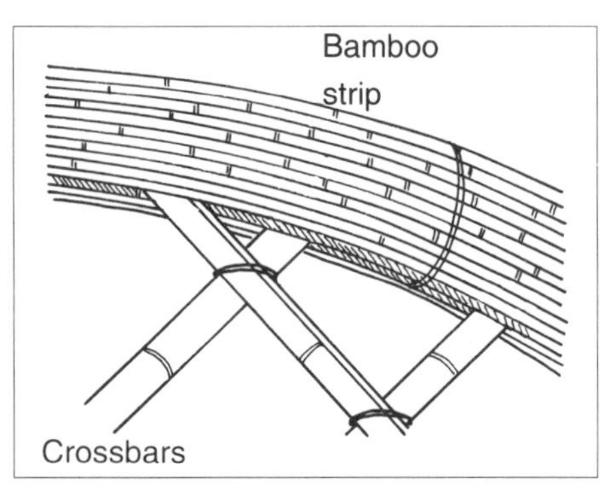

46 Shave off any section that touches the crossbar, and bind tightly as shown.

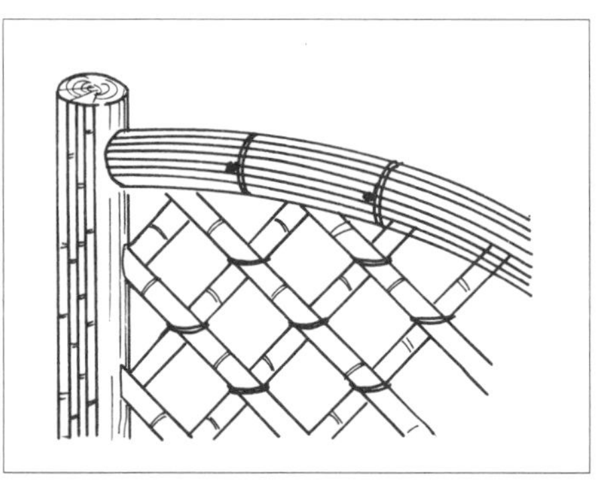

47 In the same manner, cover the post with strips of bamboo, nailing occasionally.

48 Prepare the horizontal crossbar. Wash a thick *madake* bamboo using a brass brush.

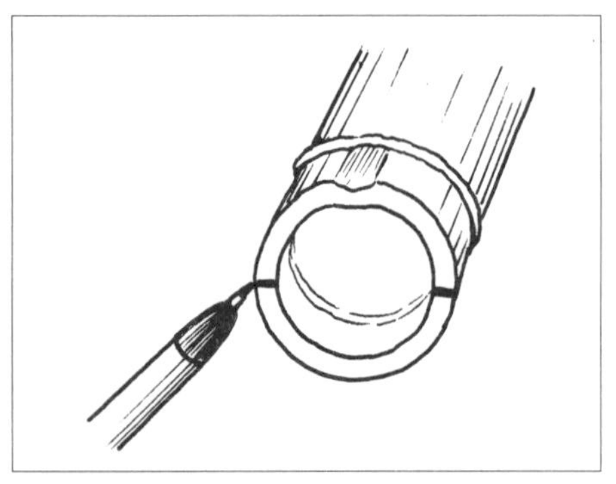

49 Mark on one end to split precisely in two.

50 Apply a hatchet onto the marks, and cut into the bamboo checking each width.

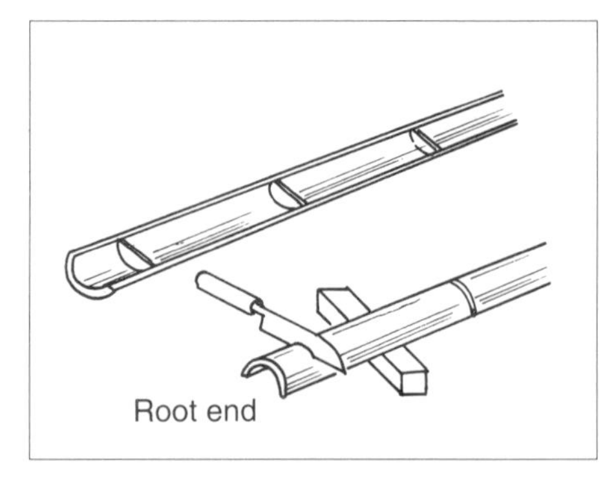

51 Cut the root end near the joint, to keep away from rainwater.

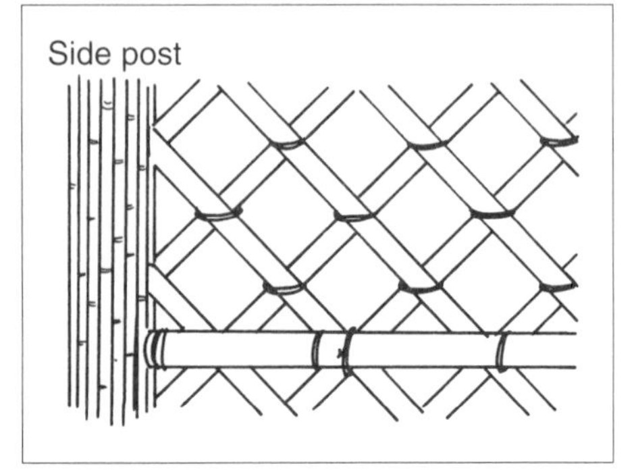

52 Set the horizontal crossbar. Putting the root ends at the post, set each half sandwiching the bottom crossings.

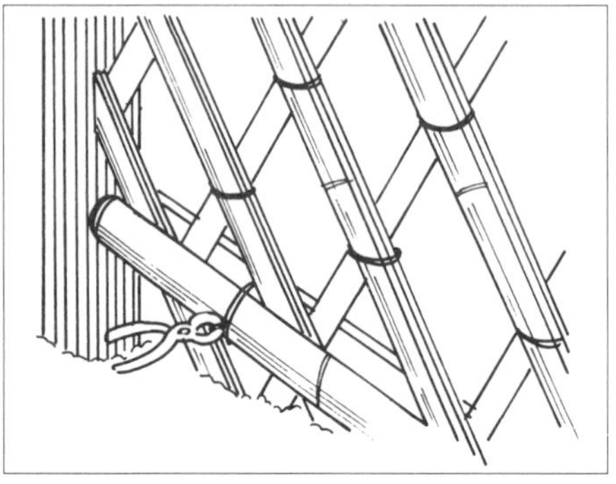

53 Using wire, bind the horizontal bars together.

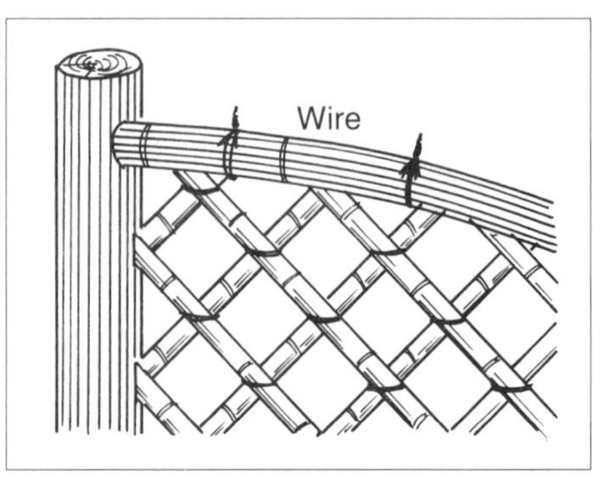

54 Bind the beading with wire at an interval. Then tie with hemp rope between the wire bindings. See page 35 for a decorative knot.

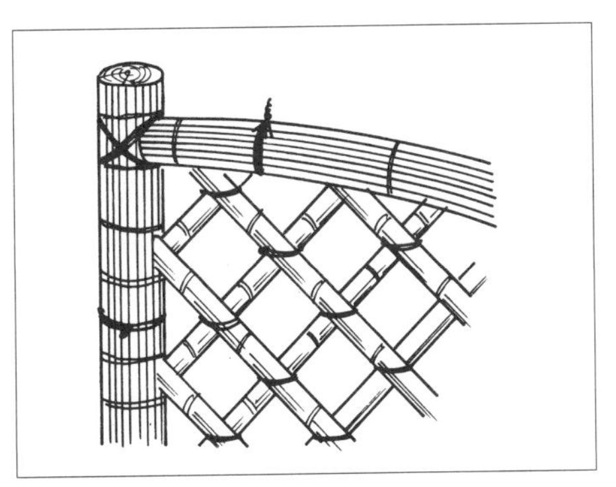

55 In the same manner, bind the post with wire and then with hemp rope.

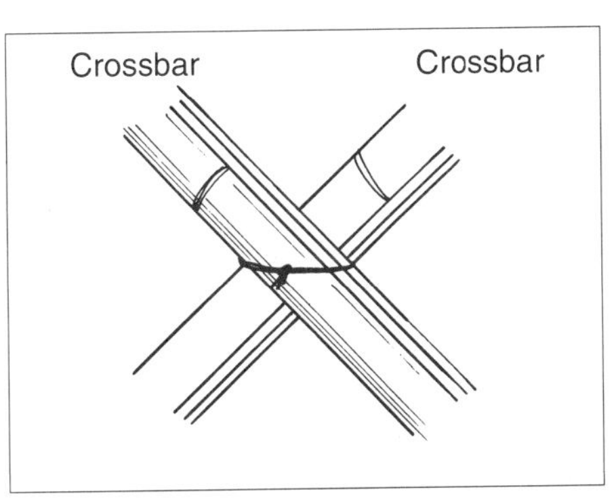

56 Tie the crossings with hemp rope, covering the wire.

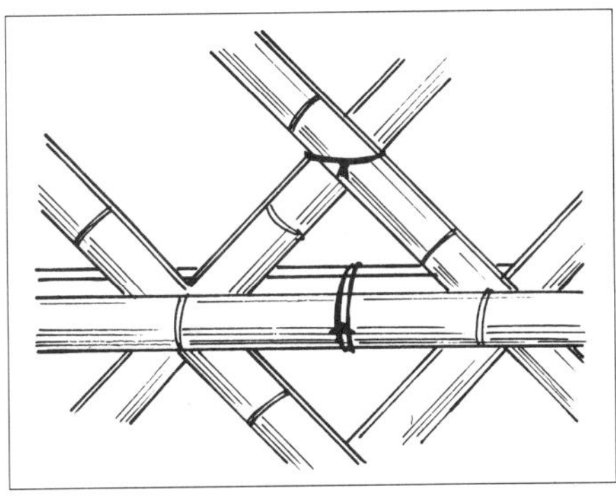

57 As for the horizontal bar, tie with hemp rope over the wire.

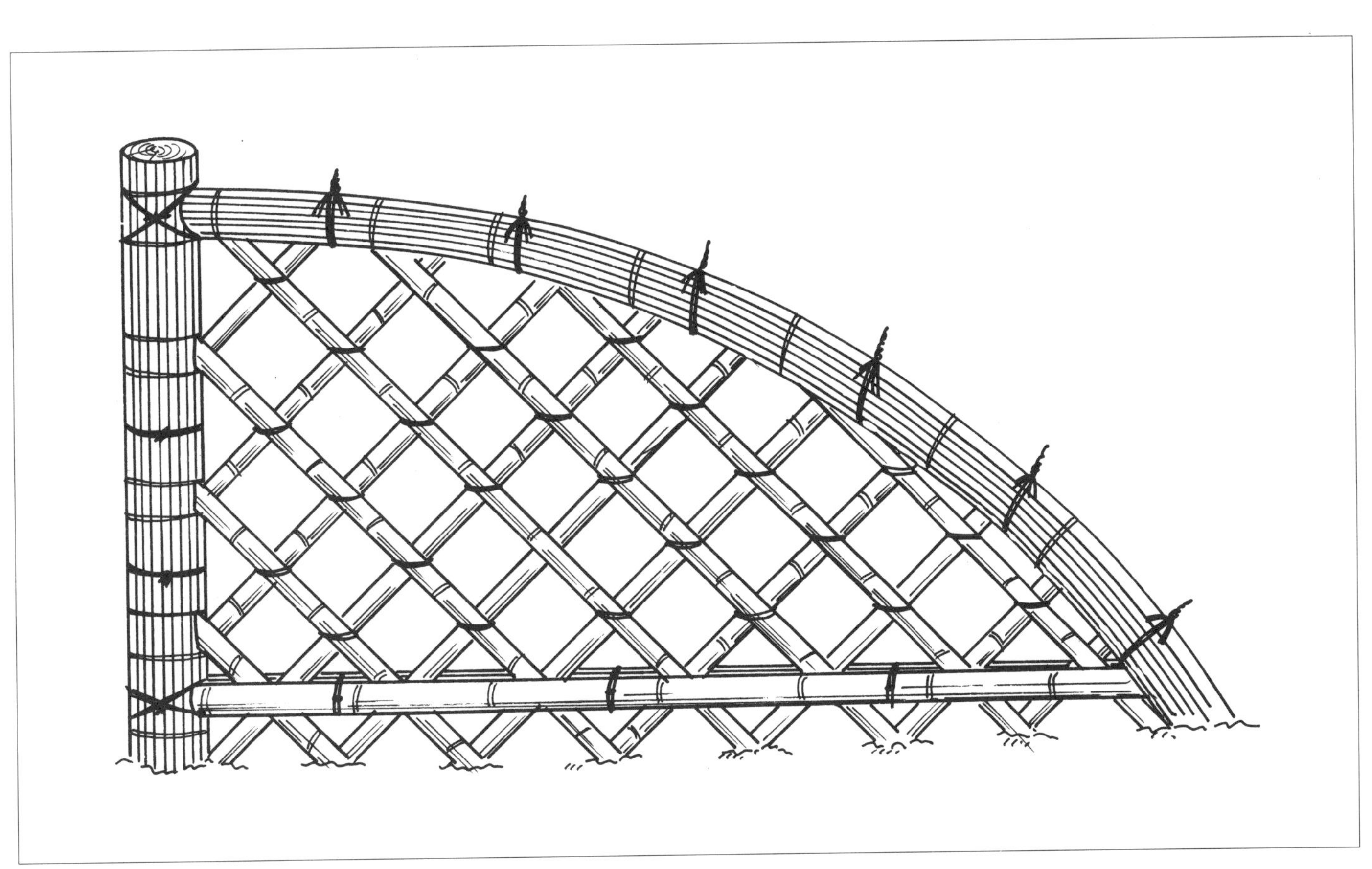

58 When all the ties are finished, wipe off dirt. In making *Koetsu-gaki*, the wire is not removed.

HOW TO MAKE *TSUBONIWA* OR SMALL GARDENS

Now challenge yourself to make an actual garden in your yard using our gardening techniques. Whatever kind of garden you are making, the preliminaries are the same: measuring, planning, preparing the ground, etc. Once the preparation is done, procedures are very important because if you work in the wrong order, you will find the later work difficult or have to repeat the same procedure all over again. Generally speaking, follow the procedures below, starting with the ground work. However, be flexible with the order and think of the ground condition or the time you are going to spend: for example, when deciding whether to build a bamboo fence before or after building a drainage system, even garden specialists have diffuculty in planning and often make the decision on the spot. Another point you should keep in mind is combination - always relate each garden element. For exapmle, keep in mind the relationship between the drainage and the water basin, the bamboo fence and the wall, or the stone lantern and the gravel bed. Relax and feel free to make changes to your original plan.

Standard Procedures

- **Ground care**
  Preparing the ground
  Dividing the ground
  Making a drainage
  Making mounds
- **Setting garden accents**
  Setting stones for arrangement, paving, stepping, or edging
  Setting a bamboo fence, stone lantern, or water basin
- **Planting**
  Planting trees, grasses or mosses
- **Finishing**
  Cleanup

For each procedure on the following pages, instruction pages are given in parentheses.

HOW TO MAKE GARDEN 1 - PAGE 6

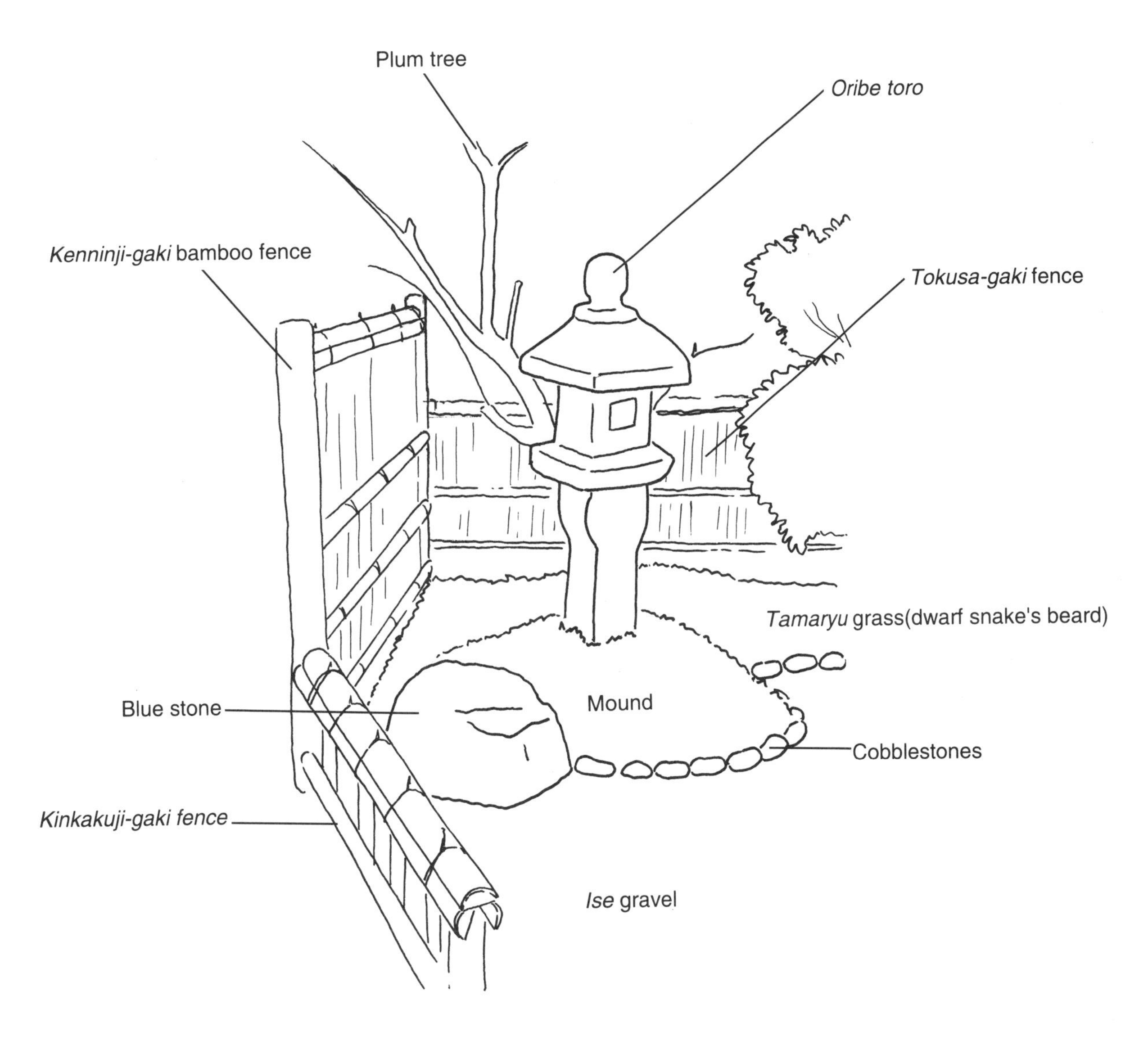

Procedure

1 Make *Kenninji-gaki* fence (See page 72).
2 Set blue stone (p58).
3 Set cobbles (p53).
4 Build mound. (p52)
5 Make drainage (p50).
6 Implant *Oribe toro* (p54).
7 Make *Kinkakuji-gaki* fence (p28).
8 Make *Tokusa-gaki* fence (p84).
9 Plant plum tree (p68).
10 Lay *Ise* gravel (p64).

Additional notes

- Use the blue stone as an object, the cobbles for edging the mound. Lay the blue stone on its longer side.
- Implant the *Oribe toro* in the mound.

HOW TO MAKE GARDEN 2 - PAGE 6

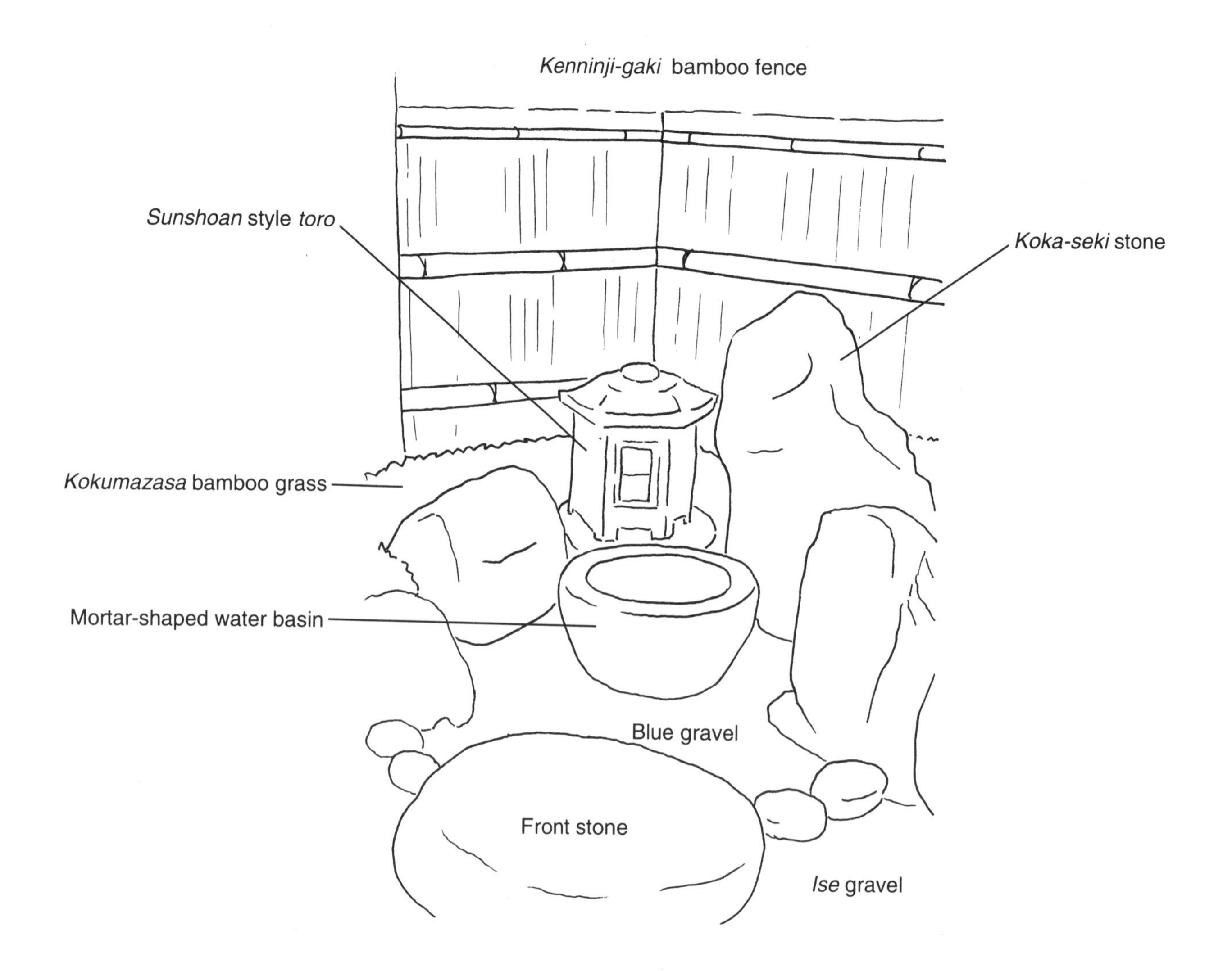

Procedure

1 Make *Kenninji gaki* fence (See page 72).
2 Set *koka-seki* stone (p58).
3 Make basin front (p56).
4 Set *Sunshoan* style *toro* (p54).
5 Plant dwarf snake's beard (p70).
6 Lay *Ise* gravel (p64).

Additional notes

- Since this garden is constructed on a porch with a drainage system, no extra drainage is needed.
- This basin front is called *nakabachi* style, in reference to the position of the basin, in the center of the "Sea". Granite is used for the front stone.

HOW TO MAKE GARDEN 3 - PAGE 6

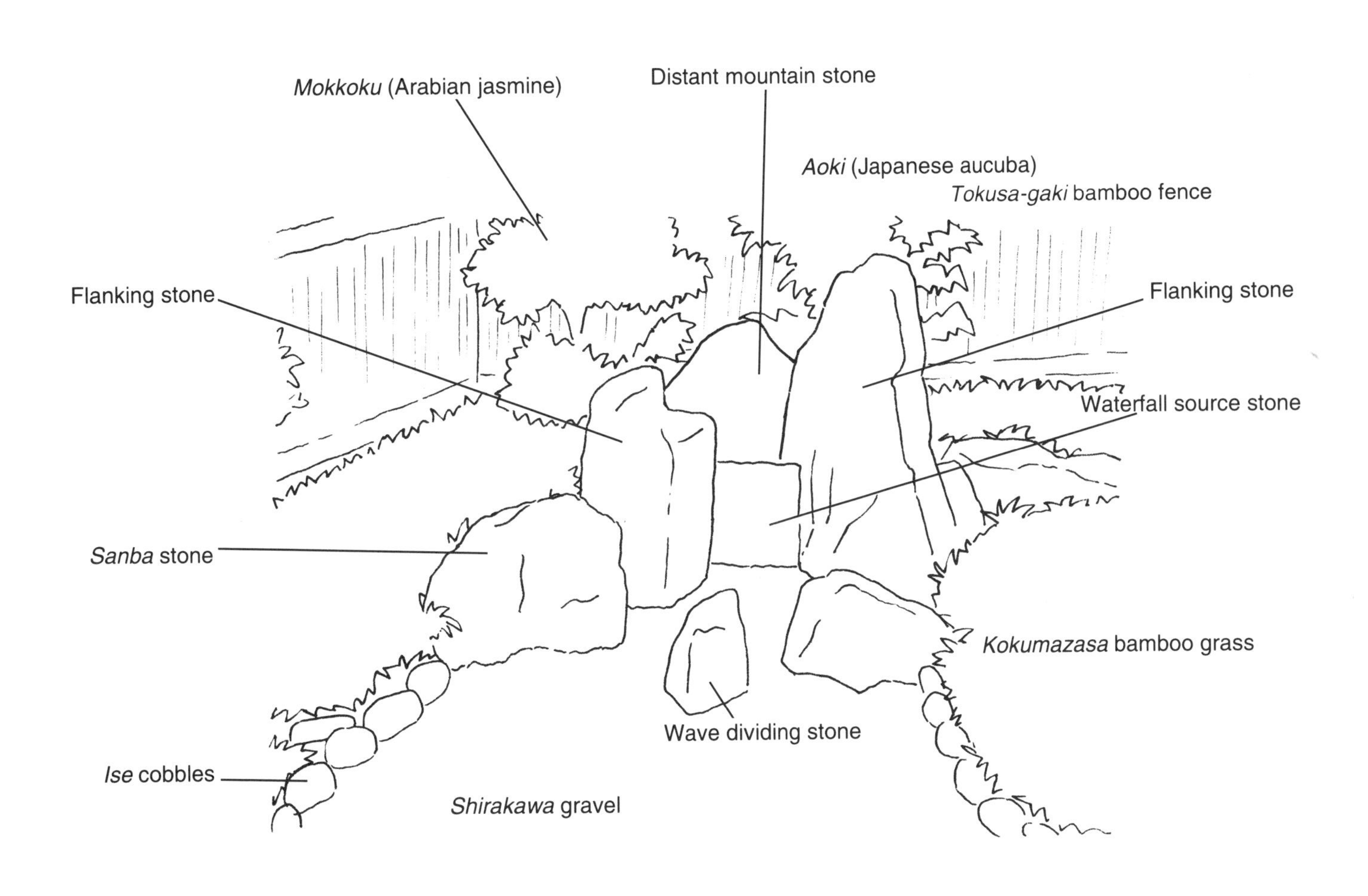

Procedure

1. Set *Sanba* stones (See page 58).
2. Build mounds (p52).
3. Lay *Ise* cobbles (p53).
4. Make drainage (p50).
5. Plant *aoki* and *mokkoku* (p68).
6. Plant *kokumazasa* bamboo grass (p70)
7. Make *Tokusa-gaki* fence (p84)
8. Lay *Shirakawa* gravel (p64)

Additional notes

- *Sanba* stones are used for the waterfall stone grouping, and *Ise* cobbles are for the edging of the mounds.
- The *Tokusa-gaki* fence is built on the wall.

HOW TO MAKE GARDEN 5 - PAGE 7

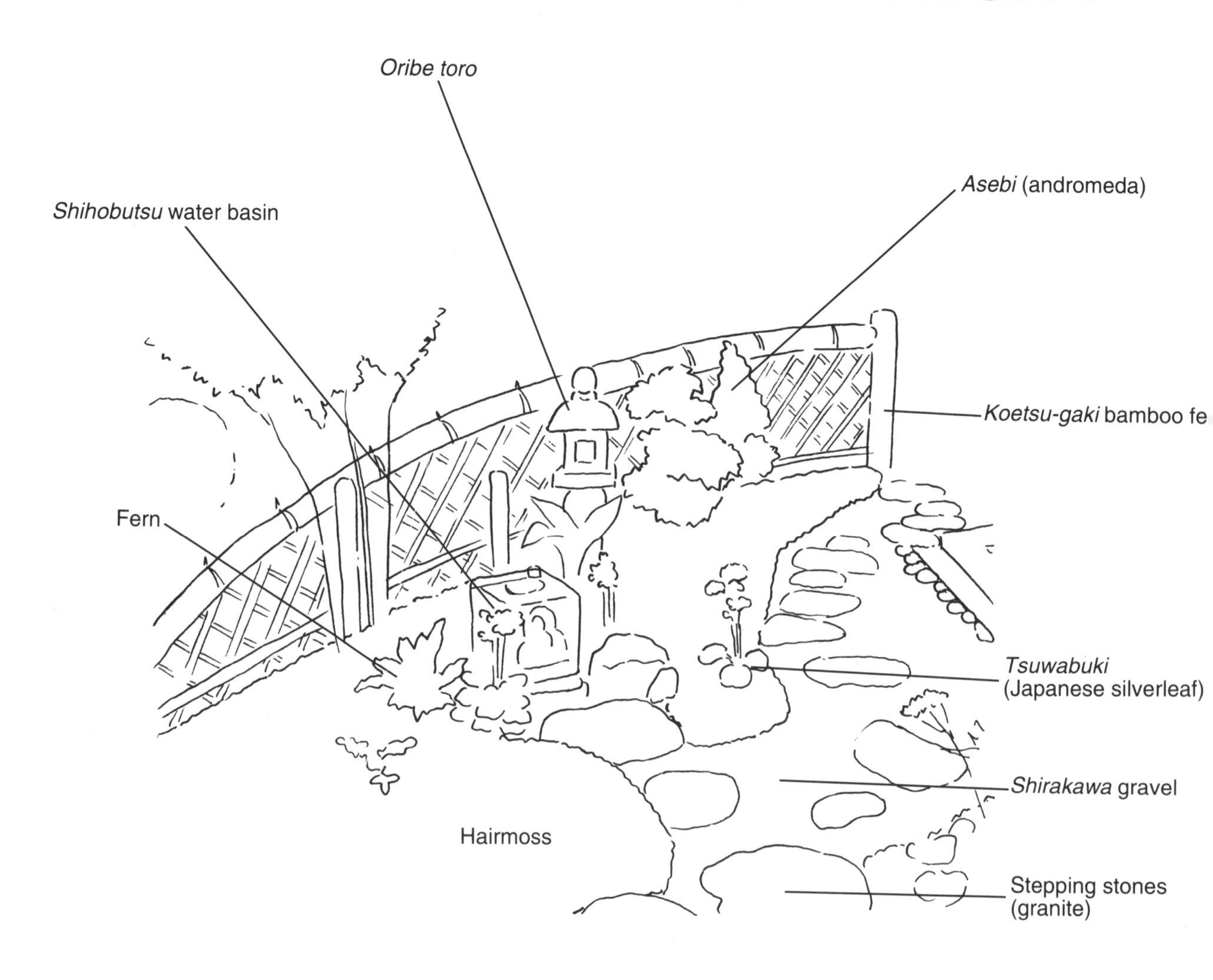

Procedure

1 Make drainage (See page 50).
2 Make *tsukubai* basin front (p56).
3 Build mounds (p52).
4 Set granite stepping stones (p62).
5 Build *Koetsu-gaki* fence (p98).
6 Set *Oribe toro* (p54).
7 Plant *asebi* (p68).
8 Plant fern and *tsuwabuki* (p70).
9 Plant hairmoss (p71).
10 Lay *Shirakawa* gravel (p64).

Additional notes

- The stepping stones are made of granite.
- This basin front is called *mukaibachi* style in reference to the position of the basin, on the edge of the "Sea".
- The *Oribe toro* is implanted in the mound.

HOW TO MAKE GARDEN 6 - PAGE 7

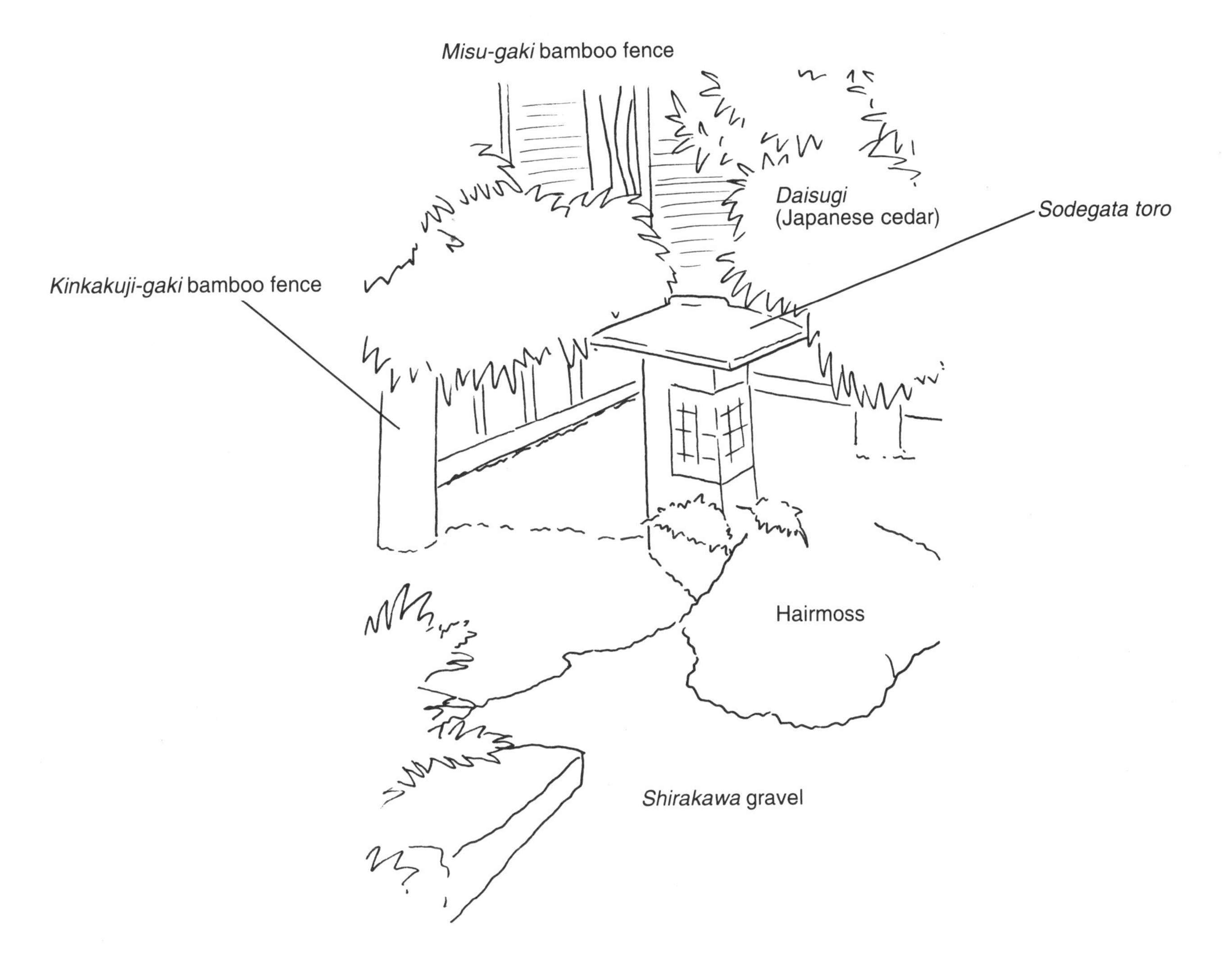

Procedure

1. Build a mound (See page 52).
2. Plant *daisugi* (p68).
3. Set *Sode-gata toro* (p54).
4. Build *Kinkakuji-gaki* fence (p28).
5. Plant hairmoss (p71).
6. Lay *Shirakawa* gravel (p64).
7. Build *Misu-gaki* fence (p90).

Additional notes

- The *Sode-gara toro* is implanted in the mound.

HOW TO MAKE GARDEN 7 - PAGE 7

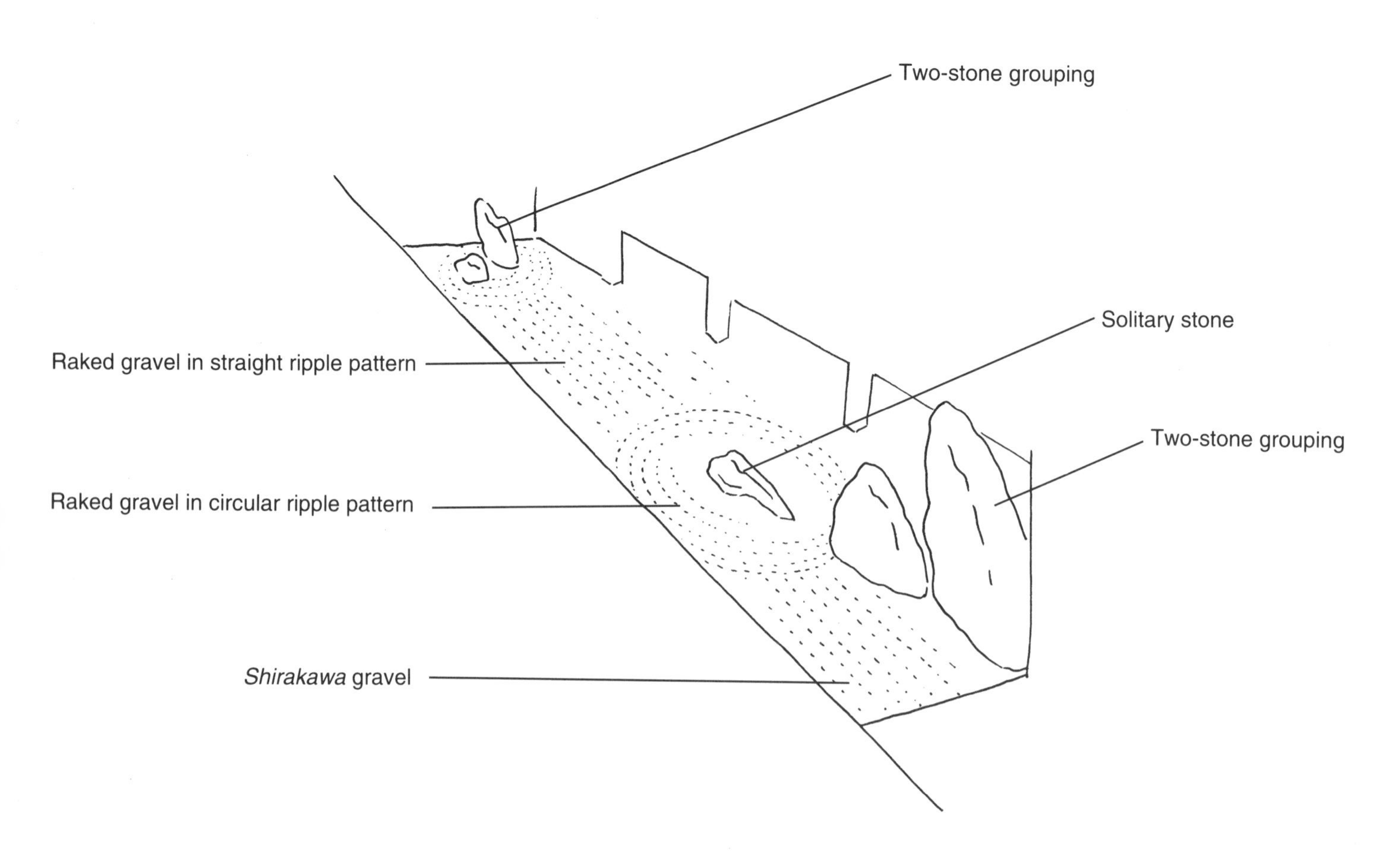

Procedure

1 Set stones (See page 58).
2 Lay *Shirakawa* gravel (p64).
3 Rake gravel into patterns (p66).

Additional notes

- Stones are arranged, from the top, in two-stone, one-stone, and two-stone groupings.
- The straight ripple pattern is called *mizu-mon*, and the circular pattern is called *sazanami-mon*.

HOW TO MAKE GARDEN 8 - PAGE 8

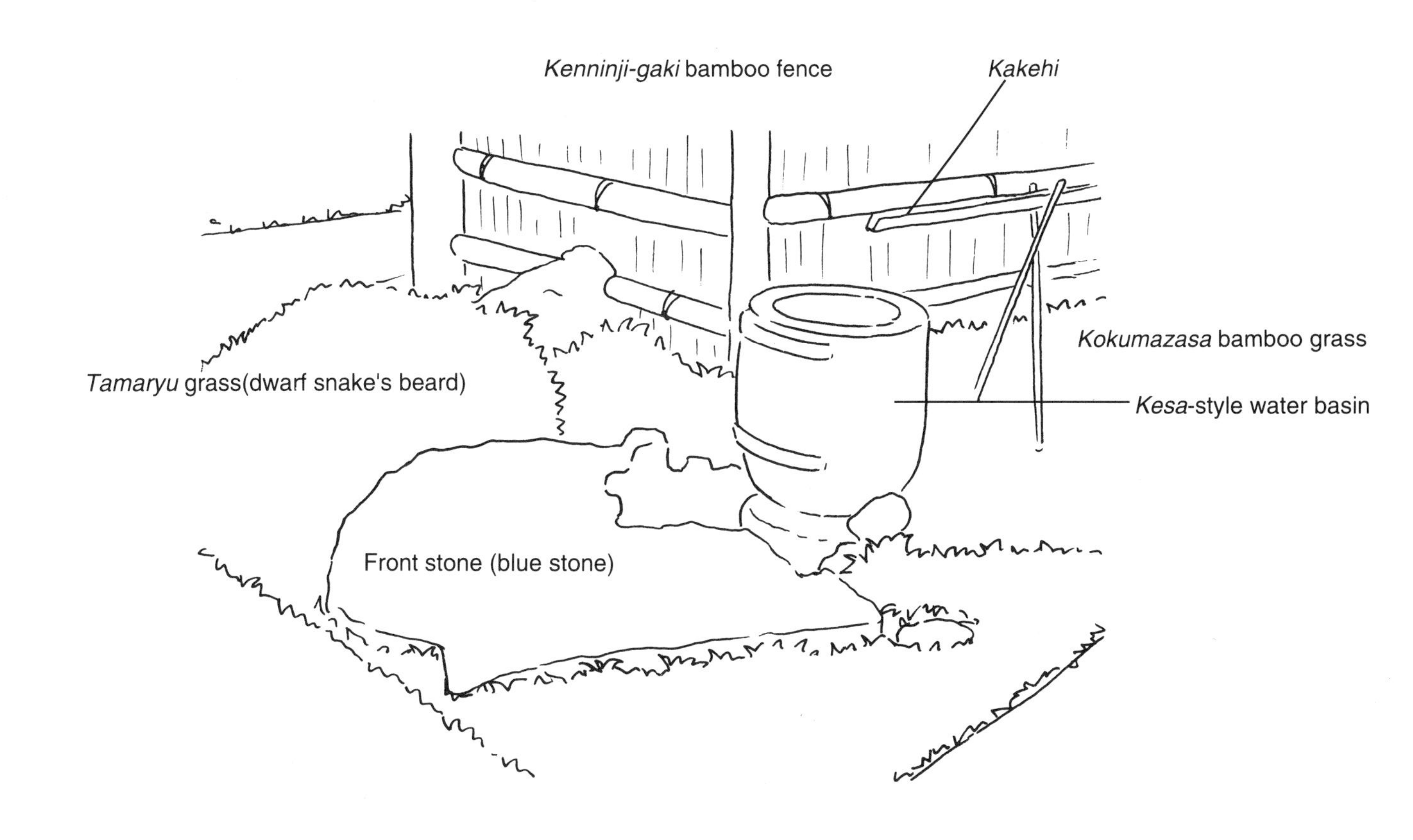

Procedure

1 Make drainage (See page 50).
2 Make *tsukubai* (p56).
3 Build *Kenninji-gaki* fence (p72).
4 Plant *kokumazasa* and dwarf snake's beard (p70).

Additional notes

- This *tsukubai* is called *mukaibachi* style, in reference to the position of the basin, on the edge of the "Sea".
- The spout of *kakehi* is cut at a slant.

HOW TO MAKE GARDEN 9 - PAGE 8

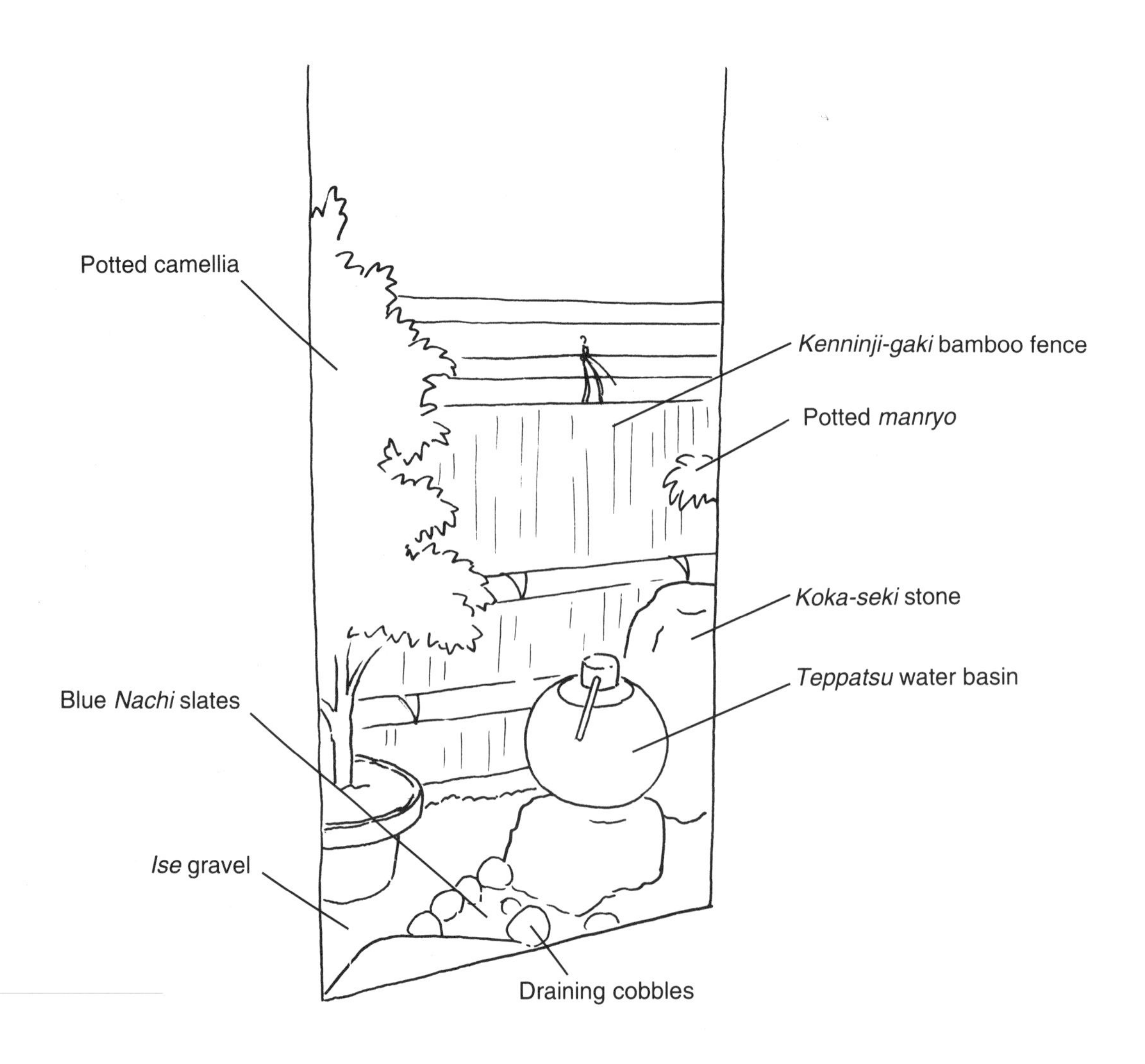

Procedure

1 Build *Kenninji-gaki* fence (See page 72).
2 Make *tsukubai* basin front (p56).
3 Plant *manryo* in pot (p70).
4 Lay *Ise* gravel (p64).

Additional notes

- Since this garden is constructed on a porch with a drainage system, no extra drainage is needed.
- This basin front is called *mukaibachi* style, in reference to the position of the basin, on the edge of the "Sea". Blue *Nachi-ishi* are laid as draining cobbles.

HOW TO MAKE GARDEN 10 - PAGE 8

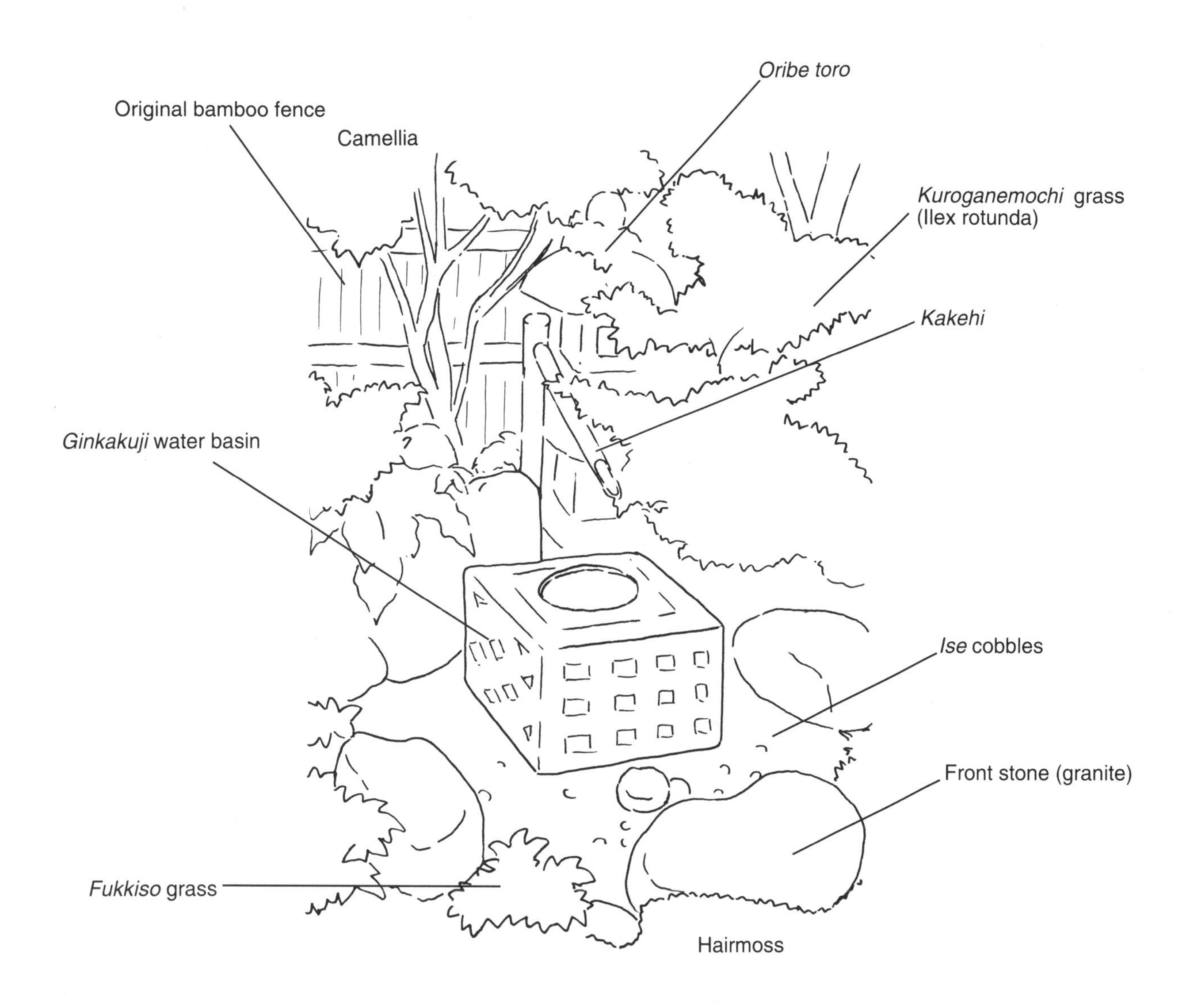

Procedure

1 Build original fence (See page 72).
2 Make drainage (p50).
3 Make *tuskubai* basin front (p56).
4 Plant *kuroganemochi* and camellia (p68).
5 Plant *fukkiso* (p70).
6 Plant hairmoss (p71).

Additional notes

- This original fence is inspired by *Kenninji-gaki.*
- This basin front is called *nakabachi* style, in reference to the position of the basin, in the center of the "Sea".
- Use *Ise* cobbles for draining area and granite for the front stone.

HOW TO MAKE GARDEN 11 - PAGE 8

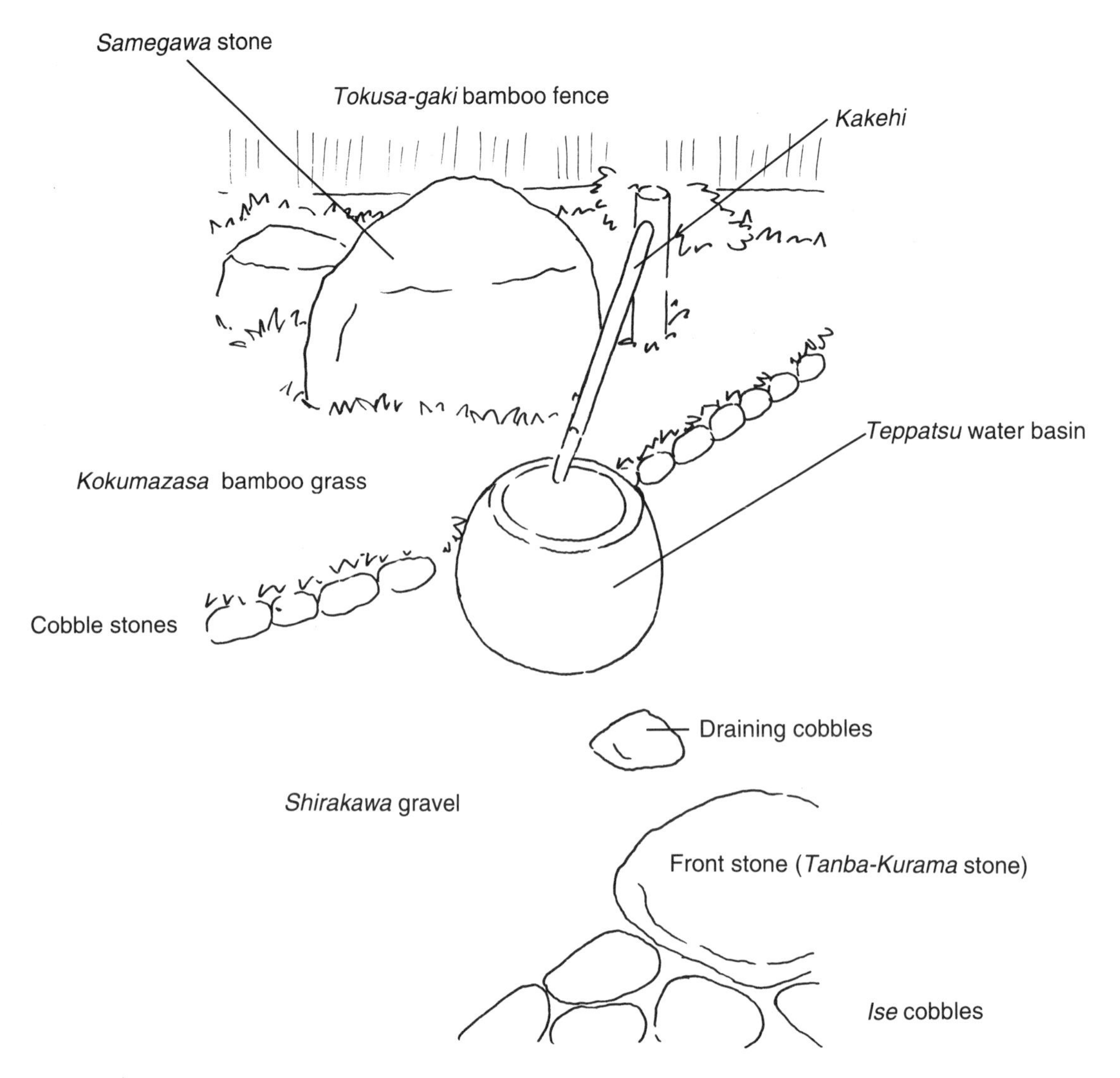

Procedure

1. Make drainage system (See page 50).
2. Set cobble stones (p53).
3. Make mound (p52).
4. Set *Samegawa* stone (p58).
5. Make *tsukubai* basin front (p56).
6. Plant *kokumazasa* (p70).
7. Build *Tokusa-gaki* fence (p84).
8. Lay *Shirakawa* gravel (p64).

Additional notes

- Use cobbles to edge the mound, *Samegawa* stone for an object.
- Use *Tanba-Kurama* stone as the front stone of the basin.
- The spout of *kakehi* is cut at a slant.

HOW TO MAKE GARDEN 13 - PAGE 9

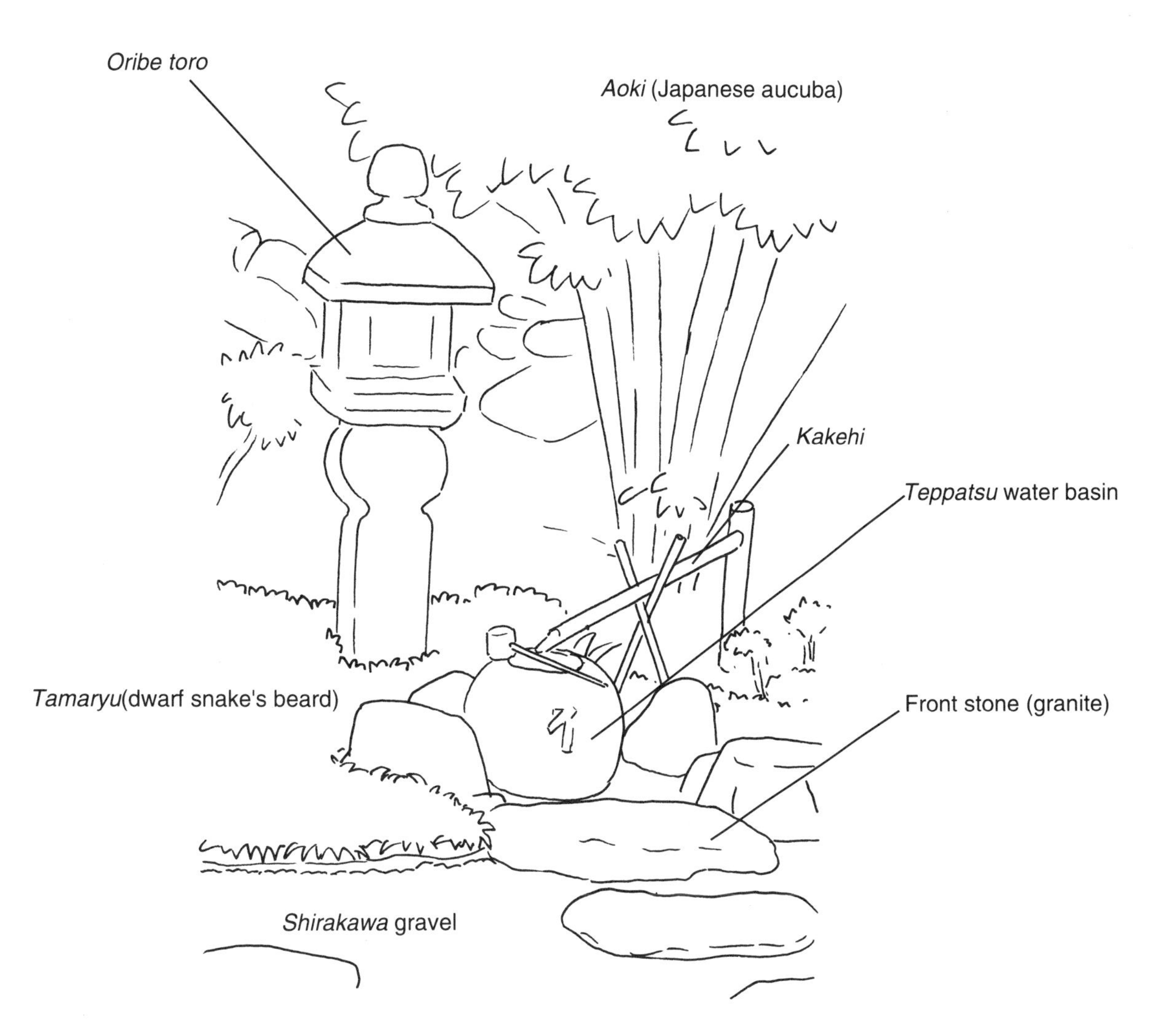

Procedure

1 Make drainage (See page 50).
2 Build mound (p52).
3 Make *tsukubai* basin front (p56).
4 Set *Oribe toro* (p54).
5 Set granite as front stone (p62).
6 Plant trees (p68).
7 Plant *tamaryu* (p70).
8 Lay *Shirakawa* gravel (p64).

Additional notes

- All stones used in this garden are granite, including accessory stone in basin front and stepping stones.
- This basin front is called *nakabachi* style and the basin is positioned in the center of "Sea".
- The spout of *kakehi* is cut at a slant.

HOW TO MAKE GARDEN 14 - PAGE 9

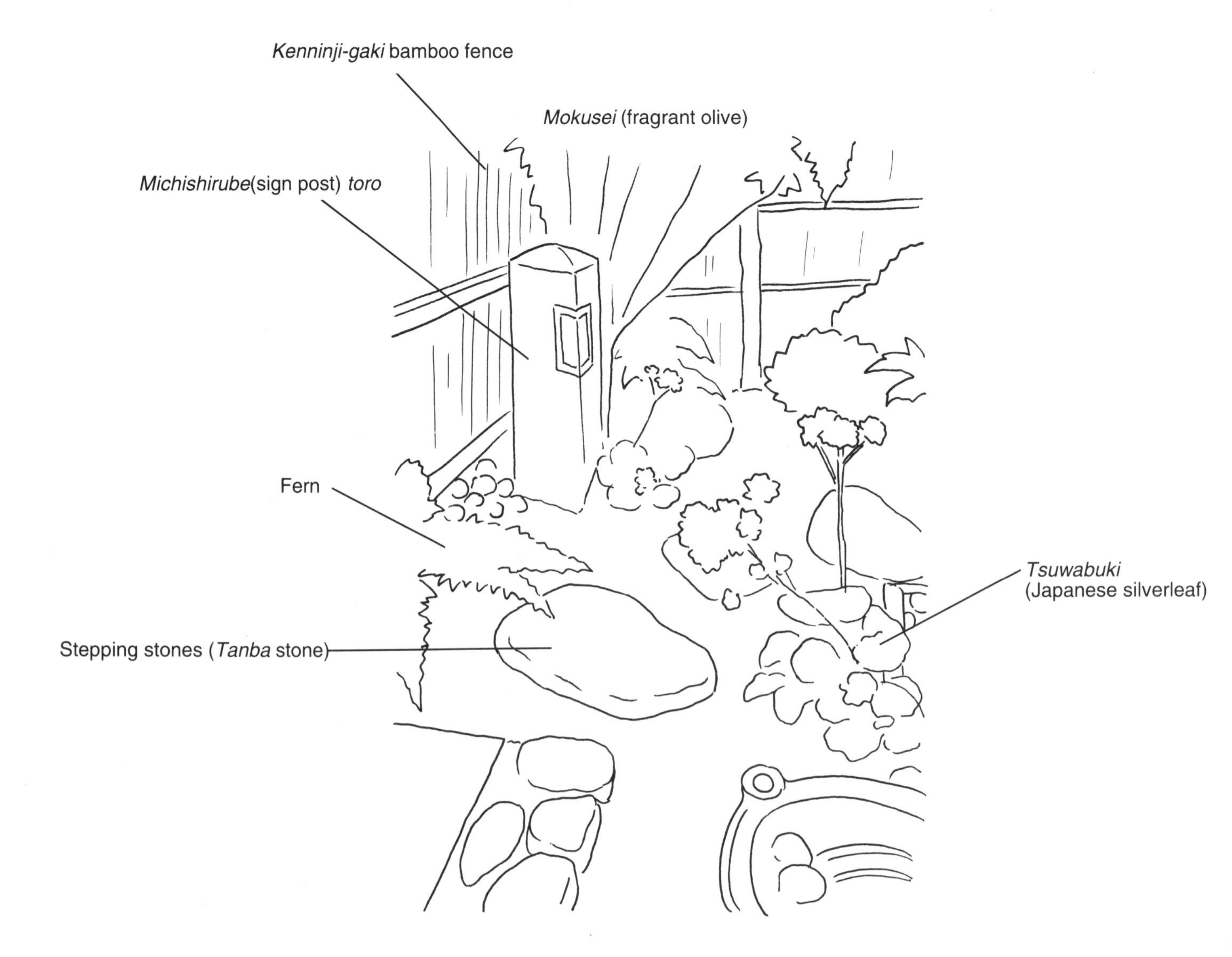

Procedure

1. Build *Kenninji-gaki* fence (See page 72).
2. Plant *mokusei* (p68).
3. Set *Michishirube toro* (p54).
4. Set *Tanba* stones as stepping stones (p62).
5. Plant fern and *tsuwabuki* (p70).

Additional notes

- Implant *toro* in the ground.
- Use *Tanba* stone for stepping stones.

HOW TO MAKE GARDEN 15 - PAGE 9

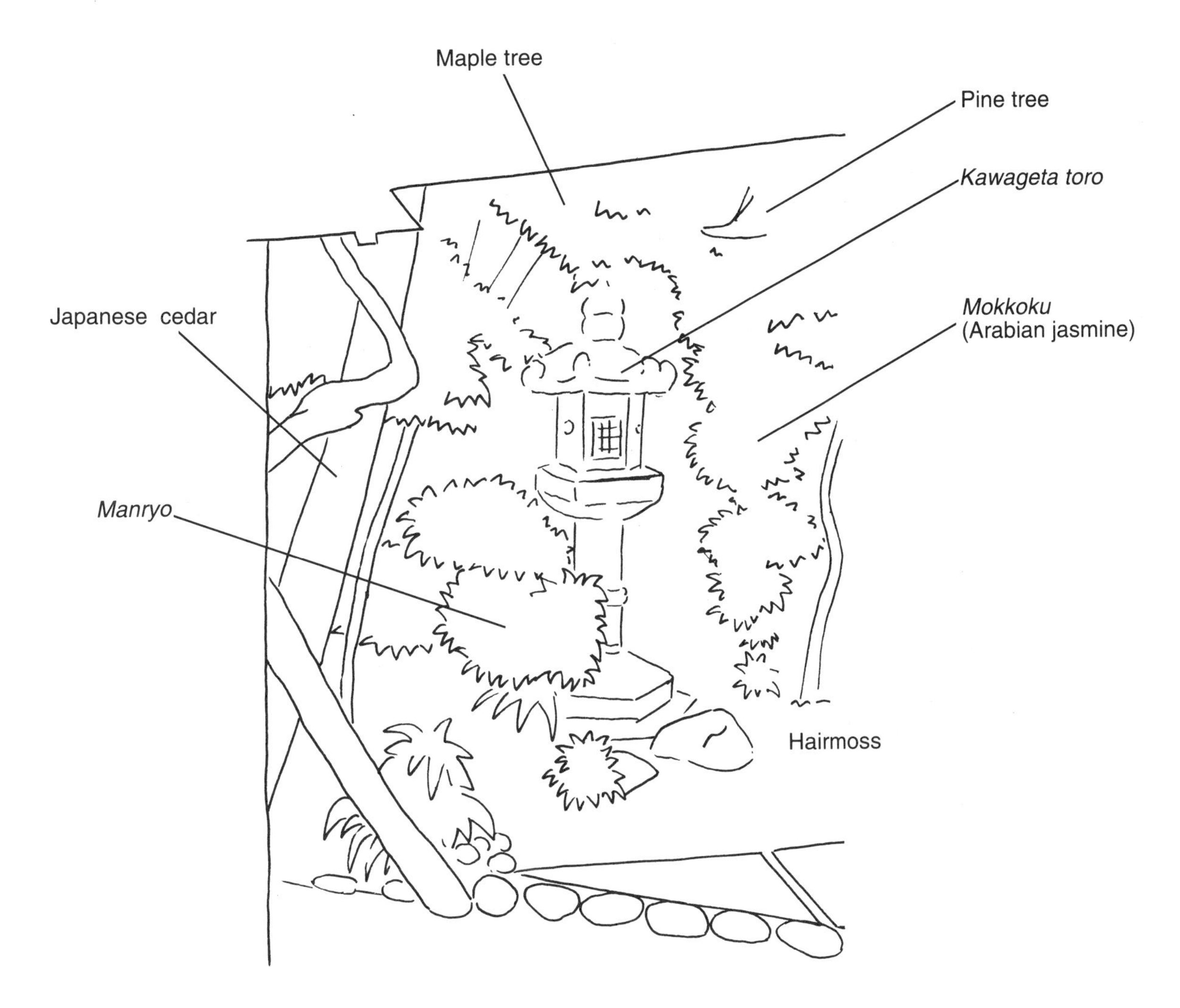

Procedure

1 Set *Kawageta toro* (See page 54).
2 Plant Japanese cedar, pine, Arabian jasmine and maple trees (p68).
3 Plant *manryo* (p70).
4 Plant harimoss (p71).

HOW TO MAKE GARDEN 16 - PAGE 10

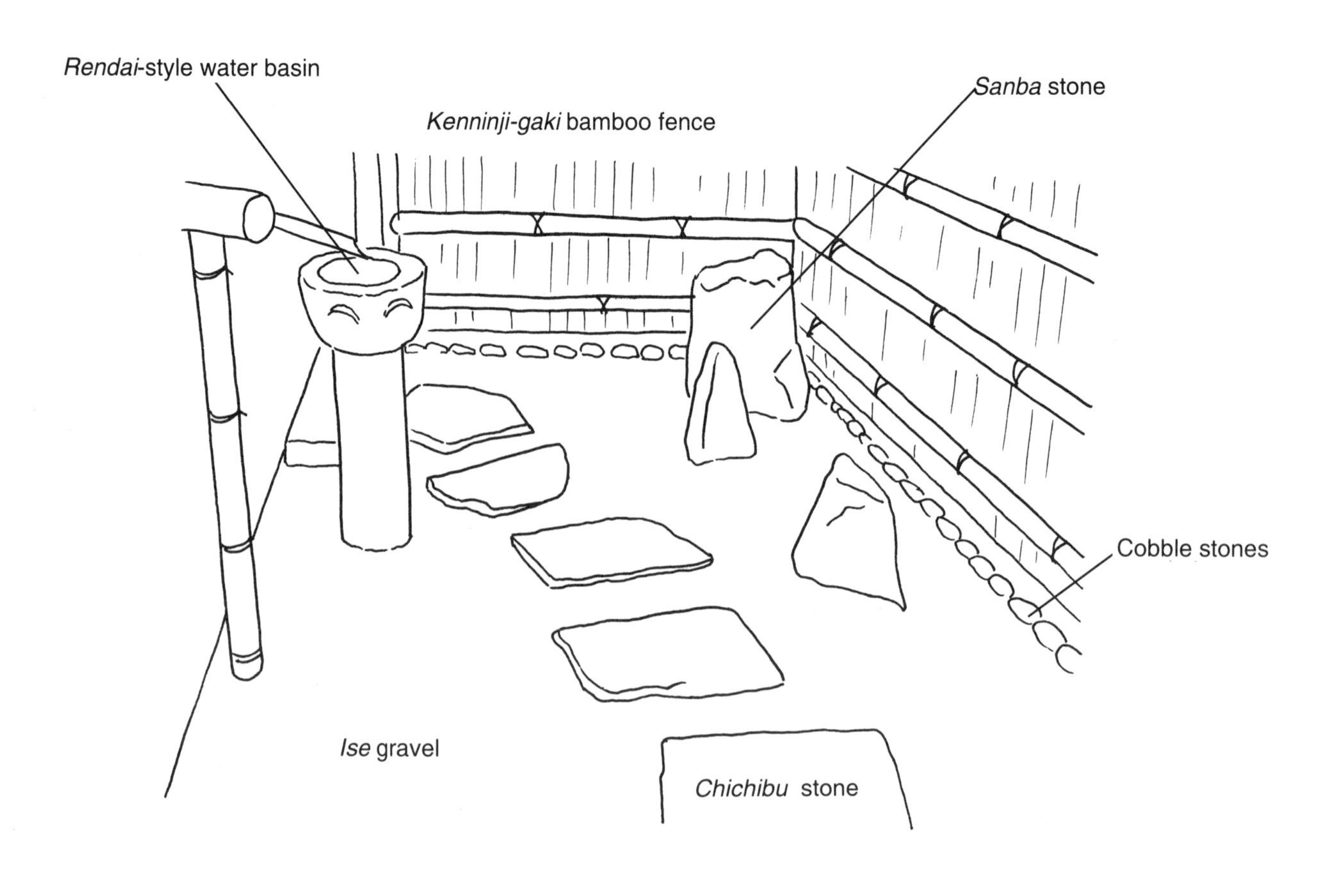

Procedure

1 Make drainage (See page 50).
2 Build *Kenninji-gaki* fence(p72).
3 Set *Sanba* stone (p58).
4 Lay cobble stones (p53).
5 Set *Chichibu* stones(p62).
6 Set *Rendai*-style basin (p56).
7 Lay *Ise* gravel (p64).

Additional notes

- Use *Sanba* stones for objects, *Chichibu* stones for stepping stones.
- This basin is set as an *ensaki* basin which is set under the eaves at the edge of the veranda.
- The spout of *kakehi* is cut at a slant.

HOW TO MAKE GARDEN 17 - PAGE 10

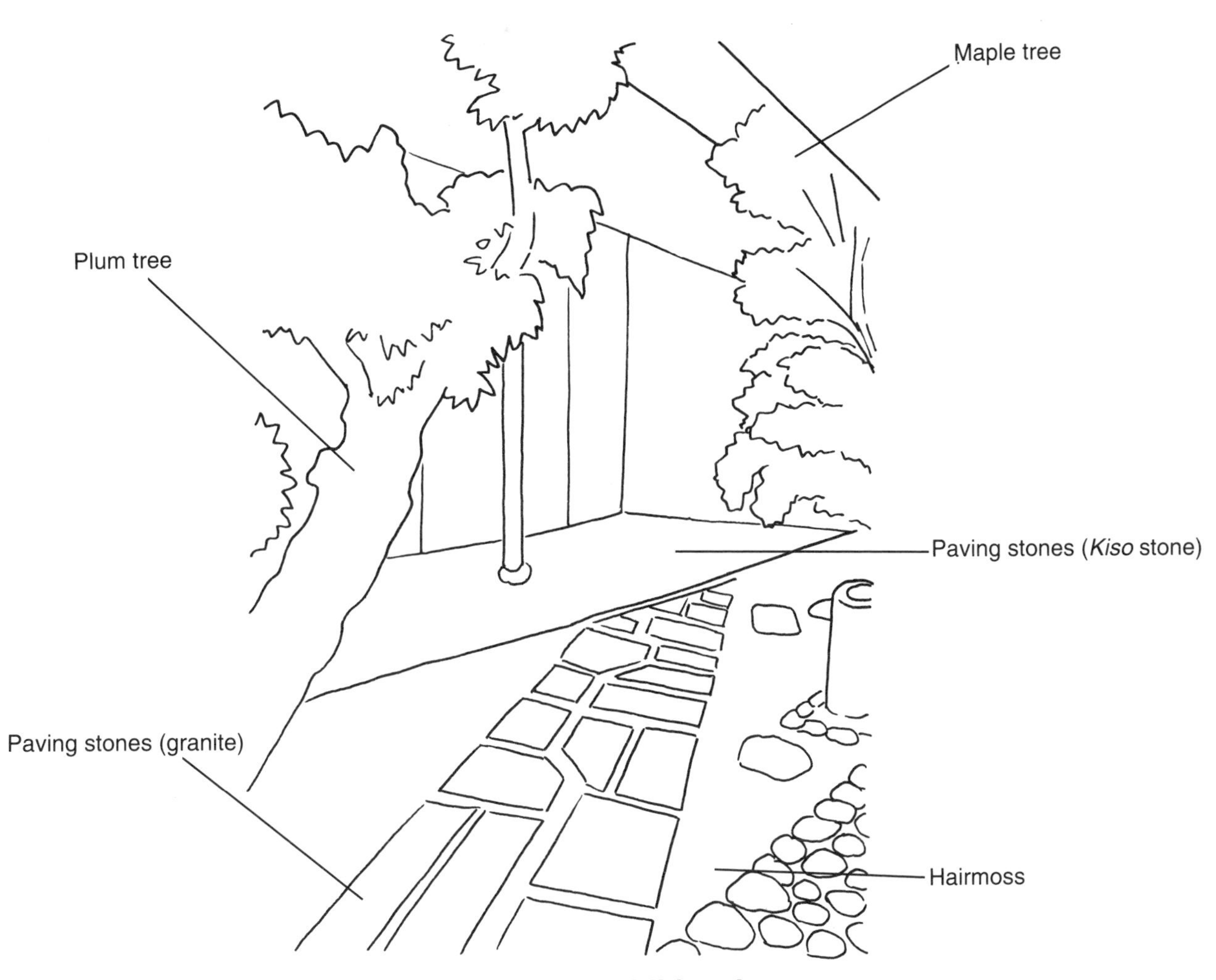

Procedure

1 Plant plum and maple trees (See page 68).
2 Lay *Kiso* stones (p58).
3 Lay granite (p60).
4 Plant hairmoss (p71).

Additional notes

- For the inner pavement, use partially processed *Kiso* stones in "*gyo*" style.
- For the passageway, use cut granite in "*shin*" pattern variation.

HOW TO MAKE GARDEN 18 - PAGE 10

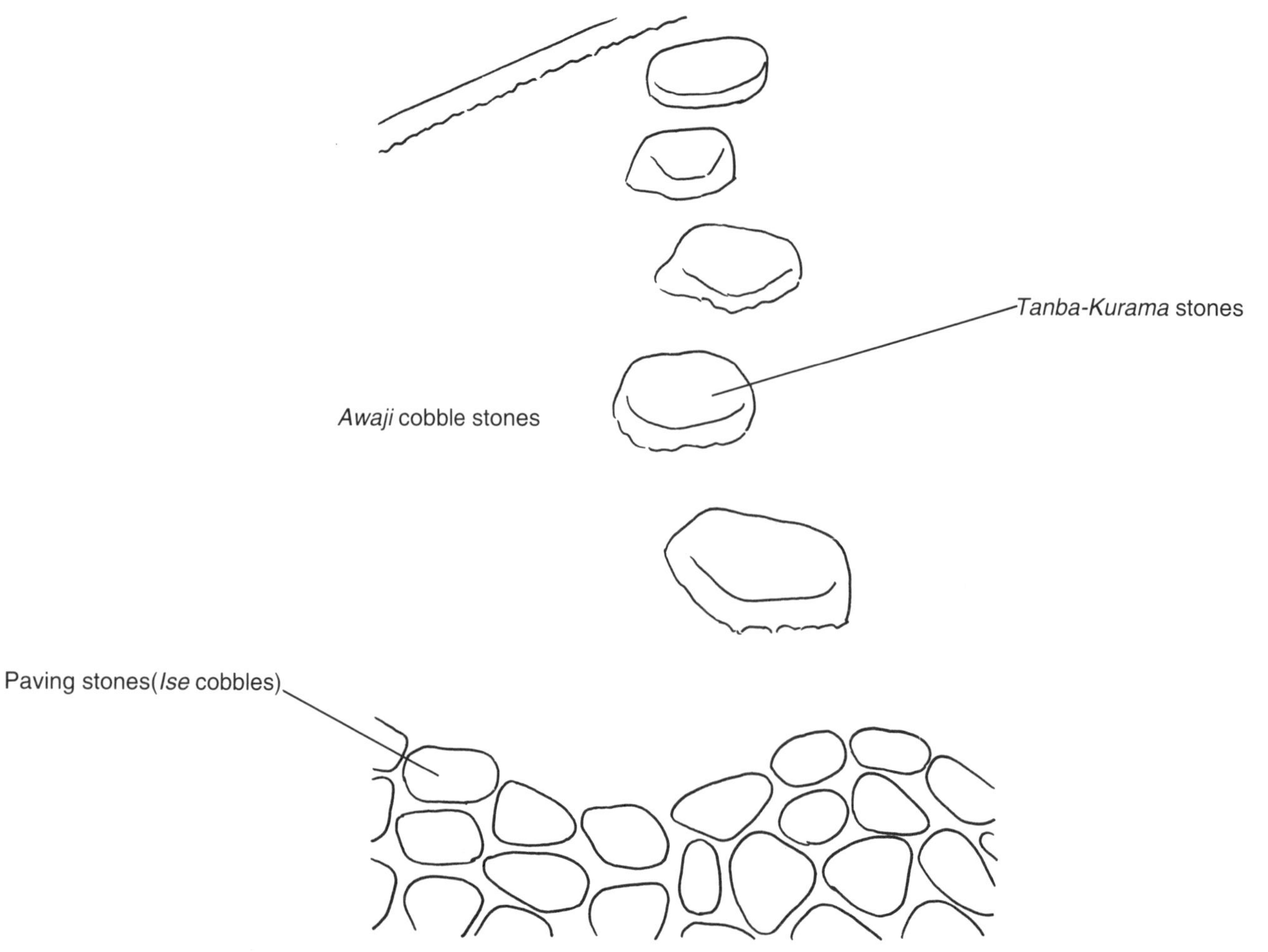

Procedure

1 Make drainage (See page 50).
2 Lay *Ise* cobbles (p60).
3 Set *Tanba-Kurama* stones (p62).
4 Lay *Awaji* cobble stones (p64).

Additional notes

- Use *Tanba-Kurama* stones for stepping stones, *Ise* cobbles for paving stones, and *Awaji* cobbles for the ground cover.
- Lay stepping stones in *chidori* (bird step) pattern.

HOW TO MAKE GARDEN 19 - PAGE 10

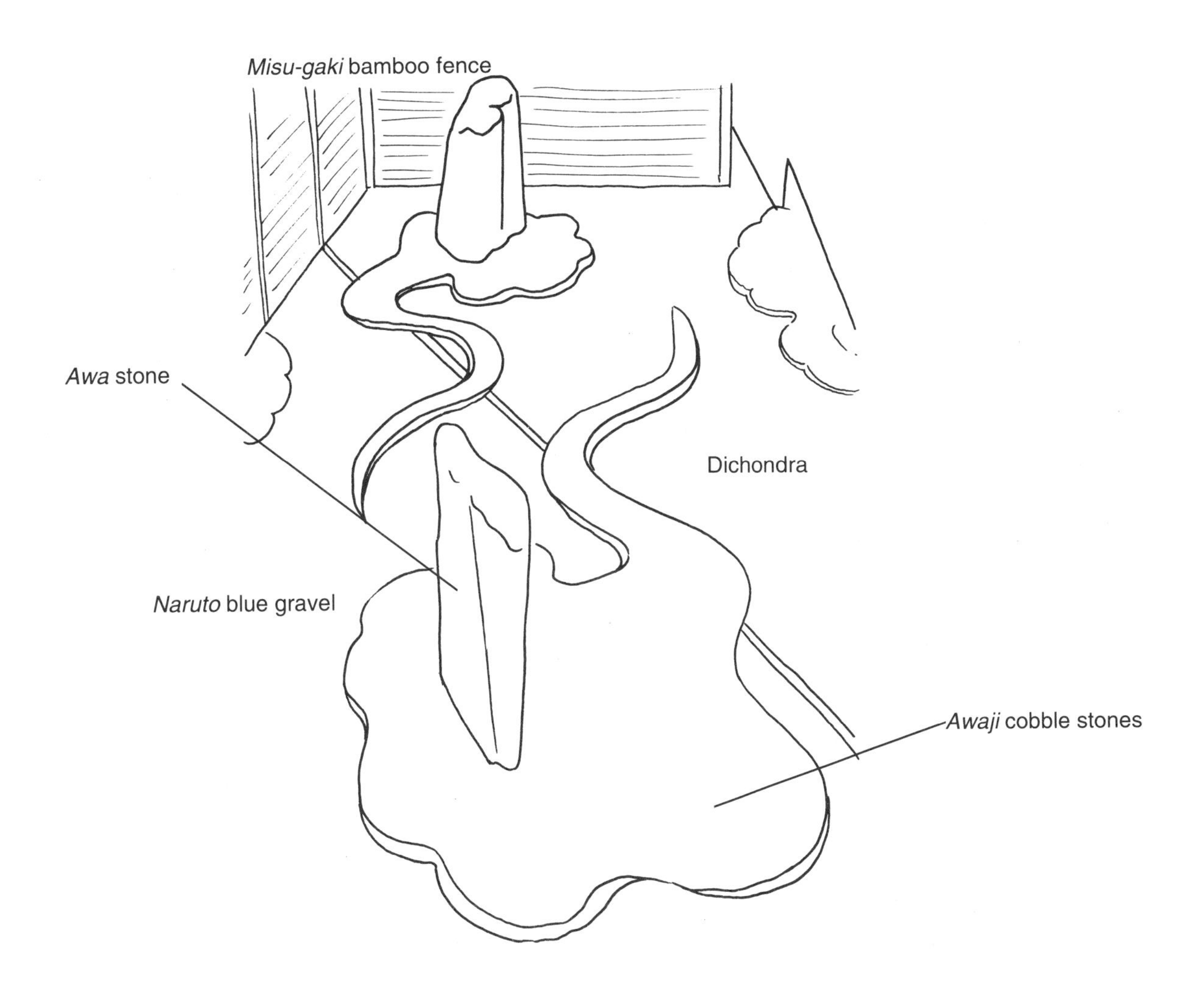

Procedure

1 Build *Misu-gaki* fence (See page 90).
2 Set *Awa* stone (p58).
3 Lay *Awaji* cobble stones and *Naruto* blue gravel (p60).
4 Plant dichondra.

Additional notes

- Use *Awa* stone as the object, *Awaji* cobbles and *Naruto* blue gravel as paving stones.
- Form cloud shapes with *Awaji* cobbles joining with white cement to resemble white clouds.

GLOSSARY

A

Aboshi-gaki
A kind of bamboo fence. P15

Accessory stones
Assorted stones positioned to enhance the main stone in a stone arrangement.

Ao-ishi
General term for blue and green stones, chlorite schist and its variety.

Ao-nachi-ishi
A kind of cobble stone. P26

Awa-ishi
Garden stone produced in Tokushima, mainly in blue color, but also white shades and others. *Tokushima-ishi.* P25

Awaji-kuri-ishi
A kind of cobble stone. P26

B

Beading
Bamboo stalks or splits covering the top of bamboo fences. *Tamabuchi.*

Bird step pattern
A stepping stone pattern. P62

Bushoan-gata toro
A kind of stone lantern. P17

Candle stone
An accessory stone in *tsukubai.* Used to put a candle on to wash hands at evening tea ceremonies. *Teshoku-ishi.*

C

Chozubachi
Hand washing basin usually made of stone. Originated by tea masters to be placed in gardens in *Momoyama* Period. P18-19

Chloride schist
A schist consisting of chloride.

D

Decorative knot
A kind of rope tying, used to both binding and decorating bamboo fences. P35

Dipper stone
An accessory stone in *tsukubai*, set on either side of the basin, on which to put a dipper filled with hot water to be used by the guests in the cold of winter. *Yuoke-ishi.*

Dry stream
Symbolic stone arrangement representing brooks, by spreading cobbles and gravel. Some are similar to rapid dry waterfall made by stones. *Kare-nagare.*

Dry waterfall
Arranged stone group symbolizing a waterfall. Used not only for *karesansui* but for gardens with ponds or fountains. *Kare-daki.*

E

Edging stones
Stones set along the sides of walkways or dividing lines of gardens. Small angular stones of 15-20cm(6"-8") are most suitable for this purpose.

Ensaki-chozubachi
General term for taller hand washing basins placed outside studies or toilets. Sorted into practical ones and mere decoration. *Renndaiji-gata chozubachi* belongs to this type in this book.

Enzan-seki

An accessory stone symbolizing distant mountains, positioned behind waterfalls, mound, or the whole gardens.

F

Front stone

An accessory stone set in front of *chozubachi* in *tsukubai*. The guests step on this stone to wash their hands.

G

Gagyu-gaki

Another name for *Koetsu-gaki* bamboo fence. The form of this fence resembles *gagyu*, or a lying cow, hence the name.

Gara-dake

Bamboo stalks thinner than *madake*, of standard thickness.

Garden stone

Stones used to create landscapes in gardens. Granite, andesite and blue stone group are used for this purpose.

Ginkakuji-gata chozubachi

A kind of hand washing stone basin. P18

H

Hedge

A row of closely planted shrubs forming a background of the garden, a boundary between houses, or partitioning a garden. Evergreen trees which are aggressive in budding are most appropriate, although some deciduous trees do a good job.

Hemp rope

Rope made of hemp fibers. One dyed black is used to bind bamboo fibers. Palm tissue is widely used for this purpose today.

Ho-kyo-in-to

A Buddhist stupa erected for the repose of a dead person's spirit.

I

Ishiusu-gata chozubachi

A kind, of hand washing stone basin. P18.

Ise gorota-ishi

A kind of cobble. p26

Ise jari

A kind of gravel. p27

Ibo musubi

One of the most basic knots used to bind bamboo fences. Also called "*Ibo*", "*Yuibo*" or "*Otoko-musubi*".

K

Kakehi

Originally a flume made of natural bamboo or wood, conducting river water to houses. The style was loved so much that it remained in gardens. Nowadays it stands for a device of pouring water into *chozubachi*, using bamboo stalks.

Kenninji-gaki

One of the most popular designs of screening bamboo fences. P14

Kesa-gata-chozubachi

A kind of hand washing stone basin. P18

Kinkakuji-gaki

A kind of bamboo fence. P14

Kishu-ishi

A kind of blue stone produced in Wakayama. Chloride schist. Its muted blue green color and clear ridges especially suit to gardens inspired by Indian ink paintings of mountains and streams. Easily splits into slab and used to make stone bridges.

Kiso-gata chozubachi
A kind of hand washing stone basin. P18

Koetsu-gaki
A bamboo fence design. P14

Kurama-ishi
Stones produced in the Mt. Kurama area, Kyoto. Known as a good material to make stepping stones or shoe stones. Extremely fast to acidify and the dark brown tones are loved by tea masters.

Kuri-ishi
General term for cobble stones of chestnut size. Mainly used to cover the ground of gardens.

Kuro-nachi-ishi
A kind of cobble stones. P26.

M

Main garden
A larger sized garden to be viewed as the center of interest.

Michishirube-gata toro
A kind of stone lantern. P17

Mikawa shirakawa suna
A kind of gravel. P27

Misu-gaki
A kind of bamboo fence. P15

Movable *toro*
A kind of stone lantern shaped like a portable lantern. *Sunsho-an toro* and *Busho-an toro* belong to this type.

N

Naruto-ao-jari
A kind of gravel. P27

O

Oribe toro
A kind of stone lantern. P16

Original *chozubachi*
Specially designed hand washing stone basin. *Ginkakuji-gata chozubachi* and *Zeni-gata chozubachi* are shown in this book.

R

Reformed *toro*
A kind of stone lantern made from objects which were used for other purposes.

Reiganji-gata chozubachi
A kind of hand washing stone basin. P19

Roppo-seki
A kind of stone. P27

S

Sarashi-dake
Product name for processed thin bamboo stalks. Grilled to remove oily substance.

Sarashi-gaki
A kind of bamboo fence. P15

Scorched log
Hard log such as cypress, with burnt surface. Used as a supporting post of bamboo fences.

Sea
A draining space between *chozubachi* and front stone, covered with cobble stones.

7-5-3 stone arranging
Stone grouping pattern using the positive numbers which have been loved in China since ancient times.

Shihobutsu - gata chozubachi
A kind of hand washing basin. P18

Shikaku-gata toro
A kind of stone lantern. P16

Shimizu-dake
A product name for processed narrow bamboo, mainly used to construct *Shimizu-gaki* fence. Cut to the same length after being polished and oil is removed.

Shin, Gyo, So
A categorization of styles originally used in Japanese calligraphy.

Shoe stone
A flat stone on which to remove shoes before entering a house, high enough to climb onto the floor of the house. Although *Kurama-ishi* was popular to use for this purpose, other stones including blue stones are used today.

Sode-gata toro
A kind of stone lantern. P16

Soseki-gata chozubachi
A kind of hand washing stone basin. P19

Sugikawa-gaki
A kind of bamboo fence. P15

Sunshoan-gata toro
A kind of stone lantern. P17

T

Tachi chozubachi
General term for taller basins in comparison with *tsukubai*, where you have to crouch down to reach the basin. *Rendaiji-gata* basin is shown in this book.

Takeho-gaki
A kind of bamboo fence. P15

Tama-ishi
Small stones worn smooth and round by erosion.

Tanba-ishi
A kind of stone. P27

Tea garden
A garden adjacent to tea ceremony house.

Teppatsu-gata chozubachi
A kind of hand washing stone basin. P18

Three-stone arrangement
One of the basic stone arranging styles. Three stones of different shapes and sizes are combined to form a scalene triangle.

Tokusa-gaki
A kind of bamboo fence. P14

Toro
Lighting equipment to offer votive light to God or Buddha. Made of metal, china, and stone, out of which the stone lanterns are most common.

Tsuboniwa
Courtyard gardens or small quadrangles.

Tsukubai
The basin front including the whole area surrounding *chozubachi*, a low basin where you have to crouch down to wash hands. Includes a drainage system, front stone, candle stone, and dipper stone. Often mistaken for *chozubachi* itself.

Z

Zeni-gata chozubachi
A kind of hand washing stone basin. P19

GARDENS IN THIS BOOK